A SCOTT NEARING READER

The Good Life in Bad Times

Edited and Introduction by Steve Sherman
Foreword by Helen K. Nearing

The Scarecrow Press, Inc.
Metuchen, N.J., & London
1989

Frontispiece: Scott Nearing in Arden, Delaware, in 1930.

British Library Cataloguing-in-Publication data available

Library of Congress Cataloging-in-Publication Data

Nearing, Scott, 1883–
  A Scott Nearing reader.

   "Bibliography of Scott Nearing's major writings": p.
   Includes index.
   1. Social sciences. 2. World politics—20th century. 3. Rad-
icalism. 4. Nearing, Scott, 1883–   —Political and social
views. I. Sherman, Steve, 1923–   .
II. Title.
H83. 377 1989   300   88–29528
ISBN 0–8108–2144–3

CONTENTS

Foreword by Helen K. Nearing   vii

Chronology   ix

Preface   xiii

Scott Nearing, 1883–1983: A Good Life in Bad Times   1

1 The Solution of the Child Labor Problem (1911)   17

2 Social Adjustment (1911)   23

3 Woman and Social Progress (1912)   31

4 Social Sanity (1913)   41

5 Social Religion (1913)   50

6 Poverty and Riches (1916)   61

7 Debate: Will Democracy Cure Social Ills? (1917)   71

8 The Great Madness (1917)   77

9 The Trial of Scott Nearing (1919)   85

10 Debate: Capitalism versus Socialism (1921)   107

11 Debate: Can the Church Be Radical? (1922)   114

12 The Next Step (1922)   121

13 Oil and the Germs of War (1923)   135

14 Debate: The Soviet Polity and Western Civilization
        (1924)   143

15 Glimpses of the Soviet Republic (1926)   154

16 Whither China? (1927)   160

17 Black America (1929)   167

18 The Twilight of Empire (1930)   178

19 War (1931)   186

20 Fascism (1933)   200

21 United World (1944)   206

22 The Tragedy of Empire (1945)   216

23 The Soviet Union as a World Power (1945)   220

24 Democracy Is Not Enough (1945)   223

25 The Maple Sugar Book (1950)   234

26 Economics for the Power Age (1952)   242

27 Living the Good Life (1954)   253

28 To Promote the General Welfare (1956)   257

29 Our Right to Travel (1959)   264

30 The Conscience of a Radical (1965)   275

31 The Making of a Radical (1972)   278

32   The Good Life Universal (1974)   282

Bibliography of Scott Nearing's Major Writings   286

Index   291

FOREWORD

SCOTT NEARING was an independent thinker and a man of integrity and dedicated purpose. This shows in the excerpts Steve Sherman has made from the samplings of his books. Scott was a man before his time and blazed trails, making the way easier for the rest of us. He took chances in opening up new avenues of thought and action. He did not achieve high office or attain world fame, but he made his mark by demonstrating that purpose and persistence in research and action bring results of lasting worth to mankind.

He also had his very warm and human side which deeply touched those who met and spoke with him. At his 100th birthday (and death day three weeks after) he received over 1,000 letters, cards, and wires from strangers as well as friends telling how much he had affected their lives by his writings, speeches, and gallant commitment to principles.

Here are two samples of the many outpourings of gratitude for the life he lived and the views he had shared. Scribbled on a postcard was this poetic message from our local mail carrier: "Scott will be remembered as a man who gave forth knowledge, a way of life and a new line of thinking. When the word is received that Nature has called another, we shall listen and pause, then go on our way, knowing full well that here was a man who altered and improved the direction of many."

Studs Terkel, of radio and writing fame, wrote Scott: "When I saw you last at Harborside we chopped wood together. I tried lifting the heavy wedge and couldn't make it. I thought: what a man! And by God, you are still chopping away at cant and hypocrisy and injustice. Scott, I salute you, one of my truly American heroes. There aren't too many, unfortunately."

My own memory of him is his unselfish service and kindness to anyone anywhere; his inherent humility; his rectitude and careful attention to detail, whether in his writing or speaking, or gardening or care of his tools. He was a righteous man, with humor and a twinkle in his eye.

Now that he is gone, the home we built together here (of stone, and in our seventies and nineties) is being kept up as a Good Life Center where people can come, read among his older and newer books, see his garden, his methods of work and construction which keep green his memory. If possible, the Good Life Center may even be kept going after I leave the scene, so that students and scholars can continue to study here.

Steve Sherman has done a splendid job of working through every one of Scott's fifty books, many of them now out of print and only available to interested readers through major libraries. He has extracted the important points, well illustrating the prophetic nature of Scott's ideas and the worth of his prognostications.

May readers gain light and understanding on the path of politics and world affairs and a glimpse of the good life universal. That is what he would have wished and what he gave his life to finding for himself.

Helen K. Nearing

CHRONOLOGY

1883	(August 6) Scott Nearing born in Morris Run, Pa.
1898	Nearing family moves from Morris Run to Philadelphia.
1901	Graduates from Central Manual Training High School in Philadelphia.
1901–02	Attends law school at the University of Pennsylvania.
1903	Enters Wharton School at the University of Pennsylvania. Teaches sociology to theological students at Temple College while an undergraduate at Wharton School.
1905	Receives Bachelor of Science in Economics from Wharton School and Bachelor of Oratory from Temple College.
1905–07	Secretary of the Pennsylvania Child Labor Committee.
1905–15	Spends summers and weekends at Arden, Del., a single-tax community based on Henry George's principles.
1906	Begins teaching at Wharton School.
1906–07	Instructor in Sociology at Temple.
1906–14	Instructor in Economics in the Wharton School.

1908   Marries Nellie Seeds.

1908–12   Instructor in Economics, Swarthmore College.

1909   Receives Doctor of Philosophy in Economics, Wharton
                School, University of Pennsylvania.

1912   Son John born. Robert adopted in 1914.

1912–15   Teaches at Philadelphia School for Social Work.

1913   First lectures at Rand School of Social Science.

1913–17   Lectures on social science in Chautauqua (N.Y.) sum-
                mer school.

1914–15   Assistant professor in economics, Wharton School.

1915   (June 16) Learns of his firing at the University of Penn-
                sylvania for his work against child labor.

1915–17   Professor of Social Science and Dean of the College of
                Arts and Sciences, University of Toledo.

1917   (April 17) Trustees of University of Toledo fire him for
                his work against U.S. participation in World War I.
                (April 29) Is accused of treason by Allan Stockdale in
                pulpit of the First Congregational Church in Toledo for
                speaking against World War I.

1917–22   Member of the Socialist Party.
                Becomes staff instructor at the Rand School of Social
                Science.

1917–37   Writes more than 30 books and pamphlets.

1918   Runs for Congress on Socialist Party ticket against
                Fiorello La Guardia in the Fourteenth Congressional Dis-
                trict on Lower East Side of New York City.
                Indicted by the Federal Grand Jury for writing *The Great
                Madness*.
                Establishes Federated Press, a news service, with Louis
                Lochner.

1919   (February 6–19) On trial for *The Great Madness* under
                the Espionage Act, and acquitted.

1920   First year speaking at the Community Church of Boston
                where he spoke every year for 50 years.

1925   Separates from Nellie Seeds.
                Visits the Soviet Union for the first of nine times.

1927   Joins the Communist Party.

1929   Meets Helen Knothe.

1930   Expelled from the Communist Party for publishing *The
                Twilight of Empire*.

1932   He and Helen buy farm at Jamaica, Vt.

1943–53   Writes the *World Events* newsletter, which merges with
                Monthly Review, an independent socialist magazine be-
                gun in 1949. First of a series of 200 "World Events"
                columns that ends June 1972.

1947   Nellie Seeds dies. His father Louis Nearing dies at 86.
                (His mother Minnie died in 1943 at age 78.)
                Marries Helen Knothe.

1951   Moves to a farm in Harborside, Maine.

1952   Incorporates the Social Science Institute.

1954   Publication of *Living the Good Life* (reprinted 1970).

1956   Federated Press syndicate discontinued after 37 years.

1957–   Continues world travel, including the Soviet Union,
            China, Cuba, Venezuela, Austria.

1973   Awarded honorary degree from University of Pennsyl-
            vania that had fired him in 1915.

1973–76   Works on new stone house.

1981   One of the "witnesses" in the film *Reds* about John Reed
            and the Russian Revolution of 1917.

1983   (August 23) Dies at Forest Farm in Harborside, Maine.
            His ashes are scattered on the land.

PREFACE

SCOTT NEARING wrote *Woman and Social Progress* in 1912 (when women were second-class citizens and could not vote); *Oil and the Germs of War* in 1923 (when the two were not connected in the public mind); *Black America* in 1929 (when "Negroes" had not yet used "black" so extensively); *Fascism* in 1933 (before Hitler stunned the world); *United World* in 1944 (before much was written or spoken of a world society). Some of the 50 books and scores of pamphlets that he wrote are prophetic; all address important issues of his time and the future. Over the years his sphere of interest enlarged from the community to the nation to the world, but as a crusading social scientist he never detoured from his central concern—improving the life of ordinary people toward, as he put it, the Good Life Universal.

A teacher above all else, Scott relied on educating the people so that they could make social changes for their own democratic benefit, not for the plutocrats that he deplored. He made his writing clear, direct, and accessible, believing not so much in "Live and let live" as "Live and help live."

An independent radical in the fullest sense, he was too self-sufficient for the corporate society, too imaginative and action-oriented for academic and university administrators, too strong-minded and free-wheeling for the Communist Party. He nurtured a ruggedness of spirit seeded early in life, the kind of sturdiness and grit that we associate with singular people. A man of adhesive intelligence and energy, at ease with strong words and bold actions, he did not merely scholasticize his ideas, he lived them. At times he was pedantic, but when speaking of social justice he did so from a platform of intense political action, of immersing himself in the fight against the injustices of his time—the cruelty of child labor, the hypocrisy of academic censorship, the carnage of world war, the imperialism of unleashed capitalism, the repression of women and blacks, the despoiling of natural resources. He traveled for first-hand research and knowledge to literally every state in the Union and to Mexico, Venezuela, Japan, Britain, Germany, Spain, France, Greece, the Philippines, India, to restricted China (three times), Russia (nine times), Cuba, and Albania.

While others wrote of the personal adventures of the celebrities of war and empire, Scott wrote of the price these chieftains inflicted on the common people. He decried the business of war, which he called "organized destruction and mass murder by civilized nations." His pacifism extended to fish and animals; he refused to war against any living creature. He enslaved no animals as pets or producers, used none of their waste products, and lived the integration of pacifism, socialism, and vegetarianism because he considered these inseparable, as did Tolstoy, one of his models.

Scott was a maverick in mind and spirit, and he led a life of vigorous defiance. His radicalism was anchored in an unbreachable persistence that put other individualists to shame. He was part of the vital cutting edge of society that keeps the country alive with energy for improvement.

These excerpts reveal this edge, which was sometimes ragged but always sharp. They are arranged chronologically with brief editorial comments to set them in historical perspective. None of his wording has been changed or placed out of sequence.

Helen Nearing has been extremely helpful to me in preparing this book. I thank her profusely. She allowed me access to her complete collection of Scott's books and papers, some of which are rare and treasured. Often we would sit in the sunny kitchen of Forest Farm and eat a lunch of her steaming vegetable soup and home-grown apples while we talked of the 55 years of her life committed to Scott and his ideas. She is an energetic and cheerful woman in her eighties with her own intellectual and spiritual allegiances. Her commitment to Scott remains as strong and enthusiastic as it must have been when she met him in 1928. ("Even more so," she says.)

SCOTT NEARING, 1883–1983:
A GOOD LIFE IN BAD TIMES

IN 1883, THE YEAR Scott Nearing was born, the United States was festering under an economic depression. Industrialists cut wages to keep profits, as manufacturers had done in the hard times of 1867 and 1873, and as they would in 1893 and 1907. The Industrial Revolution, abetted by the Civil War, gained such enthusiastic momentum that by the 1880s a fever for money had infected the nation. Renowned Baptist minister Russell Conwell rode the lecture circuit preaching "it's your duty to get rich." Collis Huntington of the Southern Pacific Railroad preached the bribery of legislators. Napoleon Hill in his book *The Law of Success* taught "the commercial value of the Ten Commandments." J. P. Morgan of the U.S. Steel Corporation, the first billion-dollar corporation in the world, pushed his principles to the forefront: "Get money—honestly if you can, but at any rate get money!"

The machine age transformed skilled craft into mindless repetition, and money belonged to Andrew Carnegie, John D. Rockefeller, Jay Gould, Philip Armour, the Morgans and Mellons and Marshall Fields. Field paid workers in his famous Chicago department store $12 for a 59-hour week while paying himself $600 every hour of the year. Families lived in New York slums with rents of $10 to $15 a month on incomes of $7.50–$8.00 a week while industrialists accumulated stockpiles of wealth so that, according to the census bureau, the richest 1 percent of the country owned more money than the total wealth of the remaining 99 percent.

The social status of money and the unleashed methods of acquiring it held sway. Gilded parties at Delmonico's and the Waldorf-Astoria in New York were more than isolated aberrations; they were blatant symptoms of the society as a whole. One Waldorf-Astoria affair cost $10,000

1

for forty guests, $250 for each guest, the six-month wages of an average worker. Defenders of the system proclaimed that in this burgeoning, free-enterprising nation any poor boy could become a rich man and that riches were the signs of success and opportunity. Detractors proclaimed that the extremes were new forms of slavery by which the wealthy owned the body and soul of workers, and that claims of opportunity were cynical false hopes to keep workers in line and working hard.

Child labor was woven into the social fabric. Girls and boys 10 and 12 years old spent entire days sweeping cotton from textile mill floors; young rural women were lured by fancy promises of exciting urban life and big-city wages, only to drudge from sunrise to sunset in deafening woolen mills. In Pennsylvania breaker boys, as they were called, spent 10 hours a day hunched over conveyor-belted trays separating slate from coal. They earned 60¢ a day. They learned nothing. They grew into deformed hunchbacks, their lungs caked with coal dust and disease, spirits corroded.

Scott's grandfather, Winfield Scott Nearing, supervised the Morris Run Coal Company in Morris Run, Pennsylvania, Scott's birthplace. It was a company town, and as head of the company Winfield Nearing supervised the town for 40 years. He broke strikes by evicting workers from their homes. He earned his reputation as a strong-arm despot and union-buster—"Tzar Nearing of Morris Run."

Scott's father Louis operated the company fruit and vegetable store. He brought Minnie Zabriskie from a comfortable banker's home in New Jersey to the wilds of coal-mining Pennsylvania, and they gave birth to Scott on August 6, 1883. Five other children followed. In Morris Run, Louis remained under the privileged shadow of WSN, as the Tzar was known, and earned his living only through the good graces of Winfield, his father.

Meanwhile, Winfield took a liking to Scott and for a time became the young boy's idol, passing on his drive and ambition. Scott had the run of the town ruled by Winfield, but he was warned that, being among the favored few, he should stay away from the miners and their children. These people were clearly of a different class. So Scott grew into manhood between the extremes of wealth and poverty, and it was this discrepancy seen up close that provoked his sense of social justice. In the few years to come, the admiration, respect, and affection that Tzar Winfield sought to instill in his favorite grandson turned sour. Instead of admiring the insensitivity of corporate power over common workers,

Scott grew to despise the arrogance and ruthlessness of wealth that his grandfather represented.

In 1898 when Scott was 15, the Nearing family moved to Philadelphia in order to be near good schools, although they returned to Morris Run every summer. Scott enrolled in Central Manual Training High School in Philadelphia because, he maintained, he wanted a more useful education, one that combined theory with practice. He made a deliberate decision to stay away from the more academic Central High School.

The Nearings lived close to Rev. Russell Conwell's home in Philadelphia. Across the nation Rev. Conwell was preaching the most popular religious speech of the era—"Acres of Diamonds," a defense of accumulating money. As a teenager in search of an institutional anchor for his values, Scott attended the preacher's Grace Baptist Temple and got to know the famous man. In no way did the idea to serve religion stem from his family—definitely not from his grandfather who was an agnostic, nor from his mother who showed more interest in Charles Dickens than St. Paul. Whatever the nourishment, the growth of Scott's tenacious sense of social morality turned out to be singular in his family.

By the time Scott entered the Wharton School of the University of Pennsylvania in 1903, he had known Rev. Conwell for nine years, joined his church, became assistant superintendent of the Baptist Temple Sunday School, and worked for support of Temple College and the University Samaritan Hospital. So involved in church activities was Scott that he appeared to be prime material for a religious career: He spoke to be heard, was conscious of uplifting his fellow men and women, and had joined the Christian Endeavor Society.

*   *   *

After high-school graduation in 1901, the following year Scott enrolled in law courses at the University of Pennsylvania, but disliked the curriculum. It was increasingly clear that anything having to do with the gathering of unseemly amounts of money, and defending it as lawyers were trained to do, nettled him. He switched to economics and sociology, and in 1903 Scott Nearing blossomed.

Physically, Scott inherited a lean face with dark intense eyes, a serious set of lips that matched his eyes, low-slung thin eyebrows, a well-formed patrician nose. He parted his brown hair on the right, kept it close-cut at his ears, and left a slight natural curl high above his left eye. Behind his smooth skin and school-posed propriety roiled an argumentative, dynamo worker, a young man bursting with energy, but which had yet to find its true release. He was strong-voiced, strong-willed, fluent and plucky, a life-hungry youth favored with good stock and lucky breeding. Early shyness and a stammer gradually faded as he grew older and trained his mind for public speaking.

Intellectually, he needed the right flint to spark him to fire. For two restless years he sat through the droning classes at the University of Pennsylvania, begrudging the sessions conducted by professors who, as a matter of principle, deflected the occasional, timid student questions. Teachers demanded that lectures be copied and tests passed, and that students stick to the texts.

Then Scott enrolled in an advanced economics course taught by Simon Patten. A half century later he recalled with gratitude the moment his intellect ignited: "I was in the presence of a thinker. Discussion was his meat and drink. Intellectual activity pleased and thrilled him." Scott saw a man who not only answered but encouraged questions, longed for student response, diverted from lecture schedules for spontaneous discussion, cast his store of ideas at students as if ideas were gold and he had too much; take them and use them.

It was a simple but monumental awakening. Through subsequent classes Patten transformed Scott, and ripened his decision to become a teacher. He flourished, and under Professor Patten's example and influence his moral strain emerged.

Scott became Patten's "fair-haired boy." He could work with hands and mind both, and when Patten continued to emphasize that theory should be linked to practice, this combination appealed to young Scott and heightened his ambition. The professor made ideas exciting, he made life exciting. He instilled a sense that individuals could make differences in the world, that they could arm themselves with the powers of the mind to change society, better it, lessen the burden of the poor, improve the common good. The slight deflection of society by an individual, he taught and Scott remembered, could change the direction of entire nations in the future, like a pencil tilted an inch above the horizon, creating a huge arc if a line were extended outward from it. Patten stoked up the 20-year-old, inquisitive, contentious, coal-mine villager, and for the rest of his life Scott Nearing plunged like a fearless firebrand into the world.

*   *   *

At age 22, Scott faced his first deep intellectual disillusionment, stunning him with as much bitterness and disappointment as another youth might have encountered meeting his first atheist. After establishing Temple College and the hospital, Rev. Conwell's projects received annual allocations of state legislature money. Meanwhile, Scott, a mettlesome junior in the Wharton School, made acquaintance with Fifth Ward bosses, took notes, and wrote a paper about the muddy politics of Philadelphia for Leo Rowe's political science class. He joined a local political campaign as an underling and learned up close about inside power politics that muckraker Lincoln Steffens wrote about in *The Shame of the Cities*. Franklin Spencer Edmonds, Scott's candidate for reform of graft-ridden Philadelphia, invited Rev. Conwell to join a Ministers' Committee as a show of support to clean up smudgy city politics; Conwell accepted. The following Sunday Scott, proud of the endorsement that Rev. Conwell gave, attended the reverend's service. Rev. Conwell took the pulpit and, in the stentorian delivery that made him famous, he said he was withdrawing his support. He described Philadelphia politics as the cleanest in the country, expounding that the city was upright and just. Reform was unnecessary and so was the election of Scott's candidate.

Scott walked out of the church. He realized that the political bosses, notorious Sam Maloney in particular, let the reverend know on which side his financial bread was buttered. Scott was well aware of Conwell's "Acres of Diamonds" sermon on acquiring wealth, but this rapacious turn of events hit too close to home. Scott never returned to the Grace Baptist Temple or any other church.

In three years Scott finished undergraduate work and continued headstrong into graduate study. During this time he taught sociology to theological students at Temple College for three years beginning in 1903. In 1904 he received a degree in oratory from Temple. At Swarthmore College he taught economics for four years beginning in 1908. His experience as an assistant instructor in elementary economics at the Wharton School for Business Administration from 1906 throughout his graduate years confirmed his decision to teach social science.

Meanwhile, Scott joined the single-tax community of Arden, Delaware, and built a small house there. The community was based on theories in Henry George's book *Poverty and Progress*, which advocated highly valued land to generate a large single tax for government services. Scott joined to be among other liberal and radical activists (Upton Sinclair was his neighbor) as well as to practice what he thought.

In 1908 he had married Nellie Seeds, a school friend who eventually earned a doctorate, worked with him on child labor and women's rights issues, co-authored *Woman and Social Progress* with him, and published some of his pamphlets. Scott and Nellie gave birth to John four years after they married and adopted Robert two years later. They spent their summers and weekends in Arden for 10 years.

In 1909 at 26 he received a doctorate in economics and became an instructor in the Wharton School. He assigned students investigative projects that involved real-life issues and urged them to go "into the field" to learn directly about working conditions, pay inequality, accidents, exploitation, resource waste. Just as Patten had activated fire in Scott, he instilled his own students with enthusiasm. Students crowded his classes. He carried on Patten's professional axioms: "The place of the teacher is on the firing line of progress," and "Be sure of your facts and then go ahead."

Soon Scott accepted invitations to teach at the Chautauqua Summer School, the New York School for Social Work, the Philadelphia School for Social Work. He was tireless, totally committed to the task of righting an unjust world. He wrote popular articles on education for the *Ladies' Home Journal,* pamphlets on the distribution of income, essays on social welfare in religious programs. But the overriding issue for him was child labor.

*   *   *

Scott's first full-fledged immersion in social reform began with an appointment as assistant secretary to the Pennsylvania Child Labor Committee in 1905, the year he decided to continue graduate study. When Scott replaced Helen Marot as full secretary of the committee, he charged into the volunteer assignment with characteristic vigor. While continuing graduate studies and teaching assignments, he traveled across Pennsylvania to lecture on the abuses of child labor. He described the breaker boys in the choking coal mines, girls in textile mills, boys spending entire sunless days sorting nuts and bolts in machine shops, girls carrying bottles all day in glasswork factories. During his vacations the crusade took him out of state to Chicago, St. Louis, and Richmond. He searched for any podium he could get and sometimes lectured twice on Sundays.

He worked on his own for years to expose the horrors of child labor. News reports of his efforts circulated around the state, causing the special interests of industry and politics to join forces. Slow, steady pressure mounted on manufacturers employing children, especially that of textile magnate Joseph Grundy, kingpin Republican in Pennsylvania.

Since the University of Pennsylvania was scheduled to receive increased state funds, Grundy applied pressure on the university administration to strap Scott's mouth shut. The warning did not take. Scott continued to speak out, defiantly giving 10 lectures in the following two weeks. By 1915 the Board of Trustees voted that, after nine years of teaching at the Wharton School, Scott's contract would not be renewed. A secretary read the curt letter dated June 16 over the telephone to Scott in Arden.

My dear Mr. Nearing:

As the term of your appointment as assistant professor of economics for 1914–15 is about to expire, I am directed by the trustees of the University of Pennsylvania to inform you that it will not be renewed. With best wishes, I am

Yours sincerely,

Edgar F. Smith

Scott was surprised only at the curtness of the dismissal, and the timing. He rushed back to the campus and informed a group of eight like-minded colleagues of his summary dismissal and they in turn informed others. By late afternoon Scott and the others had written, printed, and mailed 1,500 copies of an announcement of his dismissal to newspaper editors, key politicians, and university administrators. The story was picked up and made national headlines, thus blackening the name of the hitherto respected University of Pennsylvania. Cries of a breach of academic freedom were directed at the trustees. They were cited for being narrow-minded, autocratic know-nothings. The ripples of anger erupted into a tidal wave of protest that took the trustees by surprise. Part of the anger stemmed from the realization that, if such an abrupt dismissal could happen to Scott Nearing for speaking his mind, it could happen to other professors as well.

Overall, Scott received strong support. The Philadelphia *North American* headlined its front-page article: "Nearing's Dismissal Laid to Fight on Child Labor." The *New York Evening Post* said, "The University of Pennsylvania cannot suppress Nearing." The *Chicago Herald:* "Nearing's unforgivable sin is his talk about wages. He believes that labor ought to be paid enough to support life. That is pernicious." In the August issue of *Metropolitan* from New York, among other writings by Theodore Roosevelt, John Reed, Richard Harding Davis, and Walter

Lippmann, Managing Editor Carl Hovet wrote: "That a man of such clean life, of such attainments, of such courage, and with such an influence for good on the younger generation, should be thrown out of the employment of the university without a word of thanks for past services, without a word of explanation, just as if the Trustees had been dealing with a drunken janitor, is one of the most deplorable events in a deplorable year."

Scott and his defenders were fighting abuses in a time when stupendously wealthy industrialists and manufacturers adhered to the assertion that no economics professor ever proved that poverty was unnecessary. Phoney reasons were given for Scott's dismissal: Nearing taught in his bare feet; Nearing had said once young men and women should go to parties in bed clothes to save money; Nearing was by nature a disruptor of society, an enemy of the people, a contrary, vexing, annoying man; Nearing longed for headlines. Such accusations provided fodder for the trustees' vote. Yet the central reason for Scott's dismissal was far from his ineradicable attachment to the truth and the mettle and means of speaking it. The main reason was that he seemed to be making individually conspicuous progress in the battle against child labor. Were anti–child labor legislation to be passed and, worse for the proponents of child labor, were general public opinion and support against it to be set in motion, big-moneyed interests would face dwindling profits and employee unrest. Better to fire Scott Nearing and defeat him before he defeated them.

*   *   *

News of the Scott Nearing academic freedom case spread across the country. It continued to damage the reputation of the University of Pennsylvania, created vehement essays and editorials against the wholesale disposal of opposing viewpoints on campus, and aroused defenders of intellectual freedom who disagreed with Scott's basic politics. Lightner Witmer, a long-time professor at the university, was one who stood totally against Scott's ideas and methods, but he was so outraged by the action against his colleague that he researched the affair and wrote the book *The Nearing Case: The Limitation of Academic Freedom at the University of Pennsylvania by Act of the Board of Trustees June 14, 1915.*

Scott applied for teaching positions elsewhere, and in December 1915 he left with his family for the University of Toledo, Ohio, where he became professor of Social Science and Dean of the College of Arts and Sciences. His reputation preceded him; he was the kind who wrote letters to Billy Sunday, the Bible-thumping preacher, telling the evangelist to preach about poverty and unemployment, not that capitalism should come to God, which was Sunday's topic. Toledo University welcomed Scott, and he immersed himself in teaching, lecturing, and public forums.

In Scott's second year in Toledo, the seductive glories of the European war reached this country. Although Woodrow Wilson won the presidential reelection in November 1916 on the slogan "He kept us out of the war," Scott and others saw the signs of approaching U.S. involvement. In his characteristic no-truths-barred way, Scott spoke out against such involvement. He soon discovered that Allan Stockdale, the liberal clergyman of the First Congregational Church who had welcomed him to help with the forum lectures, turned about-face. From the pulpit on April 29, 1917, Stockdale accused Scott of treason for speaking against U.S. participation in World War I. After little more than a year, the trustees herded their forces together and fired Scott, this time, for his stand on the war. Once again the church that preached peace failed Scott, and again trustees of a university figured, mistakenly, that they could silence him by firing him.

Wherever he could Scott continued to denounce the war, including five debates with Paul Douglas of the University of Chicago. He joined the Socialist Party and became a permanent teacher of the Rand School of Social Science in New York. In 1918 he acted as chairman of a meeting in Madison Square Garden before a packed house of 13,000 people who had come to hear Socialists protest the war effort, while prowar hecklers and troublemakers agitated in the audience. In the same year, he ran for Congress on the Socialist Party ticket against Fiorello La Guardia in the Fourteenth Congressional District (Lower East Side, New York). He based his campaign on opposition to war and aspects of imperialism. He lost.

Then in 1917 he wrote a 44-page pamphlet titled "The Great Madness," a long essay against U.S. involvement in World War I. The *New York Call,* a Socialist newspaper, serialized it and 20,000 copies were printed and distributed. A Federal Grand Jury indicted Scott for writing the pamphlet and the Rand School for publishing it, charging under the Espionage Act insubordination, disloyalty, mutiny, and encouraging resistance to the draft.

For the trial February 6–19, 1919, Scott took the stand and, under long drawn-out questioning by both prosecution and defending lawyers, turned the trial into a forum for his ideas. The press gave the case wide coverage; Scott already had become well known as a committed pacifist and rousing debator. His testimony was printed each day of the trial. He considered the publicity a victory for the dissemination of his opposition to the war.

Scott was acquitted, the only radical of the times to have been dismissed from these and similar war-inspired charges. Other opponents of the war, such as Max Eastman and Rose Pastor Stokes of the "Masses" journal, leaders of the International Workers of the World (IWW), and Eugene Debs (who received a 10-year sentence) were convicted and sentenced to long prison terms. The Rand School was convicted of originally publishing the pamphlet and fined $3,000.

                    *   *   *

Scott was ostracized by the teaching profession, and Macmillan Publishing Company took his books off its list and refused to publish others. Typically, he refused to fold his tent and fade away. For the next dozen years Scott traveled and lectured. He was a tireless researcher and worker, totally committed to curing the ills of society. As a popular member of the lecture circuit, he shared the platform with philosopher Bertrand Russell, criminal defense lawyer Clarence Darrow, John Haynes Holmes, minister of Community Church of New York, Hamilton Fish, isolationist Republican congressman, and other luminaries of the day. The issues that he debated were hard-core: could the church be radical; did capitalism have more to offer than socialism; was the Soviet form of government applicable to the west; who would pay for the war.

Following the war years of 1914–18, he traveled to Britain, Spain, Italy, Germany, France, and in 1925 made his first trip to the Soviet Union. In Germany he saw early signs of fascism, returned to the United States, and wrote about it as the logical result of unfettered capitalism under a highly privileged class. Fascism to the masses, he wrote, meant continued life under a decaying social order, with chronic unemployment, reduced wages, and war—"Fascism is the way of death."

In Russia he saw the revamping of the educational system, and wrote a book about it. The development of new human energies as a result of the revolution there reinforced his hope that the plight of the common workers could be alleviated in countries where poverty and degradation divided the populations into distinct classes and left ordinary people in neglected and hopeless conditions. He numbered his own country among these.

In 1927 Scott joined the Communist Party (The Workers' Party, as it was known then) after much self-deliberation and (not incidentally) deliberation by the party itself. Scott was known as an independent-minded renegade, a radical in the public eye who brought attention—and notoriety—to himself and his causes. Nevertheless, the party used him to campaign in the United States for its candidates. Scott drove across the top of the country, down the Pacific Coast, and returned to the East by way of the South. His travels through the South verified his understanding of the vicious segregation and poverty there; he took hundreds of photographs and wrote *Black America,* which contained scores of these photos.

In the interim, a former student of his had gained authority in the Chinese government and in 1927 invited him to be economic consultant to the Chinese Railway Administration. Since he had separated from his wife Nellie two years earlier, and was free to go, he boarded a ship for China for what he anticipated to be a job of many years. He arrived in the midst of a national political split and revolutionary fever. His employment there was out of the question; Chiang Kai-shek's forces were killing any dissenters they could get their hands on. Scott left China and, at the request of the U.S. Communist Party, traveled by the Siberian Railroad to an international conference in Moscow.

Everywhere he went he collected material for his books. He wrote many during the 1920s and 1930s, including *Dollar Diplomacy* (1925), *Russia Turns East* (1926), *World Labor Unity* (1926), *The Economic Organization of the Soviet Union* (1927), and *Whither China?* (1927). In 1929 he wrote *The Twilight of Empire* and submitted it to International Publishers, the official publisher of the Communist Party U.S.A. for examination and acceptance. The manuscript was sent to Moscow where it was reviewed and rejected. Scott had written *The Twilight of Empire* as a history of imperialism and related it to modern days, tracing imperialism from earliest Roman times. The official party line took its text from Lenin's *Imperialism,* which referred to imperialism from 1870. Who was Scott Nearing to challenge Lenin? Scott protested that Lenin himself had said that during his exile in Switzerland where he wrote *Imperialism,* his resources limited him to 1870 onward. It did not matter. The party ordered Scott not to publish his book.

He faced the dilemma of having his book suppressed because of ideas and facts that he knew were perfectly acceptable and accurate, or of taking the manuscript elsewhere for publication. If he followed the latter course, he would be rejecting the party line, and the party demanded strict discipline. By profession and training, Scott considered his loyalty to any discoverable truth a higher priority. He decided to leave the party and go his own way. The party would have none of this. No one resigned from the party. It expelled him, and printed a long explanation in the January 8, 1930, *Daily Worker,* the party newspaper. The party said, in effect, that Scott was too independent and not subject to the disciplinary action required of social and political parties to make revolutionary changes.

As for Scott, his hesitancy about joining the Communist Party in the first place centered on the issue of intellectual disciplining, which to him implied intellectual compromise totally anathema to his background and life. Not the least of his personal convictions was pacifism and work to change society by rational persuasion, not violent power. Holding to any evolved party tenet of the violent overthrow of a government could never be strong enough when balanced by an overall commitment to peaceful change for improvement. At root he was a teacher who believed that the education of the people led the people to educate themselves for bettering their own society. By leaving the party he lacked the support of an organization, but he regained his freedom. In 1930 Vanguard Press published *The Twilight of Empire.*

In subsequent years Scott changed his opinion of the Communist Party in Russia, but only in private, not in print. Although he spoke against the choking Communist bureaucracy and dictatorial methods, in his books he wrote none of it in order not to flay the new hope and promise that other parts of Soviet Russia symbolized. This public blind spot of the murderous Stalinist "purge" trials in the 1930s cost Scott severe criticism. He justified this lack of public condemnation on his part by declaring his refusal to join the packs of capitalist intellectuals attacking the Soviet system through Stalin. He chose to emphasize the good that the system achieved for the workers and their education. It had taken Russia very few years to enter the modern world as a major power, he pointed out. The blockade by the Western powers to strangle the new Russia economically and politically had failed.

*　　　*　　　*

The Great Depression was eroding the economic and moral lifeblood of common people and turned Scott's attention toward the cause of this nightmare—the shocking imbalance of wealth and power. As he did, he foresaw the seeds of a second world war germinating in tandem with the general economic malaise. In 1931 he wrote *War*. Later he considered this his best offering and hoped it would be his most remembered book. It was subtitled *Organized Destruction and Mass Murder by Civilized Nations*. The word *civilized* connoted less irony than it did direct judgement, for as the years passed, Scott increasingly viewed civilization and its imperialistic traits with horror. The book takes a detached look at the plutocratic planning and business of war, and gives an acerbic analysis of this cancer of civilization.

At about this time he met Helen Knothe, a vivacious, attractive musician 20 years younger than he. She came from a well-to-do family in Ridgewood, New Jersey, and knew nothing (she acknowledged later) about politics and economics before meeting Scott. A life-long vegetarian, a prospective concert violinist, an adept of Eastern philosophies, she developed a strong intellectual outlook in her own right. She spent 1921–25 with Krishnamurti, a renowned Hindu spiritual leader, plus a few self-searching years in Australia before settling in with Scott, eventually marrying him in 1947. They made a curious pair—she imbued with a Pythagorian strain of mysticism and the arts, and he with an Aristotelian vein of rationalism and science. Their marriage lasted, however, for 53 years, until the day he died.

In 1931 Scott took Helen for her first visit to Russia; it was his fourth. They returned to New York, and lived in the poverty that the Depression continued to produce. So poor were they at one point that they had to burn Scott's pamphlets in their stove to heat the cold-water flat in the Lower East Side.

They decided that it was better to be poor in the country than in the city and searched for a rural locale. In 1932 the couple bought a farm near Jamaica, Vermont, for $300 down payment and an $800 mortgage. There they refurbished a dilapidated farmhouse, rejuvenated the garden soil, and eventually purchased adjoining land with productive sugar maples.

They spent what winters they could in traveling to Germany, Russia, Austria, and Spain. Then as Scott had predicted, World War II came to a head in Europe and Britain, and the United States entered the conflict. In 1944 Scott wrote *United World* and offered a blueprint for a federal world based on the governing structure of the United States. Local autonomy would be preserved while a federated system of nations maintained the peace on a planetary basis. He saw the trend toward world trade and banking, world communication, world travel, world law, world sports, world arts, world education, even a world language. The next step, he argued, was a global parliamentary government to balance the distribution of natural resources and agriculture in order to eliminate poverty. This in turn would remove the need for economic aggression and domination.

In subsequent books and pamphlets, he expanded this idea of a federated world, urging cooperation to replace competition, the natural social instinct of sharing to replace greed. From 1943–53 he wrote and distributed the newsletter/journal *World Events* before it merged with *Monthly Review*, a national independent socialist magazine begun in 1949. For this magazine Scott wrote a series of 200 monthly columns, again titled "World Events."

On August 6, 1945, Scott's 66th Birthday, President Harry Truman ordered the bombing of Hiroshima. The advent of atomic war became another reason that Scott turned his back on the U.S. government. He wrote to Truman, "Your government is no longer mine."

*   *   *

Meanwhile, he and Helen kept their Vermont country life highly productive by daily scheduling four hours for bread labor in their garden, four hours for individual intellectual pursuits, and four hours for service to the world community.

Scott and Helen worked the maple orchard so efficiently that it became a cash crop each spring. They produced maple syrup and maple sugar to supplement their meagre income. Soon they turned their expertise into coauthoring *The Maple Sugar Book* in 1950.

By this time magazine and newspaper articles brought hundreds of visitors to Forest Farm. Coupled with the development of nearby Stratton Mountain for skiing, the traffic of visitors overwhelmed the Nearings, disrupting the core of their chosen life. After 19 years in Vermont, they bought a 140-acre abandoned farm in Harborside, Maine, still another backwater of New England. They moved there in 1952.

The two of them had ten years of relative quiet until once again they were "discovered." During these years Helen and Scott coauthored *Living the Good Life,* a modest-selling book for a few years. With the dawning of the Back-to-the-Land movement, the 1954 book turned into an alternative lifestyle bestseller. This time thousands of visitors trekked to Forest Farm at Harborside to work with, talk with, and be in the presence of the Nearings. Helen and Scott found themselves the mentors of those disenchanted with the Vietnam war mentality of the administration, the materialism of society, the chemicalization of food, and the degradation of the natural world. The vegetarian, pacifist, socialist Nearings were prototypes for a younger generation, and once again Scott (throughout his seventies and eighties) was a teacher.

Living as he preached inspired young people in search of meaningful values. At the same time, Scott's tenacious hold on a particular view of life and how society should be developed became so single-minded at times that some of his personal relations suffered. He maintained that he regretted none of the major decisions of his life, and carried no chip on his shoulder, but in the end he wished he could have softened relations with his family. So neglected and angry was his son John Scott that for World War II he sold Liberty Bonds and announced that, unlike his pacifist father, he was a proud militarist. Later John legally removed "Nearing" from his name and went out of his way to criticize Scott publicly. His other son Robert was more gentle and private as a casualty of a controversial father, but still the distance remained. Robert ended up working in a bank, a business that represented the antithesis of Scott's life.

During these later decades Scott kept writing books and pamphlets, speaking and traveling. In 1972, at the request of friends and acquaintances, he wrote *The Making of a Radical,* his political autobiography. At age 90 he and Helen started to build a two-level stone house. And in 1976 they finished, continuing the good life there—gardening, researching, writing, and receiving thousands of visitors a year. In 1973, the University of Pennsylvania declared:

> In recognition of a singular career begun as a member of the Faculty of the Wharton School, and for adhering to the belief that to seek out and to teach the truth is life's highest aim, the Trustees have designated Scott Nearing honorary Emeritus Professor Economics.

This was the university that had fired him 58 years earlier.

In 1981 Scott appeared as one of the "witnesses" in the film *Reds* about John Reed, the American journalist who was in Moscow during the Russian Revolution. He had known and corresponded with Reed. In his tough, crusty way Scott was not going to let a movie crew tell him what to say. "Uh-uh. Don't fool yourself," he said on film, obviously in answer to questions about Reed's personal life. "No, sir. I'm not a purveyor of neighborhood gossip. That's not my job." Instead, Scott described Reed in words that could have described himself as well: "He stirred up trouble for the capitalists, and he also wanted to arouse the working masses to the necessity of some kind of effective united action."

At 99 Scott's body slowly wore out after a lifetime of hard physical and mental labor. On August 24, 1983, without pain or pills or hospitals, and three weeks after his 100th birthday, he breathed his last, quietly at home and ready to go.

1 THE SOLUTION OF THE CHILD LABOR PROBLEM (1911)

F ROM 1905–07 SCOTT NEARING worked as secretary of the Pennsylvania Child Labor Committee. With youthful vigor (he was 24 years old), he focused his energy on the plight of children working long hours in monotonous textile mills, stultifying mines, and back-breaking cotton fields. One example he used for this book was a factory man who was fired from his $2/day job and replaced by his own son at $1 for the same work. In 1910 (the year the Boy Scouts of America was founded) the U.S. Census reported child labor increased to 20 percent of those 10–15 years of age.

In his first book *Economics* (1908) coauthored with Frank Watson, a colleague at the University of Pennsylvania, the last line reads: "Knowledge creates zeal, and zeal will bring to pass the transformation that knowledge opens up." The words were addressed to students, for whom the text was written, but they may as well have been an epigram for Nearing himself. He coupled his work against child labor with a drive to publish his findings and conclusions for the general public. This combination aroused the wrath of authority, in this case trustees of the university. Some of these trustees came from the ranks of manufacturers and industrialists that Nearing criticized for employing children.

The solution to child labor, Nearing asserts here, lies not in excluding children from factories but in eliminating the financial necessity of families to send children to factories and mines. He also calls for improving a poor educational

17

system that offered no incentives for children to remain in school. He states his remedy directly: "The axe must be laid at the root of the tree," namely, the basic economics of American society.

On one mill hang two signboards:

SMALL GIRLS   SMALL BOYS
WANTED   WANTED

For years the signs have hung there, until they are old and worn, and meanwhile the manufacturer has secured and is still securing the merchandise which he desires. Every morning the children come trooping along the road and into the mill. Many of them answer well to the description of the sign. They are "small." While this mill is the exception, and while few advertisements for "Small girls" are seen, yet the low standard set by the "small girl" manufacturer must, in the competitive struggle, be accepted by other manufacturers; hence the "small" ones secure employment everywhere.

In 1900, of the 1,750,178 working children between ten and fifteen, 60.7% were in agriculture; 16.2% were in manufacturing and mechanical pursuits; 15.9% were in domestic service; 6.9% were in trade and transportation; and 0.2% were in professional service.

In animals, we respect this period of growth. What farmer is there who would hitch a colt to the plow and compel it to work ten hours a day? "Assuredly not," you exclaim, "that would be such folly." And why? Simply because the body of the colt is still plastic and unformed; as yet it is not prepared to meet the physical strain involved in plowing. The farmer has learned this fact traditionally and perhaps by experience; but he has learned it, and he respects the period of growth because lack of respect for it will almost inevitably mean money loss.

The child of fourteen years is still developing, with a body plastic and unformed like that of the colt. Yet such children are expected, as indicated by the laws of nine-tenths of the states, to work ten, eleven, and in some extreme cases, twelve hours a day in a factory, at tasks which prove as burdensome as is the galling plow collar to the colt.

Why such a sharp distinction between the treatment of a growing colt and of a growing child? Is the child better prepared to do the work? The body of the child of fourteen, like the body of the colt, is developing and rounding out, and that it is, therefore, as readily ruined in one case as in another. Why the contrast? It would seem that the money element is the chief consideration. In one respect the colt differs from the child,—it possesses cash value. It requires an outlay of money to replace a colt; a "wanted" sign will replace the child.

To grow in mind, the child must play. He must construct and evolve; at first houses of blocks; then whistles; then games; then school problems; and finally engines, and books, and theories, and truths. The child who sits for eleven hours a day and guides a piece of cloth as it rushes past him on the machine, neither constructs nor evolves; his mind sleeps—and too often it is the sleep of intellectual death.

Play is to the child what poetry is to the man. Deprive either of this essential element, and from the misdirected sowing is reaped a harvest of misdirected lives. Instill into a boy's mind learning which he sees and feels not to have the highest worth, and which cannot become a part of his active life and increase it, and his freshness, spontaneity, and the fountains of his play slowly run dry. Such is the fate of the average child who spends his play time feeding with hand and body the modern industrial mill. Premature work and premature decay of moral fiber are kindred forces running hand in hand toward the almshouse.

In the social fiber, in family life, in taxes, child labor is costly. It breaks down the individual, it destroys the family life of the present, and threatens the family life of the future, and last, probably least in importance, it adds to the number of incompetent that the community must support. From any social viewpoint, child labor is costly.

What are the causes of modern child labor? (1) industrial evolution; (2) greed; (3) necessity; (4) ignorance and indifference.

The meanest, hardest, cheapest employer sets the pace. One such can force nineteen others to provide for their employees the most rigorous of working conditions, or fall behind in the race for business.

It is to protect the children from this class of employers that child labor laws are enacted. They are men hungering after profits,—and when they take them in the form of children, the community balances the account. But competition is disappearing from industry, and is being replaced by combination. Moreover, manufacturers are coming to see, more and more, the undesirability and the unprofitableness of child labor. Child labor has ceased to be an industrial benefit and has become instead an industrial detriment. And the thinking manufacturer recognizes this fact. But even granting for the sake of argument that the average employer is a profit-hungry, child-grabbing ogre, it would be impossible for the children to get into the mills unless they were willing to go, or unless their parents were willing to send them. The manufacturer may provide the means for child labor, but he cannot secure the children without their consent, or that of their parents.

The statements which are constantly made, laying the entire blame for child labor upon the manufacturer, are, therefore, unfounded and unfair. The employer may, as in the case of industrial evolution, make child labor possible, but he does not actively cause it.

There is still another factor—the greedy public. "Give us dividends," cry the stockholders, "give us dividends, and big ones!" and the president of the company, with his salary at stake, turns in the children. "Give us bargains," cry the consumers, "give us bargains, and cheap ones," and the retailer, his business at stake, turns to the sweat shop and child labor.

A demand for cheap finery, for bargains, for cheap goods of all kinds, is a demand on the sweat shop and on child labor. Child labor goods are cheap goods. The South has found this true to her cost. It requires skill to produce quality as much as it ever did before the invention of the machinery which is doing the heavy and mechanical work of the world.

But the public, by its insatiable demand for cheapness, furnishes the manufacturer with the incentive for cheap production. He, in turn, advertises for child labor. One factor is the complement of the other.

An investigation made in 1903 by the United States Department of Labor covered 25,440 families, among which the average total income was $749.50.

The discrepancy between the minimum physical efficiency standard, $900, and the wages actually received, is startling.

Here, then, is a real cause of child labor. It is clearly a social and economic one; social in so far as society is responsible for maintaining its children—economic in so far as the smallness of the income of a definite group in the community does not enable the man to provide adequately for the needs of his family. In no sense is it an individual cause.

The second important cause of child labor to which allusion has been made is the desire of the child to go to work. The average child has two alternatives—work and school. Few children choose the school. A little questioning of school children will show that most of them—particularly the boys,—detest school and long for work. The causes of child labor are primarily economic and social.

Two other factors enter prominently as causes of child labor. They are the moving causes that are actively operating to send children to work. First, the wages of the average workman are so low as to preclude the possibility of his bringing up a family without some outside aid. This is often secured by sending the children to work. Second, the school system with its ancient curriculum, rigorous discipline, and low-paid, inexperienced teachers, is heartily detested by the average boy, and probably by the average girl, who take the first opportunity to escape from its monotony and confinement to the freedom of work.

Briefly summarized, the facts are these: The manufacturer does not need the child. The work of the children can be done with equal if not greater cheapness and efficiency by mechanical devices or by adults. The child does need a school training that will fit him to participate efficiently in some form of life activity. A great number of parents need the earnings of their children. They would not starve to death without them, but they would be deprived of a part of the food and shelter necessary to maintain bodily vigor. Society needs the child, developed eventually into an efficient worker, a good citizen, and a thinking, social being.

How can this desired end be attained? What steps are necessary? (1) To insure proper training of children for life and work; (2) to give to society thinking, efficient, social men and women; (3) to keep families above the line of malnutrition; (4) to prevent the premature employment of children.

This problem has been extensively dealt with abroad, where three methods have been devised which, directly or indirectly, assist in the maintenance of family standards: (1) the minimum wage; (2) compulsory insurance; (3) school feeding.

For national defense two schools are provided, one at Annapolis and one at West Point. In these schools, food, clothing, and the most painstaking training are provided for the boys who are expected to become the military defenders of the nation. It is seldom that the nation is compelled to resort to the military in order to maintain itself, but every moment of every day the nation is absolutely dependent upon industry for that maintenance.

Is it a necessary thing to give food, clothing, and training to the military defenders of the nation? How much more imperative that the necessaries of life should be provided for its industrial defenders. The military struggle is an occasional one, but the industrial struggle is a constant one, and far more depends upon it than upon military events.

The foregoing discussion makes the Programme for Child Labor Reform almost obvious. The programme revolves around three steps:

1. The guarantee, by the public authorities, of a minimum standard of living that will provide for all children a quantity of food, clothing, and shelter sufficient to enable them to develop into efficient members of the community.

2. A reform in the school that will:
   (a) Make a child want the school.
   (b) Develop efficient citizens.
3. The passage of legislation requiring school attendance and pro-
   hibiting factory work.

It is only when the child has been physically and intellectually provided for, in the manner indicated, that any permanent good can be
done by the modern child labor legislation which merely forces children
out of the factories.

2 SOCIAL ADJUSTMENT (1911)

TOWARD THE END of this book, Nearing proposes that education is a critical antidote for poverty and family misery, that if ordinary hard-working men and women understand basic sanitation, nutrition, and normal rising living standards of other Americans, they will have a frame of reference to act for improvement. Always the teacher, Nearing urges knowledge; always the activist, he incites action for improvement. He quotes his beloved teacher Simon Patten as saying that heavy ineffectual tomes on economics for intercampus reading should be dismissed in favor of generating widespread public opinion through newspaper and magazine articles.

Nearing wrote articles and lectured extensively. He also produced one book a year for six years beginning in 1911. The subjects dealt mostly with the income of workers and how wages seldom kept up with the cost of living. He had received his doctorate in economics in 1909 and, among other reasons, was assuring himself that he would not perish if he did not at least publish.

This year of *Social Adjustment* was also the year of revolution in China and the fall of the Manchu dynasty, the introduction of the National Health Insurance Bill in England, and the dissolution of the Standard Oil Company by the U.S. Supreme Court. Changes were occurring throughout the world, and Nearing, ever conscious of the grand scale, saw the changes as beneficial to workers who provided the wealth for the corporate owners.

There are three popular beliefs which rise like mountain chains across the trail of progress. The first is the belief that things are sacred because they are old, or, conversely, that things are dangerous because they are new. The second is the belief that the submerged class wants to be submerged; that it enjoys dark rooms and revels in filthy alleys; that it gloats over insanitary plumbing and thrives upon malnutrition. The third, no less preposterous, is the belief that the submerged class is poverty-stricken because it is degenerate; that those who wish can rise; and that the fact of their remaining submerged is proof conclusive that they are innately incapable of improvement.

This book marks, I hope, one step in the advance of scientific truth that is being directed against these mountain chains of misbelief. In the course of the work I have attempted to make seven points:

1. That maladjustment exists in numerous virulent forms, in many parts of the United States.
2. That maladjustment is (1) due to economic causes, (2) involving social cost, and (3) remediable through social action.
3. That maladjustment can be, and in many instances is being, eliminated by efficient education plus wise remedial legislation.
4. That the vast majority of children are born normal and are made abnormal, degenerate, and diseased by their defective environment.
5. That recent investigations demonstrate conclusively that the proportion of genius, mediocrity, and defect does not vary materially from one social class to another, and hence all are capable of the same uplift.
6. That progress is impossible so long as society maintains the fatalistic viewpoint which condemns men because of the sins of the fathers and is blind to the transgressions of the brothers.
7. And finally, that it is through the promulgation of the new view of the universality of human capacity, the remediability of maladjustment, and the advantages of universalized opportunity, that maladjustment will eventually be eliminated and adjustment secured.

Social adjustment is in any age an approximation to the normal; but with invention and progress, education and evolution, the potentiality of each age is one step in advance of the normal of the past age. As possibilities increase the normal standard of society moves forward. Each age must, to complete its adjustment, realize all of these possibilities, and when the normal possibilities of any age are realized, its adjustment is complete.

Under the old, hopeless view of the human race, some men were depraved, sinful, wicked; others were shiftless, lazy, inefficient, and poor. These conditions were regarded as natural—as the results of God's efforts to purge the human race; men were being rewarded according to their deserts. If they were sick and poor, it was because they deserved it; if they were shiftless, it was because they were worthless; and if they were vicious, it was because they were naturally depraved.

The development of modern thought has created an essentially different attitude. Men were formerly regarded as naturally inefficient or vicious or lazy. Modern discoveries have clearly demonstrated the fallacy of this view, by showing that energy, efficiency, and adjustment are normal, while laziness, inefficiency, and maladjustment are subnormal.

A man must be hungry to know what hunger really means, and he must have lived on a starvation wage to understand fully what a starvation wage implies; yet the wages of Perth Amboy and Pittsburg, the hungry school children of Chicago, express in some measure the social cost implied in low wages and standards. These conditions constitute a portion of our national life, and their elimination becomes a part of the duty of every citizen.

A group of men and women, ignorant of American standards, accept wages far below the level of family efficiency, and by so doing, establish a basis to which the wages of all labor must approximate. In so far as immigration is synonymous with ignorance, it is responsible for the reduction in life standards,—it is a prime cause in creating low wages. On the other hand, the exigencies of competitive industries, coupled with the cupidity, ignorance, or indifference of employers, are an equally effective force in lowering wages. These two groups of causes, sometimes working independently, sometimes in conjunction, are responsible for the low wages and standards which are continually resulting in social cost.

The cause of low wages and standards being, therefore, economic, and the effects being measured in terms of social cost, what remedies will be efficacious in raising the minimum standard of wages to a standard of efficiency and thus removing social cost? The remedies for low wages and standards group themselves under five heads: 1. labor unions; 2. small families; 3. minimum wage laws; 4. restriction of immigration; 5. education.

Labor unions perform their chief function as educators of the low standard workmen. The immigrant who reaches America has no other agency from which he may derive a knowledge of American customs and standards. In so far as it is successful in the educational effort, the union stands as a strong bulwark between the standard of American labor and that of the immigrants.

Mere congestion per acre does not present a serious problem,—it is the evils which accompany acre congestion that make the social reformer hesitate and ponder. Men and women in the New York tenements suffer, not because they are living close to their neighbors, but because the tenements are so constructed as to exclude from large numbers of rooms any adequate air supply, and to prevent the entrance of sunlight into many corners of the building. To one who has seen a seven-story East Side tenement, it is perfectly obvious that the sunlight cannot penetrate below the fifth or fourth story through the narrow air shafts and courts which the law requires. Overcrowding per acre is therefore a serious problem in New York, and a less serious one, but still a problem, in many of the large cities of the United States.

The other form of congestion, overcrowding per room, is a problem which exists in practically every industrial section of the country, whether it be rural or urban in character. Not only do the Italians and Jews sleep five or six or seven to a room on the New York East Side, but the Slavs and Huns in the small industrial towns scattered through the East live under equally congested conditions. It is true not only that the amount of air space reserved per inmate in these New York tenement rooms is far below 400 cubic feet, the minimum necessary to maintain physical efficiency, but that similar conditions prevail in all of the cities or towns which have an immigrant or pauper population.

The instances of overcrowding, discovered in Pittsburg and surrounding towns, are startling in their intensity. These Pittsburg tenement rooms were small,—as large as a small bedroom,—yet a man, his wife, and baby and two boarders lived in one room. Another apartment of three rooms contained a man, wife, and baby in the kitchen, two boarders in the second room, and the third room was sublet to a man, his wife, and child and two boarders. In this last room, "a small one," there were two beds, a stove, table, trunks, and chairs.

These conditions of overcrowding in private houses were only surpassed by the overcrowding among the single men in the Slavic lodging houses. Beds stood as close as the floor space would permit, men sleeping on the floor, two shifts using the same bed, one shift by day and another by night.

The overcrowding among the steel workers of Pittsburg is paralleled by the congestion in New York construction camps, a description of which appeared in the *Survey* for January 1, 1910. Bunks are built in tiers, and men are huddled together in unventilated or ill-ventilated buildings, without sanitary conveniences, or even sanitary necessities.

Either congestion per acre or congestion per room, or both of them, constitute a maladjustment of the first importance,—providing it can be shown, first, that the causes of congestion are economic; second, that it results in social cost; and third, that adjustment may be secured through some form of social action.

It is often stated that people stay in the tenements because they wish to; that they live several persons to a room because it conforms to their idea of living; and that they would not leave either condition were an opportunity afforded. This is in many cases true. The inertia due to underfeeding and ignorance are serious barriers to any reform which has for its purpose the elimination of congestion.

Acre congestion would not be seriously affected by education, but a proper standard of education could establish a personal standard of decency that would not tolerate the conditions of modern room congestion, and would not accept wages which led to such conditions.

Congestion is a problem presenting itself to every industrial group in the United States. It is caused by factors which are clearly economic. Its effects are social cost and its remedies are apparent. It therefore constitutes a maladjustment to which public attention must be directed, and against which public opinion must be aroused to the enactment of legislation, which will result in the amelioration of the conditions surrounding acre congestion, and in the elimination of room congestion through restriction of immigration, and through an education that will lead to a higher standard of work and life.

The large family in 1910 is a menace because each additional child in a wage earner's family lowers the family standard, and renders it less probable that the members of the family will elude the clutches of poverty. In 1903 the United States Commissioner of Labor reported on 11,156 families of workingmen. In the families with one child, the average income per person was $212.76; in the families with three children, the average was $133.18; while in the families with five children, the average income per person was $94.97. In the average workman's family, each additional child means additional hardship.

The state must assert its authority through legislation, but it must also exercise its influence through education. If certain things, such as phosphorus matches, necessarily involve sickness or death in their manufacture, the public should substitute another product (in this case safety matches) and should refuse to take goods which involve human sacrifice. The worker, in every trade, should be intelligent enough to use wisely the safety appliances provided, while the employer should recognize his social duty and reduce to the veriest minimum the loss of health and life incident to dangerous occupations.

Dangerous trades have received little attention in the United States. The public recognizes certain trades as dangerous, but the extent of the danger, the numbers of workers involved, and the cost to society in decreased vitality are not definitely established. One fact alone has been proved beyond dispute,—the mortality in some trades is far higher than the mortality in other trades, and the excess of mortality in the first group is due to the inherent danger of the trade under consideration.

How severe is the danger involved in the dangerous trades? The marble and stone cutters, the tobacco workers, and the cutlers and grinders show a very high degree of mortality, but what is their length of life? When do these workers die? What opportunity do they have to realize their full potentiality? No general answer can be given to these questions. If a definite answer were possible, the public might the sooner demand remedial legislation.

It is a known fact that lead poisoning affects young female workers more seriously than any other group, and it may well be that there are other industries, a careful analysis of which would reveal like results. For the present it is possible to say only that the industrial mortality is three times as high in one trade as in another, and that those trades in which the death rate is highest present an unparalleled example of social cost.

The victim of a dangerous trade loses in part or in whole the ability to gain a livelihood; those dependent upon him must go elsewhere for support; and society loses the working capacity so vitally necessary for its maintenance and perpetuation.

Dangerous trades are the outcome of economic causes; they result in social cost, and remedies, proved and found successful elsewhere, are at hand. It remains only for the public to demand and secure these remedies in the form of effective legislation, in order that this maladjustment be permanently eliminated.

There is one effective way to remedy the conditions which permit of accidents, and that is to make accidents very expensive. The employer does not at present bear the weight of industrial accidents,—he is in all probability insured in a liability company which fights his accident suits for him.

The employer is largely exempt from liability, and he permits the continuance of conditions which create accidents. If each accident incapacitating or killing a man cost the employer $10,000, there would be fewer accidents. It is because accidents are so cheap that they are so numerous.

The investigation conducted by the Pittsburg Survey showed conclusively that the injuring and killing of men is a cheap affair,—involving little real expense to the employer. So long as it is cheaper to have accidents than to provide safety devices and exercise ordinary care, accidents may be expected.

If accidents were expensive,—really expensive,—there are certain things which every employer would do. He would adopt all available safety devices and safety appliances, such as guards on exposed gear wheels and knives and on belting and shafting. The mine manager would see to it that props were not lacking, that rock did not fall, and that lamps were covered and blasts properly fired. In every direction such steps would be taken as are enumerated in the average factory and mine law.

The author who is to be effective must stop writing treatises and state popularly a few plain simple truths. In his presidential address before the American Economic Association in 1908, Dr. Patten makes this point clearly and emphatically. "A three hundred page thesis not only does not fit a man to be an economist; it really incapacitates him for work." On the positive side Dr. Patten says: "He [the economist] should cultivate visual expression by using charts and diagrams and arouse the imagination by striking phrases and vivid contrasts. His vehicle should be the newspaper and the magazine, not the scientific journal. The public want what we have, and if we have something it does not want it is not worth having. To be scientific is to be popular. There is no renown worth having but that of the newspaper and the magazine and the class room. . . . The place of the economist is on the firing line of civilization; his product must be clear, concise, and impersonal, instead of being submerged in bulky volumes and formal treatises. Our real affinity is with the journalist, the magazine writer, and the dramatist, and not with writers who, separated by time and space from what they describe, function as critics of persons and events instead of being actors in the momentous struggles of the present."

This truth applies, not to economics alone, but to all the social sciences as well. Popular attention can be called to maladjustment and the desirability of eliminating it in only one way,—by placing before the public in a striking, unanswerable way the facts of human capacity and the possibilities of social adjustment.

Journalism can well be made the vehicle of great educational influence. It can be so used, however, only by men of ability who are familiar with modern economic and social facts and who will state them clearly and decisively.

Journalism and authorship are the two tools upon which every movement must rely for the education which alone can firmly establish its contentions. The facts of investigation and the theories of reform alike depend upon clear, definite statements for any public influence they may have.

All of the maladjustments thus far analyzed are the result of ignorance regarding personal standards, a failure to intelligently perform parental duties, or a lack of an intelligent feeling of social responsibility. A uniform, inefficient form of education is accepted because the community is not intelligent on the school problem; low wages are paid because the employer does not recognize his social responsibility for the payment of living wages; congestion exists because families are willing to live under insanitary and unhygienic surroundings, and because of land speculation and an ignorance of the elements of city planning; women are dependent because of the failure of parents to train their daughters for independence; parents have children, with no thought of the means which are to be used for their support; and accident, disease, malnutrition, ignorance, and inefficiency shorten life, and create misery, vice, and poverty.

There is scarcely a first-hand student of maladjustment who does not cry out in astonishment that a society which professes civilization should tolerate the conditions which exist in the United States to-day. The conditions exist because the society is ignorant. An enlightened society would eliminate maladjustment as an enlightened housekeeper eliminates dirt. Maladjustment is the dirt of the social household, and from it are bred the disease, misery, poverty, and wretchedness from which society suffers.

The most difficult problem confronting the schools is the teaching of a sense of social responsibility. Children should be taught that normal men and women are good, and that badness is merely an indication of abnormality. They should be shown the necessity for maintaining wages, standards, and modes of life. The schools have thus far been content with the teaching of individual morality, but it now devolves upon them to instruct in social morality. It is antisocial to pay low wages, and the school children should know it; it is antisocial to maintain unhygienic living conditions in the houses which you own, and the children should be told so; the working life should be long and joyous, and the schools should make this fact a part of consciousness of every child. In this way can the school fulfill its duty. In this way can it develop a full sense of the responsibility which every man must feel for his fellows in society.

3 WOMAN AND SOCIAL PROGRESS (1912)

N EARING WROTE THIS BOOK with his first wife Nellie
Seeds, a studious young graduate of Bryn Mawr College and a coworker against child labor. Undoubtedly, she provided valuable perspective in this comprehensive and early book on women's rightful place in society.

In typical Nearing way, the book places the subject in historical context before explaining the progress of women's rights and offering detailed prescriptions for improvement. After analyzing male and social dominance of women, the Nearings write about opportunities for women in industry, education, and social service. They end the book on the importance for women of securing the most education possible in order to develop an individual's full potential and to put this potential to use.

The book appeared when the legacy of the Victorian woman lingered in America. Although the Victorian woman may have reigned in the home, her influence in politics to affect widespread societal changes held little sway, and the timetable for securing this power stretched through the decades. The first women's rights convention was held at Seneca Falls, New York, in 1848. Sixty-four years later at the publication of this book, women still had no right to vote in the United States. This was the year in which 25,000 textile workers of the American Woolen Company in Lawrence, Massachusetts, went on a daring, dangerous strike that ended in violence against parents and children leaving town for food and other supplies. Three months passed

31

before the company agreed, through national hostility at the situation, to a minimal wage increase.

At this time, the country was still in formation (New Mexico and Arizona became states this year), and the Nineteenth Amendment to the Constitution granting women the right to vote was eight years away from ratification.

The editors of a great encyclopedia inserted in their first edition, which appeared in the latter part of the eighteenth century, this definition of Woman: "Woman, the Female of man. See Man." Her attributes, capabilities, and powers were included in his—she was not an individual, but an attachment to an individual. For information about woman, there was but one source—man—"the fountain-head of all her being." In subscribing this heading the editors were interpreting the general thought of the age.

Men and women are different. Certain characteristics are more strongly marked in men than in women; certain others are more strongly marked in women than in men; but concepts of "better" or "worse," "superior" or "inferior" are, as Havelock Ellis puts it, "absolutely futile and foolish." Hence they have no place in our discussion.

In this discussion of Woman and Social Progress, we are not at all concerned with the relation of woman's capacity to man's, but with the relation of her capacity to her opportunities and to her achievement.

"Women have taken little part in the history of the race," you protest. True they have not even written about it. If they had, history might read differently. History, as written, is a record of masculine achievement,—wars, battles, intrigues and dynasties constitute the great bulk of historic data. In these, it is true, the women played little part.

Neither have women made literature, nor painted, nor carved, nor discovered, nor invented. But was opportunity open to them? What has been the position of women during the last ten centuries?

With but few exceptions, since the dawn of human intellect, women have apparently been in subjection—physically, politically and socially. Some boys were born into a world of achievement, but all girls were born into a world of subjection. From their cradles they were taught their subject position—taught in terms that permitted of no gainsaying. Women must obey; must conform; must follow the precepts laid down by men.

Is it true that men have broader mental reach, and that they think more fully? We can arrive at a tentative conclusion by analyzing history. Yet historical analysis is necessarily inconclusive because, while our basis of judgment in history is achievement, women have been denied, throughout historic epochs, any opportunity which might lead them to achieve.

Women's failure to achieve in the past is no more argument against her achievement in the future, than the failure of men to fly in the nineteenth century is an argument against their success in the twentieth century. Precedent can never effectually bind the future either of man or of woman.

The nineteenth century was barely aware of woman's capacity: the twentieth century is sure of it. The nineteenth century did not ever expect women to achieve, but the twentieth century is already pointing out the line of her progress.

Capacity for achievement, then, has finally been conceded to women. But achievement requires more than capacity. Opportunity is also essential. Therefore, since the achievement of the future depends in part upon the opportunities of today, it is pertinent to ask first what is the character of the environment surrounding the twentieth-century American woman; and second, what opportunities are afforded for converting her capacities into a form of achievement that will make for Social Progress.

Perhaps the most curious tradition by which women are bound,—curious, because it is the most insistent,—is that concerning women's occupation and sphere. How often do we hear the self-satisfied man declare that the place of woman is in the home. Women have, from time immemorial, been forced to occupy themselves exclusively as housekeeper, wife and mother. If the individual is so unfortunate as to be unable to become a mother, she must content herself as the housekeeper, for the term wife itself implies no stated occupation.

Masculine dominance was so vigorous an offspring of the age of conflict that it still persists in spite of the obviously complete change in the test of social survival. It is no longer the biggest or strongest, he who can use his hands and arms most effectively, who survives. Man has thrown off the dominance of brute strength, and mental, not physical power is the test of survival today. The accumulated civilization of the ages has advanced far beyond the dreams of our remotest ancestors, but like a child with an outgrown toy, we still cling to the sex dominance of the days of primitive culture.

Not only is masculine dominance physical—it has likewise become moral and social and political. In his moral ascendancy, man has been most clever in his method of maintaining his control. He first insists that woman is innately better than man, but requires of her only the virtues which he does not desire for himself, and limits her to the immoralities of which he does not greatly disapprove. By man's continual insistence upon honor as the great virtue of woman, he has led her to place an artificial value upon it, and to sacrifice all other virtues to this one, a virtue which strangely enough may be possessed only in a negative sense. Cicely Hamilton's adage of the thief is an apt one. Woman may keep her honor only so long as chance is kind enough not to throw in her way a man so brutal as to deprive her of it. But when once deprived of it she may not cry out her theft upon the housetops and demand the pursuit of the thief. Her lack of strength to resist the theft is deemed a disgrace, to be hidden if possible and greeted with contempt when revealed. The thief, on the other hand, rejoicing in his superior strength is rather admired by the world, and pursues his way, untouched. In France, a law still survives from the Napoleonic code forbidding *"qu'on cherche le père."* One could hardly conceive a more desirable code of ethics from the man's point of view.

Even in marriage a double standard of morality still prevails for the sexes. Framed by men alone, the laws indicate most clearly their intention to subjugate the female by restricting her sexual freedom while leaving that of the male practically unlimited.

But while the honor of the individual woman is required to be unquestionable, and that of men is almost unquestioned, the violation of the honor of a group of women whose number is legion, is not only sanctioned but rendered a perpetual institution in this society which men have evolved. In order to justify the existence of prostitution, men have at various times invented the one-time plausible excuse of "physical necessity" and have even been upheld by prominent medical men in their insistence upon this opportunist plea. They have, moreover, so applied the doctrine of innate immorality to their unfortunate victims, as to prevent, until very recently, any pity among the more protected women for their fallen sisters.

Professing to have the highest respect for the so-called "superior" sex, men have never ceased, since they first began taking over industry from the home to the factory, to thus limit the sphere of women. Carefully selecting all the qualities which they deemed undesirable for themselves,—purity, constancy, devotion, reserve, self-sacrifice, sweetness, gentleness, jealousy, cowardice,—men have abandoned them to the so-called weaker sex. "Woman once the superior, now the equal of man" is a common phrase in the mouths of those who thus try to suppress the efforts of a few women to assume the qualities which men desire to reserve for themselves.

Men, from time immemorial have been allowed to choose their trade or occupation. Even the members of the proletariat may at least choose the method by which they shall be exploited,—the manner in which they shall labor for their subsistence. But women, excluded from the field of industry, often barred by custom and law from even possessing property, have had but one choice. If the individual woman could succeed in so arousing and fulfilling the desires of the male as to induce him to share his property and earnings with her, she might by a simple process of exchange, yield up her person for the means of existence. Any variation from this rule in past generations met not only with the disapprobation of the world but even with persecution and punishment. Witch-burning, commonly thought of as a relic of barbarism, was in the last analysis merely the penalty paid by women who deviated from the type of colorless wife and mother of which men approved at that time. It was not only the hag, the decrepit and the infirm who fell victims to this barbarity, it was the woman who evinced any kind of peculiarity, whether unusual beauty, mental power or the genius of Joan d'Arc.

Is it strange, then, that women are eager to marry—that, after all other trades have been forbidden them, they cling to marriage as a first and last resort,—their only hope of social salvation? Is it surprising that they learn to point the finger of scorn at the unmarried women? Far be it from anyone to cast reflection upon the bachelor!

The remedy lies in woman's own hands. There is no inherent reason why marriage should not be merely an incident in her life as it is in the life of the man,—no reason why she should not adopt a profession and follow it through life,—with the possible interruption of a few years, if she becomes a mother,—just as a man pursues his trade. True, she will have to combat the old-time tradition that women who do any work outside their homes must inevitably neglect them. But may not the home of the woman who works be the new kind of home—that based upon ideals and common interests rather than upon material drudgery? A few women have proved that it can be done. Such women as the noted singer Madame Gadski tell us that marriage and motherhood need not be a hindrance, but may rather be an inspiration to professional or industrial work. This need prevent no women who delight in domestic science from adopting that as their occupation, but it will no longer put before women as a class the equivalent of Hobson's choice—Marriage as a trade.

The effect of a college education on marriage (not motherhood) is an interesting one, and almost universally misunderstood. Statistics are usually quoted to prove that college girls do not marry; that the marriage rate among them is decreasing, and that the marriage rate of college women is less than that of non-college women. The available data do not justify any of these conclusions, but indicate that college has little or no effect on the marriage rate. Even if the assertion proves to be true,— even if the marriage rate among college girls is lower than the rate in a corresponding social group, the result is not necessarily calamitous.

College girls who fail to marry usually do so because they are economically independent, and do not need marriage as a means of support. Their ideals of a husband are high and they refuse to sacrifice these ideals for purely financial reasons. Fewer marriages, but better ones, is their motto. They usually have some concept of the meaning of eugenics and choose the husband who will be suitable not only as husband but as father.

The men who believe in sowing their wild oats cannot yet reconcile themselves to the new standard required of them by women, and consequently the better educated women may marry less often than their non-college sisters. But this is merely a transitional stage. As the demand grows,—and it is growing,—men will be compelled to meet the requirements of the college-woman standard. Until that time comes, every thinking woman,—whether college or non-college, will continue to lower the marriage rate.

Lastly, college is an important incentive to the growth of a spirit of social service. Girls learn, many of them for the first time, of the horrible maladjustments of present-day society, and gain, as a corollary to the new range of facts, the inspiration to some kind of social work. Women have much leisure,—far more than men, probably,—hence the crying need is inspiration to some really effective effort. For those forms of work which are directly altruistic, there is no stronger incentive than the ideal of social service so frequently developed by college education.

Since the spender holds the balance of industrial power, a union of all spenders could arbitrarily dictate to all producers, determining the character and extent of their production, deciding on quality, and, within certain limits, on price. The spender is the arbiter of modern industrial society.

Women are the spenders for consumption goods; all industrial effort is aimed directly or indirectly at the production of consumption goods; therefore the spenders, women, hold in their hands the power to control production.

Women may not understand the problem. They may fail to assert independence, choosing in response to clever advertising rather than to the inherent quality or worth of the goods; they may buy tawdry lace and cheap jewelry; yet by that very act, they are determining production. Failing to realize their power over industry, they prostitute their influence to their whims or fancies, instead of ruling their purchases by judgment.

As women are educated in spending, as they grow in power to discriminate, they will determine production to a greater and greater degree. Nothing in the world is so sensitive as "business." At the least indication of a change in popular favor, "business" will change its attitude to meet public demands. As women, through their buying, express public demands, business takes its cue from women.

Here, then, is a great field of opportunity for choice. Again American women must choose. They must choose between weak subservience to the influence of advertising, and a matured, trained judgment; they must choose between allowing the manufacturers to decide for them and deciding for the manufacturers. If they choose selfishly, they will take what comes on the market, careless, so long as they receive what they call "full value," indifferent to the conditions of manufacture and to the inherent value of the product.

On the other hand, the women may choose socially. Educated to a true sense of their responsibility, organized into powerful groups, these consumers may make and enforce demands. Acting on lines similar to these followed by the various "Consumers' Leagues," they may refuse goods which have been produced under bad conditions,—sweat shop goods; goods made in unsanitary factories by overworked operatives; goods made by child labor; goods which are the product of any industrial condition that is unfair or unjust to the workers in that particular industry. Following out the same policy, they may demand goods with the Union Label, ordinarily a guarantee of just working conditions. In short, by their organizations, the consumers may enforce decent treatment for the producers.

The spenders, the determinants of consumption, are women. Upon their shoulders devolves this new duty of controlling production through wise spending.

Women, therefore, must first be educated to wisdom in spending; second, they must realize their responsibility as spenders; and lastly, they must organize effectively. Coöperative effort is the only effective form of effort in modern society. The question then stands,—Will women measure up to their responsibility? Will this new generation of women coöperate to enforce the rights of the consumer? Their action will be their answer.

The most difficult problem confronting the schools is the teaching of a sense of social responsibility. Children should be taught that normal men and women are good, and that badness is merely an indication of abnormality. They should be shown the necessity for maintaining wages, standards, and modes of life. The teaching of individual morality must be supplemented by the teaching of social morality. It is antisocial to pay low wages, and the school children should know it; it is antisocial to maintain unhygienic living conditions in the houses which you own, and the children should be told so; the working life should be long and joyous, and the schools should make this fact a part of the consciousness of every child. In this way can the school fulfill its duty.

In this way can it develop a full sense of responsibility which every man must feel for his fellows in society.

The hope of progress is the school; the hope of the school is the teacher. Since nine-tenths of our teachers are women, it is obvious that upon women rests our hope of progress through education.

For ages women have been political nonentities. So complete was their subjection, in fact, that their political non-existence was neither commented on nor questioned. Unlike the Twentieth-Century suffragette, they accepted their fate in silence.

The struggle of women for political equality may be said to have begun in England toward the end of the eighteenth century. Not only was woman a nonentity politically, but she was legally disabled so as really to hinder the performance of her duties and functions as a human being. Even as a mother, she had no power over her own children and was always subject to moderate correction by her husband at his discretion. While her power over poverty was far less than that under the Roman law, she suffered especial hardship from the laws regulating marriage. Stung by the many injustices to which they were subject, women began toward the end of the eighteenth century seriously to discuss their disabilities. In 1792 Mary Wollstonecraft published her "Vindication of the Rights of Women" and Harriet Martineau soon after began writing on the subject of political equality.

That the public generally had really begun to consider the question of woman's rights, is indicated by the careful exclusion of women from the franchise under the Reform Act of 1832. "Male persons" were carefully designated as constituting the electorate instead of, as previously, "persons." John Stuart Mill, elected to Parliament in 1856, was the first to bring the matter before the body. Since that time, by successive acts, Englishwomen have secured the vote at municipal elections, county council elections and parish and district council elections. In 1907, they were made eligible for the offices of mayor, alderman, and county and town councilors. At present, the women of England lack only parliamentary suffrage.

Almost parallel with the struggle for political equality in Great Britain has been that in the United States. The agitation began here in 1828 with the visit of a Scotch woman,—Frances Wright,—to the United States. The first Woman's Rights Convention, however, was not held until July, 1848, at Seneca Falls, New York.

The social sanction given to the suffrage movement is not so general in the United States as in Great Britain. Some of the bitterest opponents of the movement are the women themselves. The suffrage is therefore rather limited. Only six of the States have granted equal suffrage to women,—Wyoming 1869, Colorado 1893, Utah 1896, Idaho 1896, Washington 1910, and California 1911.

Citizenship raises individual standards because with privileges come responsibilities,—responsibilities which impose a weight of duties and obligations. Democracy has meant for men an opportunity for the expression of opinion. It has opened a way for self development. Likewise it has opened a way for effective work. Social institutions were oppressive: the oppression was relieved; working conditions were impossible; democracy interfered; the vested interests were overbearing and grasping; they have been curbed; the government of the men by the men has broadened and deepened the stream of social consciousness and Social Progress.

Now, another change is coming. The opportunity to express opinions on public questions,—the opportunity to vote,—is demanded by women as well as by men. Where the demand has been granted, women, as active citizens, have found wide opportunities for service.

The whole field of social legislation is open to women. Children need protection; prospective mothers must not be physically overtaxed by factory work; babies require pure milk; adults need unadulterated food; streets must be clean; water must be pure; sweatshops need inspection, and the City Fathers need more careful watching. The house of the body politic needs cleaning and setting to rights. There are innumerable opportunities all through society for effective social work,—work which must finally be done by women. In the home, they have proved, by centuries of conclusive experiments, that they understand best the methods of keeping things clean and tidy; that they know most intimately the true needs of the human being.

Here then is a great field for women in politics. Men have built the house. They have constructed modern coöperative society. To be sure, women have helped,—but the chief work has been done by the men. . Now the time has come when people are ready to live in the splendid mansion. Men have built it, but they have left it littered with the inevitable accumulation of trash and rubbish. They are still pushing onward, and outward, planning and building. It is the women who realize the needs of a social housecleaning,—who are demanding an opportunity for real social service in the state.

Democracy has educated and matured men; so it must educate and mature women. Democracy has given men an opportunity to express their individual opinions and preferences in connection with the society of which they are a part; it must perform the same service for women. Furthermore, there is a distinct field open to women,—the field of social legislation, which in the next fifty years will be the battle ground of Social Progress. Women will not revolutionize society with the ballot. Men did not revolutionize society, when they secured the right to vote. Woman's opportunity in this direction is not revolutionary, but distinctively social and educative.

4 SOCIAL SANITY (1913)

A QUARTER INTO THE BOOK Nearing exhorts citizens to "Educate! Legislate! Reorganize! Adjust!" By these actions ordinary men and women will gain a satisfying livelihood. He describes the social insanity of unrelenting competition that leads to the degradation of the human spirit, especially those of the workers who support the wealth of corporation and property title holders. His emphasis is on welfare, not wealth, as the first priority, and from this will come a sane society in which to live and prosper.

This call to action coincided with radical changes in American life. In 1913 Henry Ford inaugurated the assembly line for automobile manufacture. In the same year President Woodrow Wilson pressed into legislation the Federal Reserve System as an agency to unstrap the monopoly that the gigantic private banks had on the national money system. The assembly line represented the ultimate in dehumanizing the worker, making him more of a cog in the corporate wheel than before; the Federal Reserve Board offered people more protection and regulation of their savings and investments. Wilson said at the time, "The masters of Government of the U.S. are the combined capitalists and manufacturers," a sentiment that Nearing and other reformers welcomed. The Sixteenth Amendment that authorized the federal income tax was also ratified this year.

The importance, to a troubled, questioning, partially disillusioned, unrestful, discontented age, of realizing that a society with an unbalanced mind (public opinion) may be as dangerous to itself as an individual with an unbalanced mind, can scarcely be over-emphasized. The

church, the industrial system, the institutions of representative government, the system of education, and the present type of family, have all
been made the object of recent criticism. This generation will without
question be called upon to determine the character of some of the
changes which will be made in these institutions. What principles shall
govern their decisions? Is the path leading toward social betterment
plainly marked? Certain things at least may be taken for granted. First,
the facts, in so far as they are available, must be ascertained; second,
they must be made a part of public knowledge; and third, society must
act in such a manner that the welfare of the majority is insured, while
that of the minority, wherever possible, is conserved. Careful inquiry,
through publicity and sane social action,—on these three foundation
stones the structure of a sound social progress may be erected.

Social sanity can be based on nothing less than a scientific attitude
toward the facts of social life. By what other means may society protect
and preserve itself than by determining in each case the true relations
existing between various social things?

Not once nor twice every year, a student comes to me railing against
socialism. It will destroy the home; it will break down society; it is a
menace to morals; it is organized robbery! To all of which I reply with
the pertinent question,—"What is socialism?"

First the lad bluffs, next he side-steps, then he apologizes, and finally, driven to bay, he grudgingly admits that he never heard anyone
explain the principles of socialism; that he never read a book by any
leading socialist; that he never knew anybody who had read such a
work; that his father had told him that socialists were dangerous to the
social order; that he had never talked with any really intelligent member
of the socialist party, and that, in short, while he knew nothing about
socialism or socialists, he was thoroughly opposed to both. At this
point, the average student, without more suggestion, will get a couple
of books and read up on the matter before he attempts to discuss it
further.

The question of socialism is first of all a question of fact. No fair-
minded man attempts to discuss such matters, or any other matters of
fact, until he is thoroughly conversant with the facts. In place of "fair-
minded" read scientific, and the statement is still true, for the spirit of
science requires the individual to confront all issues in a frank, open-
minded way, with an entire willingness to accept the logical conclusions
derived from things as they are.

We are no more subject to the laws of economics than our ancestors
were subject to the laws of military tactics; than we are subject to the
laws of education; or than our descendants will be subject to the laws of

the sanitary science which we are creating. There are formulas of thought called "laws" in all sciences, but Napoleon overthrew and remade the laws of military tactics; Froebel restated the laws of education; and Pasteur created the science of sanitation. There is an economic lawgiver—man, who can unmake or remake that which he has made.

The economists in the past have asked "What?" and "Why?" of economic phenomena. The time has now come when they must face the third question and discover how economics may be made to serve mankind. The discovery that opportunity largely shapes the life of the average man, determining whether he shall be happy or miserable, has led to an insistence that the economists part company with the ominous pictures of an over-populated, starving world, prostrate before the throne of "competition," "psychic value," "individual initiative," "private property," or some other pseudo-god, and tell men in simple, straightforward language how they may combine, reshape, or overcome the laws and utilize them as a blessing instead of enduring them as a burden and a curse. The day has dawned when economists must explain that welfare must be put before wealth; that the iron law of wages may be shattered by a minimum wage law; that universal over-population is being prevented by a universal restriction in the birth-rate; that over-work, untimely death, and a host of other economic maladjustments will disappear before an educated, legislating public opinion; and that combination and co-operation may be employed to silence forever the savage demands of unrestricted competition. In short, the economists, if they are to justify their existence, must provide a theory which will enable the average man, by co-operating with his fellows, to bear more easily the burden and heat of the day.

In the past, the standards of life have been constantly raised, through successive stages. The biologic world has been improved generation after generation by means of a process which eliminated the unfit and allowed only the fit individual members of a species to survive and propagate their fitness. In exactly the same way social institutions have been improved by replacing the worthless elements with newer and more worth-while forms. Without such a selection of the best, no species and no society could endure. By means of it, the best in each generation is preserved for the future, while the rest is cast away.

This is nature's method of protecting herself against deterioration. Hence all who raise the "back to nature" cry should welcome it with glad hearts, recognizing it as the conceiver of progress, the savior of civilization. In so far as man is to make a success of civilization, Nature's task of selection must be his method too. Everywhere, without regard to individual hardship, he must reject the worthless, and retain only that which is worth while. Only thus will the instruments of civilization and progress be continually improved.

The primitive man used a tool or a weapon because it had been used by his father. The modern manufacturer throws away a more desirable tool than any ever possessed by the savage, because he has found a better one. The modern navy discards expensive, intricate, murdering devices because more effective ones are to be had. The school teacher turns from the old method to the new. The doctor lays aside his dirty ways and practices antiseptic surgery. The farmer, no longer guided by the moon or the planets, reaps a rich reward from the adoption of scientific methods of agriculture. Each man is learning that the law of nature is immutable because it is right,—the more worthy alone may remain; the less worthy must disappear.

Whether in science, education, industry, or politics, this truth is getting fast hold of men's souls. They are learning that, since life is a becoming and since man may will to direct it, guided by his visions of the future, could all possess an optimistic attitude toward life, society might readily preserve itself in the present, and continually raise its standards through succeeding generations. Hence, at the basis of social sanity lie optimism and vision applied through the preservation of the best in each generation; hence at the basis of man's kingdom lies a staunch belief in man's potentialities.

Economic and social endeavor must have some goal. Shall it be wealth or welfare?

The social scientists who wrote in the eighteenth and early nineteenth centuries were inclined to the view that the chief aim of national as of individual life should be the acquisition of wealth, hence the question of welfare held a very minor place in their philosophies. Similar workers in the last half of the nineteenth century have completely revised this judgment, and, since John Stuart Mill evolved from a classical economist into a social reformer, they have replaced the "Science of Wealth" by a "Science of Welfare." Early writers maintained that economic goods were the logical end of endeavor; that the nation which produced economic goods in great abundance was the successful nation, irrespective of any other test. The newer school holds, on the other hand, that social progress lies, not in the production of goods, but in the developing lives of men and women, and that, while this end may be achieved through the production of goods, the production is merely incidental to the development of manhood and womanhood. Production, therefore, ceases to be regarded as an end in itself, and becomes a means to welfare.

In the evolution of industry, a point has been reached where the vast majority of those who labor have for their tasks clock-watching occupations. The hours never fly—they crawl. Each sixty minutes which

passes is sixty minutes nearer quitting time—the time of rest and freedom. In such labor there is no joy. In such monotony there can be no
satisfaction. Highly specialized factory work is hell raised to the nth
power. With every nerve taut, with every fiber stretched to the limit
of its capacity, these workers strain to make, in their day, enough
pieces,—perhaps a hundred, perhaps five hundred,—to buy only
this—their daily bread.

The present system of industry will not last forever. It represents only
one scene of the great industrial panorama which has been unfolding
since man first learned to use tools. No man can say what the future
holds; yet so long as specialized industry remains what it is—a hopeless treadmill for the great mass of the workers; so long as hate and
loathing, not joy and blessedness, are involved in its processes; so long
as each additional hour of labor counts one additional hour of pain; then
the less of it the better. No sane person can continue indefinitely to
demand of men eternal service of a machine. No sound thinker can
expect that human beings will love that in which there is no joy. Modern
specialized industry—a task-master armed with the sharp thong of hunger—drives men and women and even children to do things which they
prefer not to do. How soon—men and women—leaders of the great
march toward social sanity, shall we rob industry of its fangs?

One question a sane society will ask—"In how many hours of such
labor can men make enough goods to supply themselves with the necessaries and comforts of life? Can it be done in ten hours? Then ten hours
must be the day's labor. Can it be done in eight hours? Then set the
labor day at that amount." It is the enthusiasm and joy of leisure, not
the nerve-racking misery of factory labor, which is the goal of sane
living.

Since wealth depends upon industry, and since the vitalizing element
in industry is labor; it would seem that in the division of the fruits of
industry those who labored should receive the lion's share of the income
and of the pleasures of life, while those who idled should receive
almshouse fare,—the bare necessaries of living.

Anomalous though it may appear, no such relation exists between the
lives of those who labor and of those who idle. It is not true, in American society, that luxury, ease, satisfaction, and enjoyment attend on the
lives of the workers, while hardships and privation await the idlers. No
longer is the proverb held,—"He who will not work, neither shall he
eat." Indeed sometimes the exact reverse holds true. He who never
worked eats abundantly of the choicest fruits of the land.

The fruits of industry go not to the industrious, but to the fortunate.
He who labors receives not, for all of his working, while the idle man

and the idle woman, holding titles to capital or to land, reap rich harvests of wealth, and leisure. We, the well-housed, may be content with our comfort and security, with our prosperous condition and our thriving state; we may boast of our national industry and prosperity; we may preach and condemn and punish from behind our bulwarks of laws and constitutions and institutions; but until the unnatural sloughs of adversity are made dry by the leveled mountains of unearned prosperity, the nation will never be truly prosperous.

Finally, is this sanity? Can anyone suppose that when the workers—the producers of wealth—realize the extent to which their products are being absorbed by the drones, they will tolerate the continuance of such conditions?

Between the production of wealth and its use, between the expenditure of effort and the receipt of income stretch the traditions of individual ownership, which take from him who produces and give to him who holds titles to property. How wondrously have men learned to create wealth, in myriad forms, how stupidly do they blunder in the sharing of the wealth produced.

Sanity imperatively demands fairness in distributing the fruits of industry. After ages of experimentation human society has found that finally the only sane rule of conduct in dealings between man and man is the rule of equity, of justice, of fairness, of doing to that other as you would have him do to you.

Stripped of its incidental elements, apart from its traditions and its glamor, the present scheme for dividing the fruits of industry appears in its bald unjustness. Lay aside your preconceived ideas of property and property rights, look sanely, carefully into the matter from the eyrie of intellectual honesty, and find, if you can, a justification for giving to him that labors a pittance; to him that idles a competence. In that direction social sanity does not lie. Inequality in distributing the fruits of industry is the broad way that has led many nations to destruction. The path to social sanity lies along a narrow way, through a straight gate, over which is written the saying—"Social Justice."

The spirit of revolt has developed side by side with the consciousness that fair play is no longer the rule of the economic road. Men and women interested in the growth of life and the maintenance of sanity are learning that, under the industrial conditions which saw the nineteenth century out and the twentieth century in, sane living is impossible for the great mass of the population. Under this system: (1) Many of those who labor have neither the time nor the energy to enjoy life after the workday is over. (2) Welfare is the lot of so few—opportunity is so painfully restricted. (3) Aside from any nobler aim in life, such a situation does not even permit efficiency, since those best fitted to do certain tasks do not necessarily have a chance to do them. (4) Most grotesque of all, society has perfected an automatic device which takes from the producer a great part of the product, leaving him in a vast number of cases not even a decent livelihood; sets the laborer to making lace, and automobile bodies, when his children and the children of his friends need shoes, hats, dresses, and shirts; and finally which pours countless riches into the laps of an idle few.

No one can longer doubt that there are industrial and social burdens which press most heavily on the backs which are least able to bear them. Who can question the unfairness of bad milk, dark rooms, child-labor, overwork, premature death, and the host of other vultures which prey upon the common man's chance of life? The exploited has a clear case against the exploiter. The very clarity of the issue lends weight to the protest which the exploited makes.

The real wonder of wonders is not the revolt of the exploited, but their failure to revolt.

During the last two decades, prices have risen steadily, faster than wages. At the end of a period of phenomenal prosperity, many a worker is less able to supply himself with the necessaries of life than he was at its beginning. As an instrument for improving the conditions surrounding the lives of the workers, the union has succeeded, but as a means for securing a more equitable distribution of the means of livelihood, it has failed.

In recognition of this failure, the union members are everywhere turning from indirect to direct political action—from unionism to socialism. This change of attitude does not at all involve the abandonment of the union. Indeed, entire unions, like the Western Federation of Miners, vote the socialist ticket. The change does involve, however, a fundamental change in attitude. Instead of waiting for the representative of some other interest to do his work for him, the socialist sends his own representative to the legislature.

The socialist has a programme which is much larger than that of the unionist. The latter insists upon a readjustment of working conditions, while the socialist demands a reorganization of society—a reorganization which he proposes to effect through the use of the ballot. Socialism, therefore, finds its logical outcome in the formation of a political party.

Hinted at by Fourier, Saint-Simon, Robert Owen, and the other communists of the early nineteenth century, restated and symtematized by Karl Marx and the host of co-workers who have written and spoken during the past forty years, socialism is now a factor to be considered in any statement of political tendencies. In Germany, the socialist vote is larger than that of any other party; in France it is increasing rapidly; in

Belgium it is in entire control of some districts. Even in the United States, it is doubling with each presidential election, while socialist mayors, aldermen, and legislators no longer excite comment.

Socialism is an organized protest against the present system of distributing income, coupled with an organized effort to establish a new system, whereby income may be more rationally distributed. It has probably had more influence on the thought of the masses and on the political tactics of the ruling parties than any other single movement in the nineteenth century.

Whether the syndicalist movement must be taken seriously, no man can yet say. The radical wing of the Socialist Party, tired of the failure of their leaders to reorganize the industrial system in cases like that of Germany where they are in power, propose direct action. "Parliamentary government," they cry, "is a failure. The workers must take what they want by direct means." These means,—first, the general strike, and finally the literal appropriation of the productive machinery,—have been advocated freely in Europe, and the general strike has been used with telling effect.

Unionism, socialism, and syndicalism are the three current channels along which the revolt of the worker is taking place. Thus far, these movements have been reasonably quiet—almost dignified in fact. What does the future hold for them?

A group of successful young business men sat at lunch, discussing the Lawrence textile strike, when someone made this proposal,—"Suppose you were a textile weaver, destined to be a weaver till you died. You couldn't become a mill-owner; you couldn't earn more than a certain wage; you would have to live as those fellows live; and when they reached the age of fourteen, you would have to see your children go into the mill."

"Well," said a lawyer, with a strong jaw, "I should be the leading agitator of the crowd, and so would everyone else who had red blood in his veins."

Of all the revolts, the most spectacular is the revolt of the women, who, for ages, have been taught to accept the thing which is, and to be content with it. Traditionally, the judgment of women is subject to that of men in industry, education, literature, philosophy, and science. Practically in all of these fields the achievements of women have been slight. Yet the last two generations have witnessed a complete overturning in the attitude of women as a group.

Prior to that time a few scattering women had agitated this or that reform, but society still believed implicitly that the home was woman's place and that unless some untoward circumstance called her from it, she should stay there. In the transformation of social life which has forced women out of the home into spheres of varied usefulness, no factor has had a more potent influence than the woman's colleges.

The campaign for suffrage, for clean streets, pure milk, sanitary housing, safe factories, decent hours, wise regulations of the work of women and children are all part of the women's revolt. The traditionally weaker sex has become strong; the supposedly passive part of the human race has become aggressive. Women have awakened to the needs of the day, responding nobly to the call for action. A century ago, women were hardly counted in the scheme of things. Starting from a life surrounded by numberless restrictions and traditions, the women have moved fast and far in their campaign for a keener social justice and a higher social morality.

The spirit of revolt has not been felt by everyone. There are men and women in all walks of life who are thoroughly satisfied with things as they are. Yet there is not a single group in the modern world from the weariest toilers to the weariest idlers which has not somewhere in its ranks a band of "reformers," "progressives," or "radicals" who preach enthusiastically the doctrine of revolt.

Why afford opportunity? Why seek welfare in adjustment? It is true that some men are born to be hewers of wood and drawers of water, born without ambition or capacity, born without the qualities which make men run steadily. Nevertheless, the children of these men may, and frequently do, have ambition, capacity, and quality. It is for them that we provide universal opportunity. It is because of the infinite, unknown possibilities of each soul that we seek to start each man at the same mark, well equipped for the race of life. He may drop out of the race before he has completed his first lap, but he may go to the end,—a triumphant victor. The possibility that he may be worthy is the ground on which we demand opportunity for him.

The scientific discoveries of the past fifty years have led inevitably to the conclusion that the great majority of men are born with relatively equal capacities. The real differences in the achievements of their lives are made by the variations in opportunity. This necessitates a revision of the old social code, and the adoption of the newer, broader standard.

The time has come to organize a sane society,—a society of men and women who are educated, efficient, cultured; a society in which health and life are conserved; a society of which justice is the corner-stone, with ennobled manhood and womanhood the central dome, reaching to high heaven.

5 SOCIAL RELIGION (1913)

A T 30 YEARS OF AGE on publication of this book, Nearing was one of the most popular teachers at the University of Pennsylvania and a frequent off-campus lecturer in
growing demand. In addition, he was producing some
ground-breaking research and reports on worker wages in
the United States, a subject that at the time had shockingly
little serious analysis by university or federal government
economists. He published two books on the subject: *Wages
in the United States, 1908–1910* (1911) and *Financing the
Wage-Earner's Family* (1913).

He used an address he had given to the Friends' General
Conference at Ocean Grove, New Jersey, in 1910 as the
basis for this book. He enlarged the speech but retained the
"speaking" tone of it, the oratorical devices that he had
developed to rousing effect. Evidently, they worked in the
original, for the speech incited vehement protest and challenge from many members of the conference.

Nearing's thrust was to show that ignorance, poverty,
and vice were more widespread than those sheltered by
church-going had thought, that these miseries were preventable, and that the church must preach, heal, and teach for a
better society if it wished to live up to the teachings of its
founder. He pointed out that Jesus preached a social doctrine and that Christianity, to be true to itself, must be a
Social Religion.

In Jesus' time people were ignorant, sick, poor and vicious. He
taught, healed, preached, comforted and associated with the hapless
ones. "They that be whole need not a physician" were his biting words.

50

"I came not to call the righteous, but sinners to repentance." To the fault-finding lawyer, and to the hypocritical scribes and Pharisees, he told a tale of need and succor, exclaiming, "Go and do thou likewise." If ignorance, sickness, poverty and vice exist in America to-day, perhaps the "Go and do thou likewise" command still holds good.

On one occasion a lawyer came and asked Him, "Which is the first and greatest commandment?" And Jesus replied, "Thou shalt love the Lord thy God," and "the second is like unto it, Thou shalt love thy neighbor as thyself." Thus does Jesus clearly describe the foundation stone of his religion—love of God and of humanity, expressed through service to one's fellowmen. Upon such a foundation He could establish nothing less than a Social Religion—a religion of love, fellowship, brotherhood and social service.

Jesus taught a social doctrine. We profess to follow His teachings. In how far have we obeyed His command, "Go and do thou likewise" to all unfortunates? Suppose that Jesus should come to America to-night—to one of our great cities—to New York, or Chicago, or Baltimore. Would He enter the sumptuous churches? Would He teach? Would He preach? Would He heal? Would He love? Beautiful buildings, exquisite windows, divine singing—but how was that church built? Who gave the windows? Who pays the salaries? There are men working twelve hours a day, seven days a week in the steel mills of Pittsburg. Are you a stockholder of United States Steel? Did you drop an offering into the collection box? You thought that you were dropping in silver or gold, but it was the bloody sweat of a fellow being, laboring hopelessly beside the roar of the blast furnace—sacrificed on the altar of industrial progress. There are silk mills near Scranton working all night, where at midnight the children, boys and girls, are sent out together into the darkness to "freshen up" for the next six hours of toil. Do you hold silk mill bonds? They are children's bodies and children's souls that you clip with your coupons, and your tithe to the house of God reeks with the degradation of future generations. There are tenements in every city of the land, broken, squalid, without sanitation, air or sunlight. Are you a landlord? Has that fire-escape been repaired? That drainage improved? Are the cellars still overflowing with filth and disease?

It is true that the United States is a prosperous country; a land flowing with milk and honey; a billion-dollar country; a land of plenty. Tell us, girl number twenty, little undernourished Sissy Jupe, isn't this a prosperous nation and ain't you in a thriving state? There is plenty of everything in this big country of yours—plenty of ability; plenty of genius; plenty of natural resources—land, coal, oil, water-power; plenty of factories; plenty of money; plenty of opportunities; plenty of leisure; plenty of enjoyment; plenty of child labor; plenty of sweat shops; plenty of overwork; plenty of unemployment; plenty of poverty;

plenty of vice; plenty of misery. The United States is a land of great plenty, but an analysis of this plenty reveals startling incongruities.

First—Ability and genius are distributed rather evenly through all classes of the population. Thus has nature provided, in her laws of heredity, that each new generation shall start with a new standard of qualities and virtues.

Second—The natural resources, factories, opportunities, leisure and enjoyment are the possessions of the few. Here man has entered the field, enacting property laws, and laws of inheritance, which permit one man to group together, under his own control, great quantities of nature's gifts, and, after using them until he can use them no more, to hand them on to his children—to be their possessions so long as the world shall endure.

Third—Child labor, overwork, unemployment, poverty, vice and misery are the possessions of the many. They are endured by the fathers and handed by them to the children. Here and there a genius arises, and, despite the fell grip of circumstance in which he was born, pushes forward to success, raising his entire family out of the class of the many, into the class of the few. Generally speaking, however, the children assume the burdens of their fathers.

Fourth—And here lies the answer to all those who prate of American plenty—The people who have plenty of natural resources, opportunities and leisure have no child labor, poverty and misery, and, on the other hand, the people who have child labor, poverty and misery have no resources, opportunities and leisure.

Fifth—We may, therefore, summarize the situation by saying that in the United States plenty exists everywhere. Nature has scattered plenty of ability and genius through all elements of the population. Man has improved upon nature, and in his distribution of economic goods has carefully discriminated, giving to one class plenty of heaven, and to another plenty of hell; and he has founded the heaven of natural resources, opportunity and leisure—the heritage of the rich—upon the hell of overwork, poverty and misery—the lot of the poor.

Side by side these things exist; side by side stand the mansions of Fifth Avenue, adorned beautifully; and the tenements of Hester Street, squalid, insanitary, hideous. Side by side are women striving hopelessly to make the hours run—riding, driving, bridging, visiting, dressing, buying, squandering, traveling—leading lives of aimless, helpless ease; and women with seamed faces and gnarled hands rising in the twilight of the morning, at the screech of a factory whistle, toiling all of the weary day, living, striving, saving, stinting—stretching a tiny income that it may, perchance, fill a great gulf of expense. Side by side are the children—this one fed, clothed, housed, educated, sent to college, to Europe, and finally started in business with a strong body, a trained mind, and a social position that will enable him to push forward to the highest pinnacle of business success; that one, born into parsimony and misery, undernourished, half clothed, wretchedly housed, indifferently educated, and at the age of fourteen stood before a machine in a steaming cotton factory—without sunlight, or air, or play, or even exercise—and told to do his little part in the creation of national prosperity. These things exist side by side, and you, in luxury, never think of misery; you, on the bright side, never learn of the blackness of the dark side; you, in the sunlight, never dream of the shadow; you cannot know—you cannot conceive what is just behind you—if you could know, if you could secure but an inkling of the real world, perhaps you might look about and see that, because you are in the light, you cast a shadow, and that, because you take more than your share of the light, others must be content with darkness. Nay, you might even come, in time, to see that others are dwelling in the shadow which you cast. Meanwhile, you condemn those who, dwelling in darkness, bear the stamp of the darkness upon their faces and their souls. You who have made that darkness; are not its products hideous?

Three years ago a number of New York experts were asked to name a minimum amount upon which a family consisting of a man, wife and three children, under fourteen, could maintain a decent living. Sixteen experts made calculations, their figures ranging from $768 to $1,449, and centering at $950. The social workers were aghast. "What," they exclaimed, "nine hundred and fifty dollars; why, that is over three dollars a working day!"

These figures, however, are meaningless unless they can be supplemented by other figures showing what wages are actually received. It is of no moment to us in this discussion to know that $3 per working day will maintain a decent standard for a normal family unless we know, in addition, what wages are being paid to wage workers.

The federal government and a few states publish some wage statistics which permit of certain conclusions regarding the relation between a normal standard of living and the wages paid to American workmen. A summary of these available wage statistics of Massachusetts, New Jersey, Kansas and Wisconsin shows that three-quarters of the adult male wage earners employed in the industries of the New England, Middle and North Central States receive a wage so low that they are unable to provide the necessaries of life for a wife and three children; the wages of half of the same group will not provide a decent living for more than two children, while thirty per cent. receive a wage that will not provide adequately for more than a single child. In the face of such conditions, the average worker who wishes to furnish the necessaries of life to those dependent upon him will be unable to maintain the population.

Perhaps you think these statements extreme, but I believe that I can prove them. I will not cite the instance of the 166,227 anthracite coal miners in Pennsylvania, whose average wage is $503.85 annually, nor that of the 171,987 bituminous coal miners in the same state whose wage averages $525.79 a year; neither will I attempt to prove my contention by the $562.89 which goes to each of the 69,250 boot and shoe workers, and the $439.34 annual incomes of 90,935 cotton mill operatives of Massachusetts. In the first two industries foreigners, and in the last two women, compete fiercely, forcing down the wage far below a level of decent living. I will rather take my illustrations from the two leading American industries—railroading and steel making.

It is a well-recognized fact that no great industries require on the whole more skill and endurance than do these two, yet I propose to show that even in these typical, high-paid American industries wages are so low as thoroughly to justify my opening statement. In fact, that these representative industries fail to pay a family subsistence wage to the vast majority of their employes.

Each year the Interstate Commerce Commission publishes the average daily wages of about a million and a half railroad employes. An analysis of these statistics for the last available year (1909) shows that of the entire number employed in that year (1,502,823) seven per cent. (114,199) received an average wage of more than $3 a day ($900 a year); that 42 per cent. (633,674) received from $2 to $3 a day ($600 to $900 a year), and that 51 per cent. (754,950) received from $1 to $2 a day—$300 to $600 a year. The average daily wage of 210,898 "Laborers" was $1.98 per day—$600 per year, while of 320,762 trackmen the average wage was $1.38 per day, or $425.80 per year. It, therefore, appears that nine-tenths of the railroad employes of the United States receive less than $900 a year; that more than half receive less than $600 a year; while the laborers and trackmen, 530,000 in all, are paid less than $600 a year.

That the relative wages in the steel industry are almost identical is clearly shown by the investigation of the Pittsburg Survey (1908) and of the Federal Government into the wages in the South Bethlehem Steel Works and of the steel industry at large. The report on the South Bethlehem investigation includes a complete transcript of the pay-rolls for January, 1910, and covers 9,184 employes. Of this number, ten per cent. received an hourly wage rate equivalent to more than $900 per year; 75 per cent. a rate equivalent to less than $750 per year; 60 per cent. received a rate equivalent to less than $600 per year, while the wages of thirty per cent. were less than $500 per year. The Federal

Investigation of the entire industry, made in 1911, shows identical conditions for employes in all parts of the United States.

Thus, in both steel manufacturing and in railroading, two of the leading American industries, the same proportion of workmen receive more than $900 a year and the same proportion less than $600 a year.

These wage figures cannot, however, be accepted as stated. They represent the daily and hourly earnings of men paid by the day or by the hour, *when they work*. But at times these men do not work. In ordinarily prosperous years the average wage worker is disemployed through sickness, accident, strikes, and lack of orders, about one-fifth or one-sixth of his entire working time.

Therefore, I conclude as I began: Three-quarters of the workingmen in American industries cannot provide decently for more than three children; half of them cannot provide for more than two; while the wage of one-third is so low that they can barely make adequate provision for a single child. We prate about morality; we are rich, we inveigh against vice; we are comfortable; we preach against crime; we are well fed and housed; we advocate large families; but we forget to pay living wages.

Women are not only underpaid, but they are frequently over-worked. For example, weaving has always been done by women. In the early stages of machinery one woman managed one or perhaps two slowly moving looms. Then improvements gave her four or five looms to tend, and to-day, with the invention of the automatic shuttle, each woman is called upon to tend from twelve to sixteen looms. Sixteen looms cover a large floor space, and the woman must hurry from loom to loom. As a result, when night comes, she is often too exhausted to sleep. Another illustration comes from the canning industry. In the canning factory an automatic clutch carries cans of baked beans past a girl who slips a small piece of pork into each can. The endless chain of clutches runs fast, and the girl must concentrate every atom of nervous energy on the task before her or miss her can. These are but typical illustrations of the methods which are used to speed up workingwomen.

Surrounded by your atmosphere of social respectability, you pity these girls; you are infinitely above them. How much above? Suppose you started to work at six-thirty every morning; stood on your feet all day, every working day in the year; came home at night to a lonely attic room, fried a bit of bacon and ate bread and bananas, and then retired, to start at six-thirty and do it over again, six days a week, three hundred and seven days a year. Suppose you waited on splendidly dressed women and sweet-faced boys and girls; suppose, just for the sake of argument, that you were like other people and loved artistic clothes and children, and wanted recreation, expansion, life. When you looked at your paltry six dollars a week, what would you do? Would you go mad or would you go to the dance halls and perhaps ultimately on the street? You are above these girls, but how much?

Recently there have been in the newspapers and magazines numerous articles on prostitution and the white-slave trade. Did you ever think that there might be a connection between underpaid, overworked, motherless girls and the tens of thousands of women who patrol the streets of our great cities offering their bodies for hire?

In Chicago thirty of the leading citizens were appointed on the Chicago Vice Commission, which made a thorough inquiry into the matter, reporting conditions which are, to say the least, startling to the average complacent citizen. They found that the business of hiring women's bodies was "a commercialized business, organized to the highest point of efficiency, with cash registers and modern efficient bookkeeping, even with tickets, where you get $3.50 worth of service for $3.00, and have the ticket punched as the service is rendered. All sorts of business methods are used, all sorts of artificial schemes resorted to, in addition to the service rendered, to increase the income and bring in money."

Walter T. Summer, a member of the Chicago Vice Commission, says: "We were able to tell the amount of service rendered in each house of prostitution by these women. We were able to tell how many men were served. We were able to get absolute figures from the records, so that I can say to you with certainty that a woman in a house of prostitution must render service to 15 men every 24 hours, and, in times of convention, or other large gatherings, 25, 30, 50, 75, and even 100, and, therefore, we know, the earnings range from $25 to $400 a week. We know that 5,999,000 men were rendered service in the city of Chicago by 1,108 prostitutes each year, and that through this commercialized vice there was paid $16,000,000 to these 1,108 prostitutes. This did not cover the whole 5,000 women which we considered a conservative estimate of the number who are plying their trade in this business."

While Jesus taught His disciples He uttered no more solemn judgment than this: "Whosoever shall offend one of these little ones that believeth in Me, it were better for him that a mill stone were hanged about his neck and that he were cast into the depths of the sea." Nevertheless, in defiance of His warning, we offend not one, but hundreds of thousands every working day in the year. Those little children who, in the words of Jesus, "are the kingdom of Heaven" are forced on this earth to labor for their daily bread.

I have seen these children working—I have been in the breakers where the boys pick the slate from the coal in an atmosphere so filled with dust that they were forced, on a bright summer day, to wear lamps on their hats in order to see the coal at their feet; I have been in the mines and seen children of twelve working all day long, cut off from daylight and fresh air; I have gone into box factories at Christmas Time, where the girls began their work at seven in the morning, finishing at eight or nine in the evening; I have seen children preparing the dainty candies which attract you in beautiful store windows; I have been with the messenger boys all night, as they went from one house of ill-fame to the next; I have watched the exhausted faces of the cash-girls in our great department stores, as they hurried about in the August heat; I have seen these children laboring, picking, mining, making boxes and candy, and carrying messages and cash for you. You received the benefits— you may even have taken the dividends which these children were earning. If you did not buy the products, and take the dividends from their toil, you at least stood by while the legislature refused to enact effective laws for the protection of working children.

Good Samaritans, nearly two millions of America's future citizens cry aloud to you for assistance. They have been set upon at the outset of life's journey, robbed of their playtime, and left to labor in their helplessness in an inferno of grinding wheels, of snapping clutches and gears. Spiritually wounded and half dead they demand your assistance in the name of the future. Will you ever heed their appeal?

Must men always be underpaid and overworked? Must five thousand children in a wealthy city be "habitually hungry"? Must women continue to fight the losing battle that leads them to the brothel? Must society always rest upon the mangled lives of motherless girls, of haggard men, of toiling children, of overworked and underpaid humanity?

We want heaven on earth, many mansions, golden streets, crystal water, playgrounds, joyous sunshine—opportunity to grow and worship unhampered by the bonds of social maladjustment; we want heaven on earth, and we can have it if we will.

We are a wealthy nation; we can afford to pay living wages; we are an enlightened people; our women are ceasing to be beasts of burden; we are a far-seeing nation; we are protecting and safeguarding childhood. Corn will feed the hungry, and we have plenty of corn. Cotton and wool and lumber will provide clothing and shelter for the destitute, and we produce an abundance of these. Poverty is unnecessary, destitution must cease. Modern industry has created sufficient economic goods. It is merely the archaic system of distribution which has nullified our productive triumphs, creating one class with boundless possessions and another with the barest necessities of animal existence.

Jesus laid down his doctrine in unmistakable terms. "Love thy God," said He, "and thy neighbor as thyself." That is the extent of Jesus' religious theory. Formulated, His doctrine might appear thus:

I. The Theory of Social Religion
   1. Belief in God.
   2. Belief in Men.

How divinely simple; how wonderfully grand! We are to found our lives on God—good—a spirit that must be worshipped in spirit and in truth. We are to believe in God—that is, we are to believe in Good, Truth, Beauty—in all of the great beneficent forces of the universe.

This, however, is not enough. God is a spirit, and man, made in His image and likeness, is a spirit, too. Hence, we are enjoined to love our neighbor as ourselves. We are to believe in man. Indeed, our belief in God is demonstrable only through our belief in man, for, if a man cannot love his brother, whom he has seen, how can he love God, whom he has not seen? Our faith, in short, will be tested by our works.

The theory of our faith must be judged by the practice of our works. It is not enough that we believe: we must do. How shall we do? How express this theory of religion in the practical affairs of life? Let me suggest that the things needed for putting Social Religion into practice are (1) Sympathy, (2) Inspiration, and (3) Efficiency.

Those men who aim to make their religion practicable, applicable to their every-day lives, must possess these three attributes: Sympathy, Inspiration, Efficiency. It is idle to talk of the function of the church as if the church was an individual that, like Lazarus, would arise and walk. The church is an institution, the work of which must necessarily be done by men, hence it is the attributes of the men that really count in the determination of church activity. You cannot touch the hem of your neighbor's soul without sympathy—nay, without that quality, you cannot step across the threshold of his being. You must fill his life and understand his view, if you are to be to him a neighbor in the truer sense.

To do this, to live as a social being in a social group; to practice a social religion; to keep your soul open for belief in men, there must be that inspiration—that divine fire which animates every individual man and woman who is born into the world.

You do—that is something. What do you do? That depends entirely upon your belief and your inspiration. How do you do it? The answer to that question determines your efficiency. To do is well; to do right is better; but to do right in the best possible manner is best of all. No machinery can be effective unless to its inspiration and sympathy is joined efficiency.

When the theory has been accepted and the machinery evolved, there yet remains the application of our social religion. We believe in God and in man; we sympathize, longing to see our fellows live rounded, noble lives; we are inspired to help them; and we are efficient. Like the rich young man, we have kept all of the commandments. What lack we yet? We lack one thing—the power to apply our religion. We have religion—now we must do something with it.

The practice of Social Religion involves (1) clean living, (2) social service, and (3) social justice. There are, therefore, two elements—an individual and a social—in the practice of Social Religion. The individual has a machine with which he must do his work. That machine—his body and soul—must be kept in repair, cleaned, exercised, developed. "He that ruleth his spirit is always greater than he that taketh a city." The practice of Social Religion, like charity, begins at home, in the individual life.

When the individual life is clean, or, indeed, while it is being cleansed, it may, through Social Service, assist in erecting Social Justice.

Low incomes produce a living hell, and perpetuate it from one generation to the next. Why, then, are low incomes paid? Why is a system of distribution tolerated which fails to give to every family a living wage? You know why. It is because we do not really care to apply the Christian doctrine of brotherhood to the affairs of daily life.

It is entirely possible to enforce a living wage for all workers. We might follow the example of New Zealand and pass a minimum wage law, which prescribes the lowest wage that may be paid in a given industry. In New Zealand the law has been in operation for twenty years, and has succeeded admirably in raising the wages in the worst of the "sweated" industries. So salutary has been the effect of this enactment in raising industrial standards, that employers as well as employees are continually invoking it in order to suppress unscrupulous competitors.

So much the state may do to guarantee a normal standard of wages. On the other hand, it is possible to organize the workers into trade unions, as they have done in Australia, where, under the authority of law, a union can compel an employer to appear before a Board of Arbitration and settle any differences which may have arisen.

Jesus preached a social religion. He said: "Love God and serve thy neighbor." Despite the wide distribution of ability and genius, opportunities are so narrowed in America to-day that millions are condemned to a living hell of underpay, poverty, vice, and misery. This narrowing of opportunities cannot be ascribed to the anger of a jealous God, nor to the indiscretion or selfishness of a past generation. Neither omnipotent anger nor hereditary defect is responsible for maladjustments. They are the work of men, and may be remedied by their creators.

Maladjustment is darkness. Adjustment is light. What is darkness? It is but the absence of light. Turn on the light. Teach the truth. "Ye shall know the truth and the truth shall make you free." Truth is the only light that can banish the darkness of maladjustment. Teach the truth in your churches and your schools—the truth about the appalling maladjustments which threaten the foundations of civilization; about coöperative industry; about progress and brotherhood in society; about the innate goodness and capacity of men; about Social Religion. Tell the world that progress must be made, that progress is being made, and that you are helping to shape the future with its uncounted possibilities.

6 POVERTY AND RICHES (1916)

NEARING WAS DEAN of the College of Arts and Sciences and head of the sociology department at the University of Toledo, Ohio, when *Poverty and Riches* was published. The book was the first of his with photographs and reproductions of paintings, scores of them juxtaposing châteaus and tenements, steel mills and executive suites, hard workers and leisure-living millionaires. One painting, by William Balfour Ker, titled "The Hand of Fate" is captioned with: "The rich and idle pleasure-seekers at an orgy are terrified when one of the wretched laboring class who support the floor of pleasure succeeds in breaking his fist through in threat." The painting depicts a tuxedoed upper class at a sumptuous dancing party while below the floor a hand thrusts through as other workers shoulder the floor that supports the millionaires.

In 1915 Nearing had been fired from the University of Pennsylvania for his outspoken views, particularly those on child labor. At the time of his firing, he and like-minded colleagues had mailed 1,500 letters about the incident to major newspapers and professionals in education around the country. Extensive national interest arose and, later, the Scott Nearing case was credited with securing a stronger foothold for academic freedom elsewhere in the country.

On arriving at the University of Toledo in the Winter of 1915, Nearing immediately became involved in the Toledo Public Forum as its secretary and, on occasion, speaker. He also spoke at the liberal First Congregational Church, but in

61

1917 the tide turned against him. From the pulpit his progressive friend and colleague Allan Stockdale called Nearing a traitor for his pacifist speeches against U.S. participation in World War I. The trustees fired him from the University of Toledo.

Meanwhile, prowar "Preparedness Parades" were staged throughout the United States in anticipation of formal entry into the European war after Woodrow Wilson was reelected to the presidency. This was the year when General John Pershing pursued revolutionary Pancho Villa into Mexico, failing to find him, and when U.S. troops landed in the Dominican Republic to establish a military government. A military atmosphere had gained dominance.

The individualism of England was based on the law of self-interest—the dominant motive in men's lives according to the accepted philosophy of the time. The doctrine of *laissez-faire* became a weapon in the hands of the propertied classes—a weapon that was used and still is used to repress and confine the individuality of those who are so unfortunate as to have no property.

Under the individualism that developed in Nineteenth Century England, profit-seeking selfishness strangled liberty, and the individual was free in name and slave in fact. Poverty, child labor, woman exploitation, squalor and misery all flourished in the name of liberty, and they flourished because they were the basis of handsome commercial profits.

The United States has taken from Great Britain the nomenclature of liberty. She has likewise copied her machinery of exploitation. Here, as in England, squalor, child labor and beggarly wages challenge the boasted prosperity of a nation that tolerates abject poverty side by side with extravagant wealth.

The machine is the unit out of which the Industrial Régime has been built. The process of its building has reconstructed society. Machine, factory, plant, city, railroad, financial institution, are the steps in the evolution that has produced the Industrial Régime.

Before the coming of the machine, the individual craftsman was the unit in the industry. He could make a shoe, a hat, a piece of cloth, from the raw material to the finished product. Such a craftsman singlehanded could turn out industrial products.

The power-driven machine entered the field. The craftsman laid aside his hand tools, left the home work shop and went into the factory. The step was inevitable. Power was the essential element in this new type of industry, and power could be used effectively only where many machines were brought together under one roof. The factory became the new unit of industry. No individual worker in the factory made a complete product, but each one, occupied in some specialized task, worked, under the factory management, on a basis of division of labor. The craftsman disappeared, because, instead of making a shoe, he was tending a machine that performed one small operation in the whole process of shoemaking.

The factory is the unit of production, but it has built up a new social unit—the industrial city. The industrial city, depending on its neighbors for an exchange of products, becomes a unit in the industrial community. The railroads, telegraphs and telephones tie the community together. State bounderies and national lines alike become superfluous. The people of the world have been joined by their interdependent industrial activity.

The machine created the factory; the factory urbanized the village; the railroad bound together the scattered units into a closely knit community.

There is another factor, not yet considered, which is of the utmost importance. While the machine was creating the structure of modern industrial society, the business world was occupied in securing a control over it.

The combination is a union of similar industries. A number of steel industries had secured control of their raw material. These industries were merged in the United States Steel Corporation, which was one of the many combinations, or "trusts" as they were popularly called, that combined like industries. There were the sugar, oil, steel, plate-glass, harvester and many other combinations, each in greater or less control of a given industry.

Then the financial world took its last step in the organization of the Industrial Régime, by bringing together unlike industries.

The power of the Rockefeller interests and the Morgan interests is built in that way. It is neither a "trust" nor a combination, but a coordination of all of the elements in the industrial and financial world, under the control of one small group of individuals, or even around one powerful individual.

This is the Industrial Régime, and the small coterie of men who are at the center of financial control exercise whatever dominion is exercised over its affairs. Power, control, rule, government—which word must be used to characterize the part played in the affairs of the community by these few mighty ones, in whose hands there is concentrated the influence over so vast a field?

You sit down before a sewing machine that is run by electric power. You are putting the main seams in overalls. You reach over to the left of the machine, seize the two parts that are to be sewed together, place them side by side, push them under the needle, throw on the power, and for a moment the needle tears across the fabric at the speed of two thousand revolutions a minute.The piece is done; you break it from the thread, throw it into a box on the right of the machine, snatch two other pieces of goods and go on with the work as before. You are paid for the work at a piece rate that is set at a point which will enable you to make a living if you are quick and persistent at your task. There is no danger that you will loiter, for behind you, driving you to constant exertion are the want and hardship that go with low wages and perhaps the loss of a job.

There is a boy doing piece work. He sits in front of a revolving table, putting nuts onto bolts. He picks up a nut, places it upside down on the table; picks up a bolt, presses it against the revolving nut, which passes up on the thread of the bolt; picks up another nut, places it upside down on the revolving table; picks up a bolt and presses it against the nut; picks up another nut, threads it on a bolt, and so on through the twelve hours of his "shift." If he is quick, he can finish about eight hundred bolts an hour. He receives ten cents a thousand for the work.

This man is fastening the spokes into the iron eyelet that forms one side of the hub of a baby coach. He reaches for an eyelet, slips it to its place on the die, brings two pieces of bent wire that are to be the spokes and drops them into place with his right hand, drops a third piece of wire in place with his left hand, presses a treadle with his foot; the machine drops a die that fastens the six spokes securely into the eyelet; the man throws the completed work on a pile, reaches for another eyelet and repeats the process. There are seven hand motions and one foot motion required for each operation. The experienced operator turns out 20 pieces a minute; 1,200 pieces an hour, 10,000 pieces a day. In a week this machine tender repeats his series of eight motions from 50,000 to 60,000 times. What a prospect, at one week end, to contemplate for the coming week—fifty thousand repetitions of an habitual action! It is the price this man must pay for his daily bread.

The soul that should expand through the creative effort of craftsmanship; the mind that should be occupied with the educative processes of constructive work; the hand that should be trained to follow the behests of the soul and obey the directions of the mind; the stream of the man's consciousness—his whole being are prostituted to eight motions repeated, repeated, repeated until the imagination grows dizzy, as in the contemplation of infinity, with the difference that here it is affrighted by an infinity of littlenesses.

The present organization of industry makes it possible for some to live in ease and comfort without working, while the rest of mankind is engaged in hewing wood and drawing water. These people, while they use the products of the Industrial Régime, are not called upon to contribute in any way to its activity.

The device by which some of the beneficiaries of the Industrial Régime escape economic responsibility is a simple one known as "living on one's income."

No one asks how a man gets enough surplus wealth to have this property income. He may inherit it, find it, earn it. It may come from his father, uncle, or wife. Its source may be the steel business, the cotton business, the real estate market, the stock exchange or even the roulette wheel. It is not necessary for the owner of surplus wealth to explain. He simply puts his money into stocks, bonds or mortgages and draws his dividends or interest.

Those who work for wages make up the great body of the people in an industrial society. They are "the greatest number." Since democracy is based on the assumption that the welfare of the majority must be regarded as paramount, it seems evident that any system of governmental or social organization that professes to be democratic must regard the welfare of the wage-earners as of paramount importance. In so far as the community fails to give first place to the welfare of the wage-earners, who make up the greatest number in an industrial society, it fails in its efforts to establish democracy.

When the American people are willing to stand frankly for the proposition that the good things of life shall go to the favored few who hold the natural resources or some other form of monopoly power, there will be no further necessity to discuss democracy. But so long as the American government is organized as a democracy, and so long as American society is based on democratic principles, it will be necessary to insist on the fundamentals of democracy until the last bulwark of privilege is destroyed and democracy is, indeed, a reality.

The workers who carry the burdens of industrial activity should, under a democratic form of industrial organization, have its chief rewards. They do the work. They should receive the pay.

There are people—many of them—outside of the ranks of the wage-earners, who are convinced that the worker is now getting all that he is worth. Very frequently, cultured, intelligent, well-to-do people take such a position, and then, to prove their point, they cite instances of paperhangers, plumbers, gardeners and washerwomen who were paid "more than they were worth." Such statements naturally raise the question, "What are men worth?"

What is worth, and who are worthy?

Service is the only test that the economist can apply as a measure of worth. In so far as we do for others, we are expressing truth, justice and mercy in our acts. Thus the spiritual values appear in material or at least in visible forms.

Worth is measured by service. Men are worth as much as they serve.

The "useful" or "worthy" citizen is therefore the one who renders the great service. The commands, "Do unto others as you would that they should do unto you" and "Love thy neighbor" are immortal because they are founded on service, which is the first and greatest law of life.

With this service measure of worth in mind, turn to the proposition that this cotton weaver and that salesgirl are receiving adequate wages.

Here is a man who is giving the best of his time and energy—his very life—three hundred days a year, ten hours every day to the weaving of cotton cloth. As a return for this labor, he receives $600 a year. If such a man, giving three thousand hours each year to the task of making clothing that will be worn by his fellows, is worth $600, how much is the man worth who has been living since the day that he was born, thirty years ago, on the income from his father's estate?

The father and the husband protest. "Have we not a right to keep our sons and our wives in idleness and luxury if we see fit to do so?" To be sure you have. You may put your wealth into their upkeep as you would to the upkeep of any other bit of decorative finery. At the same time you must realize that they are only decorative finery, and that therefore, like any other wanton luxury, they are an offense to the community so long as there are working people who lack the necessaries of life; and furthermore, that it is unseemly, even grotesque, for such people and for the group in society which they represent to say that this or that person who is engaged in doing some useful work is "getting all he is worth."

Those who hew the wood and draw the water, those who labor with the head or with the hand in the interest of the upbuilding of the community, are in a class by themselves. In another class, distinct from the workers, are those who, because of their ownership of some natural resource or of some productive machinery, are able to take from the worker a part of the product of his labor in the form of rent or interest. The workers build society and make progress possible. The owners live, parasitically, upon the proceeds of the work which the workers are doing.

Wages are adequate when they reflect the best interests of the community. There are three important ways in which their effect on the community may be measured: (1) The wage paid must be sufficient to maintain the efficiency of the workers; (2) the wage must be high enough to make poverty, hardship or social dependence unnecessary; (3) the wage must be sufficient to enable the worker and his family to live like self-respecting members of the community.

The worker is not paid in proportion to his product. Wages are never fixed on that basis, with this single exception—that no employer can afford to pay any more in wages than a group of men are producing in product. The law of monopoly, "all that the traffic will bear," is the law which fixes the American wage.

The American wage is anti-social. The present system of wage payment fails to stimulate workers to industry and thrift because it has not given them a reward in proportion to their exertions and ability. There is no relation between product and wages. Rather wages are fixed by competition and monopoly. The present wage scale fails completely to provide a return in proportion to social needs. The simplest requirements of social progress call for ambition, for justice, and for the provision of health necessities. The present American wage scale offends even these primitive social standards.

American industry pays to the overwhelming majority of wage-earners a wage of less than $1,000 a year. Even where no allowance is made for unemployment, the wage rates of three-quarters of the men fall below $750 a year. Perhaps three wage-earners in each hundred are paid over $25 per week (a yearly rate of $1,300). Compared with the sums which are met with in the business world, the wage of the workers is small.

The Industrial Régime places a penalty on work. There is the pittance return—pitifully small, economically and socially inadequate—paid to millions of workers in exchange for their energy and time during the best part of each day and the best part of their lives. No student of the problem can escape the feeling that this wage is wholly insufficient in comparison with the contribution that the worker makes toward the upkeep of the Industrial Régime. The minimum wage and social insurance would seem to be the barest beginnings of a policy of economic justice applied to wages.

The great leader is the great server. The leader derives his commission to leadership from the special qualities that enable him to be of service to his fellows. The old method of finding leaders assumed that they must come from a select, ruling class. The new method assumes that they are to be utilized, wherever found. The old method revolved about the aristocracy. The new method revolves about the great mass of men. Under the old scheme, leaders were to be bred; under the new scheme, they are to be found. The old idea appears under the name Eugenics; the new idea under the name Education.

There is one man in the community who should do each piece of work that is to be done—that man is the one best fitted by heredity and by training to do the work. The right leader is, therefore, the man best born and best trained for leadership.

Heredity gives the quality of the steel. The training puts on the edge. Poor steel will not take an edge. But the best of steel will not cut unless it has been sharpened. How shall we determine whether a given piece of steel will cut? Sharpen it and see!

The old method rested its case with the education of the elect. Why sharpen the rest of the metal in the community when everyone knew that it was either poor steel or lead? There was no reason for extending opportunity beyond the elect.

The new plan makes it necessary to begin the sharpening of every piece of metal in the community in order to determine which is the genuine tool steel. There is no means of deciding in advance which man is best able to assuming the position of community leader. The best leaders can be picked only through a process of continuous experimentation. That process is called apprenticeship when it is applied to industry and education when it is applied to the community.

One man, who had been extremely poor in his boyhood, recently wrote an essay entitled, "Why I Believe in Poverty." But when his own son graduated from an expensive preparatory school, instead of sending him to the street, to enjoy the blessings of poverty, he picked out one of the most exclusive of the smaller colleges, and entered him there.

Men and women a-plenty have risen from poverty, but for each such case there are a dozen or a score where the balance has turned the wrong way. Of those who do recover from the effects of poverty, many bear the physical and spiritual scars of the struggle to their graves.

If poverty were such a blessing as some folks would have us believe, is it not strange that the whole community should dread it and hate as it dreads and hates no other contagious disease? And, stranger still, that for each thousand that have learned of poverty at first hand by living in it and escaping from it, not one sends his children back into the slough for the building of their bodies and the saving of their souls?

The fact is that poverty is horrible. Those who are most familiar with poverty—who have observed it and analyzed it critically, find it unrelieved by any mitigating circumstance.

There was a time when people were sent to prison for debt just as they were sent to prison for theft. The assumption was that the poor man was responsible for his poverty. He was vicious, drunken, lazy, inefficient. These things, like any other personal offenses, were punished personally.

The latest work that has been done on poverty makes it possible to say, unequivocally, that personal vices and personal shortcomings are not the chief causes of poverty. Indeed, they are insignificant when compared with the larger social causes that are responsible for poverty.

Social forces like unemployment, accidents, sickness, widowhood and the like are largely responsible for poverty.

The chief cause of poverty is low wages. People are poor because the rate of wages paid by the industries of the United States will not permit them to be anything but poor.

Those who have been in the habit of thinking of poverty as a result of personal vices, should reflect on the relations that actually exist between people in the various walks of life in present-day society. No group of people has a monopoly either on the vices or the virtues. Not all of the people who drink are poor; not all vicious people are poor; nor are all dissipated, extravagant, idle, shiftless, inefficient people poor. Such people may be found in every economic group from the poorest to the richest. There is one group of people who are always poor—the people who are paid less than a living wage. The relation between low wages and poverty is as intimate as the relation between cholera microbes and cholera. The poor are poor, in the first instance, because the wages they get are poverty wages.

Poverty is a social crime. The cause of poverty lies at our doors. People are poor because we make them poor. Children are growing up in poverty because we allow them to do it. "True enough," admit the rich, "we do not give generously. Even the largest gifts are, as a rule, paltry when one considers the amount the giver has left. At the same time, we spend our money generously, circulate it and thus make people prosperous."

That "spending" argument is very old and somewhat overlooked. Yet it is astonishing to find how many people believe it implicitly. To it there are several answers.

First, if it were true that spending makes prosperity, the cause of progress would be served best by having one person do all the spending for the community. That proposition even the most ardent advocate of the spending argument would hardly accept unless he was sure to be designated the spender.

Second, in proportion to their income, the poor spend more than the rich. Therefore, if spending were the objective desired, the most successful way to have money spent would be to give it to the poor.

Third, the assumption that spending rather than saving makes for prosperity, is based on an idea that is not necessarily correct. In a new country, the person who saves is more important than the person who spends, because it is from the savings of the careful individual that the capital for new industries is secured.

Fourth, the person who spends does not do so primarily because he wishes to be philanthropic. He spends because he wishes to have the things that he buys. The rich man's food, clothing and house decoration are bought with an eye to the rich man's taste—not to the poor man's welfare.

Fifth, when a rich man uses up food and clothing to supply himself with comforts and luxuries, he automatically denies the rest of the community those same things. There is a loaf of bread for supper. If father eats two-thirds of the loaf, there is only one-third left for mother and children. At any given time there is only a certain amount of wealth in the community. If one man uses it, other people are automatically deprived of it unless there is more than enough to go round.

7 DEBATE: WILL DEMOCRACY CURE SOCIAL ILLS? (1917)

Affirmative: Scott Nearing
Negative: Clarence S. Darrow

C HICAGO ATTORNEY CLARENCE DARROW was a noted criminal lawyer in many nationally celebrated cases. One of them was to be the 1925 *Scopes versus Tennessee* trial on the question of teaching "evolution" in public schools. William Jennings Bryan, the populist fundamentalist politician, prosecuted the case and won.

This debate was held under the auspices of The Workers' University Society, an 11-year-old organization that conducted Sunday-afternoon lectures for six months of the year at the Garrick Theatre in Chicago. In the debate, Darrow, a man of pessimistic wit and humor, declared that the purpose of man is like a pollywog that wiggles along as long as he can stay alive. Nearing took the affirmative and maintained that true democracy provided liberty today and opportunity tomorrow. Second, true democracy was designed to eliminate social ills for the mass of people, including eradicating unearned income from interest, rents, and profits, thereby preventing poverty and war.

Darrow's banter and Nearing's serious moral enthusiasm made an engaging debating pair. They drew packed crowds. In March 1921 they debated again, this time, "Is Life

71

Worth Living?" to a jammed Lexington Theatre in New York City. Darrow held that man is a traveling boarding house for microbes that eat him in the end, that our teeth fall out when we need them the most, and that the best part of life is being asleep because that is as good as dead. Nearing held that life is what you put into it, that it is worth while if it is dedicated to adventure, creation, and service.

Scott Nearing's Second Speech

Chairman: Professor Nearing will now have twenty-five minutes.

Nearing: I am glad Mr. Darrow decided to make fun of the common people instead of making fun of me. I wish, however, in his next speech he would tell us what he thinks of this crowd. There must be something wrong somewhere. Somebody must have slipped a cog. Mr. Darrow says that the man in front of the pack will be killed, and he says the man behind the pack will be killed. Then, how is it, Mr. Darrow, that we are no longer in packs, but have developed and materially advanced in our art, culture, which we call civilization? We spent a million years, maybe more or less, and during that time we have come up from pack life and we have modified, not only our method of living, but our attitude of life so completely that there is very little likeness between pack life and modern, civilized life.

If Mr. Darrow's argument were correct, the pack should be today exactly where it was a million years ago.

Mr. Darrow says the people are not intelligent; what do they know, says he, of science, philosophy and government? They are the commonplace, he says again, and like only commonplace things. I should like to condemn Mr. Darrow to live for twelve months in a society, let us say, of Spencers, Huxleys and Spinozas. If he came out intellectually and physically alive, he would be a lucky man. The saving grace of people like Mr. Huxley and Mr. Spencer and Mr. Darwin is that there are so many other people who are not like them. The fellow ahead of the pack, as Mr. Darrow so well says, is dangerous to the pack, just as the fellow behind is dangerous to himself, and so the pack eliminates the man ahead, or he is eliminated; and the pack eliminates the man behind or he is eliminated as it should very logically be in the interest of who? Why, in the interest of the pack! Thank God, the majority of people do not live in terms of philosophy, science and government. They simply live in terms of life, and if they lived in any other terms the human race could not conceivably continue.

Now Mr. Darrow says we have tried, we have failed and always will fail. That is a very interesting statement. There is only one unproved proposition in the world and that is the proposition, "It can't be done". You can not prove that. There are lots of things that you can prove, but you can not prove that it can't be done. You know that you have been proving that for about a million years. People like Mr. Darrow have said exactly that thing ever since they first began to shape the first rude implements, and to experiment crudely with the arts and crafts. Someone has always shaken his head and has said, wisely, and I hope for the sake of the crowd wittily, "Well, well, it can't be done".

During those few thousand years that we can look back to with some degree of intelligence wise men have shaken their heads wisely and they have said to Spinoza and to Spencer and to Darwin and to Jesus and to all of the rest of the forerunners, just as Mr. Darrow has said today, "It can't be done." And scientists have gone on and social reforms have gone on, and "the world do move". And the reason why, "it do move," in spite of Mr. Darrow and all he may say to the contrary, is because our human world is made up of something else except the constituent elements that Mr. Darrow seems to think are existing there.

He said ten men are idiots. They still are idiots if you bring them together. But the result of bringing a million men to the ballot box is profound wisdom. Well, you will remember that amused you when he said it, and it amused me, too, because it is true if you take ten idiots to start with, but it is not true if you go into the crowd and take ten people. Mr. Darrow should bear this in mind, and I think it is an important fact and one that we should reiterate and restate, until everybody gets it thoroughly stuck in his mind, that there are various kinds of elements in human nature. There are various kinds of genius in human nature, I know, for example, Mr. Darrow referred to home—What was that?

Darrow: Mother, home and heaven.

Nearing: Mother, home and heaven. Mr. Darrow, for example, referred to mother, home and heaven. I know women, who will never be heard of in the archives, whose names will never be written down, but who have the particular genius for bringing up children. I know men whose names will never be recorded, who have a peculiar genius for polishing wood, or setting tile, or doing some other commonplace things that are done. Now, it seems to me that where Mr. Darrow makes a serious mistake is in supposing, as he said, that a few people have done the great things of the world. This is not so. A few people have been recorded on the pages of history as having done the great things of the world. But around those few people—behind and before them—there have been hundreds of thousands of other people who have contributed a little less in degree, a little less effectively, but they have nevertheless assisted the one distinguished person whose name stands out. George Washington and the men who stood with him wrought great things, but without the men George Washington's achievements would have been impossible. The really serious proposition that Mr. Darrow raises—none of these propositions are serious—but the really serious point that he and I must face out he puts in this way: Nature, he says, knows nothing about Democracy; she works without purpose or means or ends. But, says Mr. Darrow, she must be obeyed. Let us run over that.

Nature knows nothing about Democracy. She works without purpose or means or ends, but she must be obeyed. Now, this is a very fine text because it enables me to say exactly what I want to say in the second speech. If Mr. Darrow's ancestors had followed the behests of that nature he refers to, he would be squatting in the sands somewhere along the seashore looking for shellfish. The very element which Mr. Darrow overlooks is that man has entered nature with purposes, with means, and with ends, and that it is exactly to the extent that he has purposes and means and ends that he succeeds in accomplishing the things he sets out to accomplish.

You talk about a state of nature. Compare it with the state of man and, as Ray Lankester points out in his book, "The Kingdom of Man," you have a tremendous contrast between the things that man has done for himself and the things that nature would have done if man had not butted in on the proposition. And it is just this butting in of the human race that constitutes—if you take one line of argument—one form of nature, or, if you take another line of argument—that constitutes a contravention, a denial, a subversion of nature. It is exactly this butting in of the human race that I am talking about. That is what I am here for this afternoon to try to persuade Mr. Darrow that if he and the rest of the human race will butt in with enough enthusiasm, and enough vigor, and enough intelligence, and enough of the genius that he praises so highly we can eliminate unearned income, poverty and war.

I do not mean to controvert Mr. Darrow's proposition about nature being obeyed, because I believe that, and that is one of the reasons why I am trying to make the point that I am making. Nature must be obeyed. One of the laws of nature is that we grow by experience, that we grow by activity. If you stop activity you stop life. The essential element in special privilege government is that it depends on someone else doing it for you. Monarchy, aristocracy, plutocracy, any form of government where a special group governs for the great majority, is based on the proposition that we are better off with Paternalism than with Democracy. Because we get more to eat, or because we have more to wear. I contend that we are better off with Democracy, because Democracy is a method of public expression, i.e., instead of having somebody come in and do it for you, the people are called upon to do it for themselves.

Mr. Darrow says they bungle. I should like to ask Mr. Darrow whether his friends, the lawyers, ever bungle? I know that the doctors and the school teachers bungle. I can take Mr. Darrow to any highly trained professional group in the community and I can show him a bunch of bunglers. But at the same time I can show him marvelous achievements that have been worked out in spite of the bunglers. If the lawyers, doctors, teachers and scientists were placed in an auditorium and had the Angel Gabriel lecturing to them for six hours a day, they would never become any better lawyers or doctors or scientists or teachers. But if you put them to work with the crude knowledge and tools they have and let them experiment and try and fail, and try again and fail some more, and finally work out the solution, then you are getting step by step an advance from the savage squatting on the seashore hunting for shellfish to the man in civilization with a relatively larger amount of leisure and culture and knowledge.

Mr. Darrow says the people have not even got intelligence enough to vote themselves out of the necessity of working. Mr. Darrow overlooks the fact that our ancestors did not have to work. You go down into the torrid and semi-tropics and you find people living now without working. Mr. Darrow can go and join them if he wants to.

One of the greatest things of modern life is the opportunity which some of us have to work out the things that we believe in and do the things that we enjoy. If it were not for civilization we would be squatting on the seashore waiting for the waves to roll up some shellfish. Because of civilization we can write, and we can paint and experiment scientifically; we can go on with all of the multitude of activities that the modern community offers because we have had this pack growing and progressing, advancing, developing, evolving.

My proposition is simply this, that the more opportunity you give to the pack the more rapid its advancement will be. I realize that people are stupid. I know, for instance, in our profession, we are pretty stupid on the whole; we are not a bright lot. But on the other hand I know a lot of young fellows in my profession that are trying very hard not to be stupid. Occasionally, I suppose, one or more of them succeeds in doing something that is really worth while.

That is the thing that counts effectively in eliminating the ills of society, unearned increment, poverty, war, and the other social ills with which we have to contend. A great force in the world is moral enthusiasm. And most of the men, in fact I think you can say all of the men, mentioned by Mr. Darrow this afternoon, were men who have tremendous moral enthusiasm. Men who faced insurmountable obstacles, who faced them optimistically, enthusiastically, who worked untiringly and joyously at the task they were engaged in. He says Spinoza died in a garret, that he lived on a crust of bread. What of it? He had the opportunity to practice and think out his philosophy. I submit, Mr. Darrow would have preferred to have lived on a crust and die in a garret than to sit, squatting, on the seashore, waiting for the ocean waves to roll up shellfish.

Now, do you see the issue between us? It is quite simple. Mr. Darrow thinks that it is not worth while because the people are so "doggone stupid". I think that it is worth while just because, if we will admit it for the sake of argument, the people are "doggone stupid". And I think most of us are pretty stupid. I would rather live with a lot of stupid people than with a lot of angels, I can not imagine anything more tiresome than angels, because angels are perfect people who have arrived, and all there is left to do is to sit around with crowns on their heads, read the scriptures, and sing "Glory Halleujah". I am not interested, and there are lots of other people I know who are not interested in singing glory halleujah.

We want a chance to put our energies to the wheel of progress and show what we can do in the next thirty years. We have seen other thirty year periods. For example, we have seen that brilliant period that followed the American and the French Revolutions at the end of the Eighteenth Century, and we have seen that brilliant period in the first thirty years in the Nineteenth Century when such marvelous changes were wrought in the western world. And we have seen, going back of that, other periods, in Thebes, in Greece, in Rome, in Genoa. And we have seen these wonderful spots, these bright lights in the history of the development of the human race when marvelous things were done by people, when the whole race has moved upward and onward to a higher level of development. All we ask is the opportunity to use our energy and to put our activities and our enthusiasm behind this thing, to put across Democracy, and let us see what will happen. Then if the thing does not happen that we expected, we will put across something else until the thing does happen that we expect, and we would like to have Mr. Darrow join the crowd.

8   THE GREAT MADNESS (1917)

THIS 44-PAGE MONOGRAPH was the basis for the "traitor" trial of Nearing under the Espionage Act passed by Congress June 15, 1917, for encouraging disloyalty or interference with the draft. Nearing was the only defendant prosecuted under the act during these war years to be acquitted. The monograph was published by the Rand School of Social Science, which was codefendant in the trial.

The Rand School was founded in 1906 by Carrie Rand as an outlet for educating labor organizers and workers in the ideals and principles of socialism. Nearing had delivered speeches and courses for the school beginning in 1913; he became a member of the staff and the Socialist Party in 1917. He was considered the most popular member of the teaching staff and drew hundreds of students and listeners, sometimes more than 1,000. Reserved cards for his classes were often required. He was a powerful teacher armed with research, conviction, clarity, and sincerity.

The previous summer of 1916 while teaching and speaking at Chautauqua against the "preparedness" (he asked, "Preparedness for war or peace?"), federal authorities confiscated his papers and files from his home in Toledo. For the rest of his life, he retained very few personal papers, his shock and distrust was so striking.

Organizations opposed to the war, such as the International Workers of the World (IWW), the Socialist Party, and Women's International League for Peace and Freedom, coalesced into the People's Council for Freedom and Democracy; Nearing was elected chairman.

Meanwhile, the United States officially entered the European war April 4, 1917, against impassioned revelations by Sen. George W. Norris (R-Neb.) that Wall Street members were advising their clients of the prosperity that war would bring, a central point that Nearing writes about in *The Great Madness*. The conscription law affecting 10 million men between 21 and 30 years of age (4,700,000 eventually were conscripted) was passed May 18; the first American troops reached Europe 49 days later. In the end, the year-and-a-half participation by the United States in World War I resulted in 320,000 American casualties.

The two per cent of the people (one person in each fifty) who own sixty per cent of the wealth of the United States are no different from the other people of the country,—they are no more selfish, greedy or ferocious. They realize that war is barbarous, and they would avoid it if they possibly could. They also believe that there are some things worse than war,—the confiscation of special privileges; the abolition of unearned income; the overthrow of the economic parasitism; the establishment of industrial democracy. The plutocrats would welcome a war that promised salvation from any such calamities; they would also welcome a war that promised greater foreign markets, the destruction of foreign competition, more security for property rights and a longer lease on life for plutocratic despotism.

The plutocrats, or wealth lords, are not savages, ogres or devils. They are men and women whose economic and social position makes them feel the "cohesion of wealth." Engaged in a common enterprise— the maintenance of a social system that enables them to live upon the labor of the masses—they will do anything and everything that will safeguard and protect that system.

How could the plutocracy—the discredited, villified plutocracy—get public opinion? There was only one way—it must line up with some cause that would command public confidence. The cause that it chose was the "defense of the United States."

The campaign was intense and dramatic. Japanese invasions, Mexican inroads, and a world conquest by Germany were featured in the daily press, in the magazines, on the movie screens and in public addresses. Depredations, murder and rapine were to be the lot of the American people unless they built battleships and organized armies. "Preparedness" was an argument in itself and every channel of publicity in the United States devoted a major share of attention to this argument.

The preparedness movement came from the business interests. It was

fostered and financed by the plutocracy. It was their first successful
effort at winning public confidence, and so well was it managed that
millions of Americans fell into line, fired by the love of the flag and the
world-old devotion to family and fireside; millions more trembled with
the fear of the frightful war that was coming, and other millions were
gripped by the hate and the war lust that inspire war madness.

From preparedness to patriotism was a short step. The preparedness
advocates had used the flag freely. Patriotism ran high. Enthusiasm for
the flag increased. Patriotic committees were organized, but when the
names of the patriots appeared in the newspapers they were distinguished by one outstanding fact,—the vast majority of them were the
successful business and professional men who were the center and
forefront of the patriotic movement just as they had been the center and
forefront of the preparedness movement.

The price of flags rose rapidly—the flag manufacturers took this
opportunity to get their share of the good things that were "going
round"—nevertheless, the workers by the hundreds of thousands "contributed" to provide flags for the establishments in which they were
employed. Men were discharged when they refused to make such
"contributions."

The plutocratic brand of patriotism won the endorsement of the press,
the pulpit, the college, and every other important channel of public
information in the United States. The "educated," "cultured," "re-
fined," "high-principled" editors, ministers, professors and lawyers
accepted it and proclaimed it as though it were their own. Turning their
backs upon principle, throwing morals and ideals to the winds, they
tumbled over one another in a wild scramble to be the first to join the
chorus of plutocratic patriotism.

The President hurried to the rescue with his preposterous phrase
"armed neutrality," and asked Congress for permission to place guns
and gunners on American merchantmen. While the President asked for
this authority as a peace measure, it was pretty clear that armed neutrality would mean war the first time that an armed merchantman met a
submarine.

The President's request for authority to arm American merchant ves-
sels was made in an address to Congress, February 26, 1917, in which
he said,—"I am not now proposing or contemplating war or any steps
that need lead to it. I request that you authorize me to supply our
merchant ships with defensive arms, should that become necessary, and
with the means of using them."

The armed ship bill failed to pass because a handful of senators
refused to have it rushed through during the closing hours of the session. The result was electric. The President denounced them as "a little

group of willful men." The papers cartooned them and villified them in the most shameless manner. They were called "German agents" and scores of newspapers presented them with the Iron Cross. Among those senatorial "traitors" were the few senators who had stood for the common people against the vested interests.

The patriots of plutocracy did not confine their attention to Congressmen. The term "traitor" was flung in the teeth of anyone who opposed the seven league steps that the administration was taking toward war. Radicals who had always opposed war; ministers who had spent their lives in preaching peace on earth; scientists whose work had brought them into contact with the peoples of the whole world; public men who believed that the United States could do greater and better work for democracy by staying out of the war were persecuted as zealously as though they had sided with Protestantism in Catholic Spain under the Inquisition. The plutocracy had declared for war, and woe betide the heedless or willful one who still insisted upon urging the gospel of peace.

The "patriots" wanted to ship goods to the Allied governments. Armed neutrality for them meant business opportunity. The "traitors" were those who opposed foreign entanglements and alliances and who used every effort to keep the United States out of the war.

On April 6th, with the passage of the resolution declaring the existence of a state of war, the American people found themselves in war, after returning a party to power only five months before because it had "kept us out of war."

As soon as war was declared, the administration undertook to secure,—money, conscription, and censorship. The first and most important of these was money. Congress passed almost immediately the bill authorizing a bond issue of seven billions of dollars.

The Liberty Loan was important to the American bankers who had financed the Allies, because it guaranteed Allied credit. There were other things about it, however, that were even more significant than its assistance in international business. It gave the local business men a chance to do a piece of work of the utmost importance to their own security.

Everybody who was in touch with American public opinion on the sixth of April knew that the war was not popular. People were apathetic, indifferent or actively hostile. There was little display of enthusiasm except among the business men and their immediate adherents. The Liberty Loan gave plutocracy a chance to put in every American home an economic argument (a bond paying $3^{1}/_{2}$ per cent) in favor of standing behind the government.

There was another argument in favor of selling the bonds to the people. Now that the plutocracy were the messengers of democracy in

Germany and the incarnation of patriotism in the United States, to gainsay or to question their position was to be a traitor to the Stars and Stripes, which they had taken over as completely as they had previously taken over the steel, coal, iron, wheat, cotton, water power, franchises, banks, railroads and the like. Hence, any employee could be asked by an employer in the name of liberty and democracy to buy a bond.

The President's speech on April 2nd, and the "war-vote" of Congress on April 6th, plunged the American people into the war. The Liberty Loan saddled the immediate payment for the war upon millions of unwilling common people and yoked up the next generation to a war debt over which they had no control. The war-madness was beginning to yield its bitter fruit.

The second measure of importance to the business world was conscription. When the Conscription Bill was introduced into Congress there was a general feeling through the country that it could not pass. Even the press hesitated, so un-American was this Bill, which clearly violated the spirit of the constitution and the traditions of American life.

Then courage was supplied to the press from somewhere, and the newspapers and magazines of the country went to work with a will. They apologized, explained and insisted. Six weeks after war was declared the bill had passed Congress. Within two months, more than nine million young men had been "selected for service."

The Conscription Bill paved the way for a military system exactly like that which had been so savagely denounced in Germany. It gave the American plutocracy the beginnings of a big, cheap army. It disposed of the uncertainties of volunteering and provided the possibility of military education for every young American. At the same time the way was opened for the imposition of universal service, which was all that Prussia has ever demanded in the balmiest days of her militarism. Then, too, a beginning was made toward industrial conscription, and the possibility was opened for the importation of coolie and peon labor, things which were not even thinkable in peace days.

"The United States has been suffering from an over-dose of democracy" insists one ardent supporter of the plutocracy. The censorship bill was designed to remedy this deplorable situation by sweeping aside personal liberty. The declaration of war was a slap in the face of democracy,—the censorship bill bandaged its eyes, plugged its ears and gagged its mouth.

The censorship bill, in its original form, was so drastic and far-reaching that even the newspapers denounced it. So general was the opposition that after weeks of fighting, the bill was approved by the President on June 15th in such a modified form that there was no direct reference to freedom of speech and of the press. But tucked away in an obscure corner of Section 481½ was an amendment to the Postal Laws

82

which reads,—"Every letter, writing, circular, postal card, picture, print, engraving, photograph, newspaper, pamphlet, book, or other publication, matter or thing of any kind containing any matter which is intended to obstruct the recruiting or enlistment service of the United States is hereby declared to be non-mailable."

Under this section each one of the 123,387 United States postmasters is made a censor with authority (subject to the reversal of his superiors) to exclude from the mails anything that in his judgment will "obstruct the recruiting or enlistment service." The Federal authorities were not slow in availing themselves of this immense power. The Cleveland (Ohio) *Socialist,* the Detroit (Mich.) *Socialist,* the *Rebel* of Texas, the *International Socialist Review,* the *American Socialist,* the *Masses* and other radical publications were promptly denied the use of the mails. The *American Socialist* (Chicago) had planned a "Liberty Edition" for June 30th. The entire edition and two other editions were held up by the Chicago postmaster acting under instructions from Washington. Other papers were temporarily suspended.

A storm of protest broke over the country. Within the memory of the oldest inhabitant there had been no such deliberate violation of the freedom of the press which is guaranteed by the First Amendment to the Constitution.

The President decided that the best way to "make the world safe for democracy" was to abandon America's traditional policy of isolation; to form an alliance with six democracies and seven monarchies; to mobilize the resources of the country, and to enter the world war as an active belligerent.

And the American people stood for it. Emotionalized, dazed, stupefied, and blinded by the great madness that possessed their souls, nearly a hundred millions of people cast aside their most cherished principles, sacrificed their hard-won liberties, and began spreading brotherhood and democracy with the sword.

Three years of ceaseless effort on the part of the press, the pulpit, the school, the screen and the stage had sufficed to infuse millions of Americans with the mob fear and mob hate that are the warp and woof of war-madness. The carefully planned, brilliantly executed scheme of advertising preparedness, patriotism and war, had left a great section of the American people incapable of reasoning or understanding. On April 2nd there were millions who had been worried, harried, and emotionalized through the successive stages of fear, resentfulness, bitterness, hatred and frenzy until they were sufficiently ferocious to be willing to use the knife.

The plutocrats won immunity, power and wealth, measured in seven figures. They won more. First, they secured the big navy and army for which they had worked so faithfully,—an army to menace neighbors and to preserve peace at home during the deluge of misery that will follow the bursting cloud of war-values and war-prices; a navy to guard the hundreds of millions that they have invested in "undeveloped" countries; and seven billions of dollars to be spent at once—much of it on war contracts, which afford proverbially fat pickings.

Again they had won conscription—the right to send a million Americans into the trenches of France to fight for the poor Belgians, for Lombard Street, Wall Street and King George of England.

They had established a spirit that permitted children to go back into factories from which years of incessant labor had rescued them; women to take men's jobs at a fraction of the wage, and the standards surrounding the labor of men to be lowered.

The plutocrats won another point—a point desired by every despot— they won the right to impose restrictions upon the freedom of speech, of press and assemblage, which are the foundation of democracy. The plutocracy bought the press, subsidized the pulpit, placed their representatives in control of the schools, and by the use of the police and postal censorship they restricted individual liberty.

The people of the United States woke up in 1917 to find themselves at war; subject to conscription; their liberties gone, and the business interests in control. At first they were puzzled—almost frightened. Then they began to understand.

To-day, in all parts of the United States, they are banding themselves together, politically and industrially. They are organizing. They propose to make the world safe for democracy.

Their struggle must begin in the United States. No part of the world is in greater need of their effort.

The work of the people is cut out for them—cut out in all its stupendous importance. They must:

1. Continue to meet regularly and systematically for the discussion of vital questions.
2. Publish a paper in every city that will be owned by the people and will represent them.
3. Capture the schools. The school system is the greatest single asset now in the hands of the plutocracy.
4. Establish industrial and political solidarity.
5. Educate! Educate!! Everywhere and upon every possible occasion in home, shop, street car, meeting hall.
6. Take all profit out of industry.
7. Guarantee and maintain equal opportunity and justice for all.

Those steps taken, this end achieved, and a beginning will have been made for a safe democracy in the United States and an example of immense importance will have been set for the world.

The people are learning. The events of the past few months are teaching them with lightning-like rapidity. They are filled with the bitterness and hate which the press and the pulpit has planted there; it is only a question of time before they discover their real enemies in New York and Washington—and then the "victory" of the American plutocracy will be turned into a sweeping triumph for the common people of the United States.

9 THE TRIAL OF SCOTT NEARING (1919)

T HE RAND SCHOOL FOR SOCIAL SCIENCE published the
transcript of the trial of Nearing and the American Socialist Society (not the Socialist Party), publisher of Scott's
44-page monograph "The Great Madness." The brief ques-
tion-and-answer section excerpted here shows how adept
Nearing was on the witness stand; his statement to the jury
at the end of the trial summarizes not only his motivations
for writing the pamphlet but also much of his philosophy of
socialism and pacifism.

During this era other similar trials occurred, including
those of Eugene Debs (sentenced to 10 years in prison),
Rose Pastor Stokes, Max Eastman and colleagues of the
"Masses" journal, and leaders of the International Workers
of the World (IWW). Nearing was the only one acquitted.

The indictment charged that Nearing, through publication
of the monograph, had inspired disloyalty to the country
and urged resistance to the draft, causing insubordination
and mutiny. Curiously, not one enemy agent was convicted
under the Espionage Act. U.S. government prosecution,
however, sent many American radicals and pacifists to
prison.

Nearing was 35 years old at the time of the trial. The year
was filled with social flares—4 million steelworkers,
miners, dock workers, and others struck to reduce the average 68.7-hour work week and increase wages, the Red
Army made advances in Russia, Benito Mussolini established his Fascist party, the U.S. Senate refused to ratify the

Treaty of Versailles, race riots broke out in Chicago, and
the Eighteenth Amendment (Prohibition) made alcohol illegal in America.

Q. And when you sent this manuscript, "The Great Madness" to the
Rand School, you realized if it was published, it would be distributed
and circulated, didn't you? Throughout the country, didn't you?

A. Certainly.

Q. And that it would come into the hands of men who were subject to
induction into the army under the Selective Service Act, men between
twenty-one and thirty?

A. I suppose so.

Q. And you wanted to persuade your readers to your own point of
view about the war, didn't you?

A. I wanted to present to my readers my opinion regarding the whole
incident of the war, yes, sir.

Q. And you did that for the purpose of persuading them?

A. If they saw it my way, I expected them to accept it.

Q. And you wanted them to accept it, didn't you?

A. Yes.

Q. You wanted them to believe this way, that this was an unjust war,
didn't you?

A. I wanted them to believe that this was a capitalist war.

Q. And that it was an unjust war?

A. As all wars are unjust, yes.

Q. You wanted them to believe that it was waged in the interests of
selfish plutocratic classes, didn't you?

A. Primarily so, yes, sir.

Q. And that it was not a war to make the world safe for democracy,
was not that what you wanted them to believe, that it was not a war to
make the world safe for democracy?

A. I did not then believe that it was a war to make the world safe for
democracy, and I wanted other people to see that it was not a war to
make the world safe for democracy.

Q. You wanted these people to read your pamphlets?

A. I wanted the people to read the pamphlets and realize that it was a
war that was being continued by the plutocrats, and for their own selfish
ends to fasten their hold on the American people.

Q. And you used the best arguments that occurred to you to prove
your point?

A. Yes, sir, I got the best data I could.

Q. Did it occur to you that you might persuade some of your readers
to your point of view?

A. I hoped somebody, after they read it, would see my point of view.

Q. You thought they would, didn't you?

A. They usually do, some of them.

Q. You thought your arguments were pretty good, didn't you?

A. I still think so, and I did then.

Q. Was it your belief, or was it not your belief, that if it might persuade, that is, if you might persuade by your pamphlets, some of these people to your point of view with regard to the war, men who were within the draft age, and who were subsequently inducted into the army, that they would become insubordinate?

A. I should say on the contrary, sir, that the millions of socialists who fought in this war, and who held that view, were not any less insubordinate than the other fellows, certainly not more so.

Q. Yes, but I know, they were not American soldiers, were they?

A. No, but a Socialist is a Socialist, whether he speaks American or French. The Socialists who had been fighting in the war, to my knowledge, were just as reliable as the other fellows they were fighting with in the war. I see no reason to believe that a man who had these convictions would make any worse soldier—I think he would make a whole lot better brother for the great brotherhood that is coming later on in the world—but I do not know that he would be any worse as a soldier in this country.

Q. Don't you think and didn't you think that a man believing this way, that the war was a selfish capitalistic war for the capitalistic interests, and that he was being brought into it, that he would be apt to be disloyal to his country, in the sense of the word ordinarily used, of the word disloyalty?

A. On the contrary, I know many men who were drafted and went, and others that certainly had that point of view in their minds.

Q. And you did hope, that by reading this, they would get your point of view about the war then, and then you say you think that they would be just as loyal soldiers?

A. I was not attempting to make either loyal soldiers or disloyal soldiers.

Q. I didn't ask you that sir, I asked you whether you gave any thought to the subject?

A. I don't recall that I did.

Q. Then you did not think anything about it?

A. I don't recall that I did.

Q. Did you not believe, Mr. Nearing, that this pamphlet would probably fall into the hands of men who were debating as to whether or not they would enlist in the army, voluntarily?

A. I had no such knowledge either way.

Q. Didn't you think about it?

A. I do not recall that I did.

Q. That never occurred to you, is that right, it never occurred to you?

A. I don't recall that it did. I might say again, Mr. Barnes, that I wrote this pamphlet to try to educate people. I had no particular point of view with regard to men or persuading soldiers or anybody else, I wanted the people to understand what was going on.

Q. But you would feel, would you not, that if this were to fall into the hands of a man who was contemplating enlisting, was turning the matter over in his mind, and he was persuaded by your arguments, he would not enlist, you feel that way about it? That would be its natural effect, wouldn't it?

Seymour Stedman: I want to object to that as incompetent, irrelevant and immaterial, and improper.

The Court: He may ask him if that was his belief. Did you so believe?

The Witness: I don't recall that I had any such belief, no, sir. In other words, I was not aiming this pamphlet particularly at the army. If I had been, I would have printed a different kind of leaflet. I would not have sold it through the Rand School where it went out for general circulation to a very small number of people, about 20,000.

Q. Went out to a group of people, however, who were subject to the draft?

A. Possibly. I was not in a position to know whether they were or not, sir.

Q. To a group of people who would be eligible to enlist?

A. Possibly. I was not in a position to know that either, any more than I would know whether one of my text-books would be read by man, woman or child, whether they were under forty years of age, or over forty years of age.

Q. Do not you know, that most of the Socialists in this country are between the ages of 18 and 40 years?

A. I have not ever seen a statement as to their ages.

Q. Don't you know that as a matter of fact, that most of the Socialists in this country are between 18 and 45?

A. Most of the people in this country are between 18 and 45.

Q. And most of the people who are in the circle of your acquaintance are between the ages of 18 and 45?

A. I am also between 18 and 45.

Q. And so am I.

A. And most of your friends are between 18 and 45 then, I may assume.

Q. You still feel that you were right in the position you took, in this pamphlet, Mr. Nearing?

A. I certainly believe—I do believe that the American plutocracy wanted the war, and they advocated it, and made the war, and they had the war, and it was an imperialistic war, for the purpose of enhancing the imperialistic point of view in the United States.

Q. You still believe, do you, that you were right in the position that you took in this pamphlet?

A. That was the position of the pamphlet.

Q. Cannot you answer the question yes or no, then?

A. Well, the trouble in answering a question like that yes or no, is that my own position in the pamphlet maybe is not clear, and I wanted to state my position in the pamphlet.

Q. You think that your position in the pamphlet is not clear?

A. It seemed to me that it was, sir.

Q. I think it is very clear. You still believe you were right in the efforts you made to spread this view among the people during the Summer of 1917?

A. Yes, sir, I believe that is the correct view, for the people of the United States to take.

Q. You think you were right in spreading it?

Seymour Stedman: He has said so.

The Court: He has not yet.

The Witness: Yes, sir, I thought I said yes.

Q. Well, would you again, in case we had another war, advise them in the same way?

Seymour Stedman: Oh, I object to that as highly speculative as to whether he would do it again.

The Court: Objection sustained.

Mr. Barnes: That is all.

Scott Nearing's Address to the Jury

Gentlemen, I am on trial here before you, charged with obstructing the recruiting and enlistment service to the detriment of the service, to the injury of the service, and with attempting and causing insubordination, disloyalty, mutiny and the refusal of duty within the military and naval forces. That is the charge of the indictment and that is the charge upon which I am being tried.

The prosecution has not been able to show a single instance in which recruiting was obstructed. They have not been able to show a single instance in which insubordination, disloyalty, and refusal of duty were caused.

It has been seventeen or eighteen months since this pamphlet was published. During that time there have been about nineteen thousand

copies of it loose in the country, and the prosecution was unable to bring
before you a single instance where these things have actually occurred.
How then do they seek to make out their case? Mr. Barnes said, in his
opening:

> It is not necessary for the Government to show that there was an actual
> obstruction in the sense of a physical obstruction; it was not necessary for
> the Government to show actual mutiny and disloyalty, but the publication
> of this book in itself is sufficient to result in a conviction.

In other words, the Government maintains that the publication of this
book, and the intent showed by the publication of the book, and by their
surrounding evidence is sufficient to warrant a conviction.

So that the only act that is alleged against me is an expression of my
opinions: writing in this book and expressing my opinions on the St.
Louis Proclamation, of the Socialist Party platform.

The act and the intent are both to be construed from my expressions
of opinion. It has not been shown that I obstructed enlistment, that I tore
down enlistment posters, that I told men not to enlist, it has not been
shown that I went among soldiers and asked them to mutiny, or to be
disloyal or to refuse to perform their duty, none of these things are
shown.

I am charged with writing and having sent that writing to a publisher
and had it published. I am charged, furthermore, with expressing further and other opinions in the pamphlet on militarism and in certain
other ways, so that the whole crime of which I am supposed to be—
according to the prosecution's case—guilty, the whole crime consists in
my expression of opinion, and the intent which they propose to show,
both arising out of my discussion of public questions.

Now as to this book, you have heard it read or have read it, and I
suppose all of you have or have had or will have copies. This book was
written in order to present a view held by many people—held by me
among that number—on the greatest public question that has come
before the American people, I suppose, since the Civil War.

It is a book written on the greatest issue that we have viewed in our
generation. It was written openly, sent to a publisher, sent to Washington and copyrighted and sent through the mails throughout August,
September, October, November, December, January, February and
March and until the indictment was found in April.

During all of those nine months, this pamphlet went through the
mails, and as some of you know, the Post Office Department has been
very rigorous in enforcing its decisions with regard to unmailable matter; and all through those nine months that pamphlet went through the
mail and it was never once stopped to our knowledge. It was copyrighted, it was sent through the mails for nine months, it was sold

openly in the Rand School bookstore and in other parts of the United States. So far as I know, (and I am in touch with the situation), it never was given away, but sold for ten cents, openly, without any attempt at concealment.

In other words, gentlemen, I took on this great public question, a certain position; I presented my views in this book, and I am indicted for writing the book because the prosecution alleges it caused—it was an obstruction or it caused, or it was an attempt to cause disloyalty and mutiny, therefore if I am convicted under this indictment I will be convicted for an expression of my opinions. There is no other evidence before you except my opinions.

The District Attorney has not shown a single act except those involved in the expression of an opinion, either on the witness stand or in the various writings of mine which he has brought before you.

So that by convicting me for writing this book you convict me for public discussion, and you draw my intent from my discussion. On the same ground I think all of the opponents of any administration during the war might be convicted for opposing in any way the administration, because in opposing an administration, any opposition to it tends to dampen the ardor, and to hold back and to check enthusiasm.

All through my life, I have been interested in preserving the institutions of democracy. That has been one of the things, as I tried to point out on the witness stand, that seem to me fundamentally important. I believe that democracy is a better form of social organization than aristocracy, or monarchy or any other form of Government that the world has ever known. Discussion is one of the purposes of democracy. Democracy means that a people talking a question over, thinking it out and reaching a decision upon it, may then register that decision.

The only way to have intelligent public opinion is to have discussion, and the moment you check discussion you destroy democracy. When any administration, whether in Russia or Germany or England or the United States, stops any discussion and puts its opponents in jail, that has destroyed the institution of democracy because democracy rests on discussion; and the only way in which we can preserve democracy is to reserve to every citizen of the democracy the right to express the convictions that he has: the right to be right and the right to be wrong.

The Constitution does not guarantee us only the right to be correct, we have a right to be honest and in error. And the views that I have expressed in this pamphlet I expressed honestly. I believe they are right. The future will show whether or not I was correct, but under the laws, as I understand it, and under the Constitution as I understand it, every citizen in this country has a right to express himself, subject always to the law, subject always to the limitations which the law prescribes, has a right to express himself on public questions. The moment any administration enters and shuts down that right, that moment democracy ceases to exist.

Now the principal question that enters into this thing is the question of intent. Mr. Stedman, I imagine, will talk to you about the law, or about the legal consideration, and the Judge, I believe will charge you with regard to the legal aspect of the problem of intent.

I am not a lawyer, and I cannot speak to you regarding the legal phases of the case, but I should like to say a few words about this problem of intent.

We have tried to produce evidence to prove to you that for the last twelve or fifteen years I have been a student of the institutions, standards and ideals of American life. Ever since the time that I entered college and indeed from the time I was in High School, I have been profoundly interested in seeing a certain thing done in the United States: I wanted to see liberty first, because I believe liberty is fundamental in society; then I wanted to see justice. I wanted to see that people got opportunity, that the boys and girls that were born had a chance to be well born and well brought up.

And during these twelve or fifteen years I have been busy with that problem; that has been the thing to which I have devoted all of my life thus far; that is the thing in which I have been profoundly interested— profoundly interested because I came to the belief many years ago that with the resources of America and the opportunities in America we could have a very much finer and a very much higher standard of life here than we actually have.

My studies and my investigations have led me to certain conclusions: for example I believe that economic forces are fundamental forces. I tried to point that out in the course of my testimony, just as plants in a garden draw their nourishment from the dirt, so men and women in a society draw their life from economic sources. They eat, they wear clothes, they live in their houses, and every time that the sun rises they have got to do those things, we are thrown back to that life. In the garden you get roses, you also get lettuce and turnips, fruits of almost all kinds—all products out of the same dirt.

And so in society you get different minds, different thoughts, different ideas, different standards of life, and they all reach back to the same dirt: to the food, clothing, shelter, and the necessary economic things of life.

If you cannot get these economic necessaries you cannot live. Therefore in that sense, economics is fundamental in the minds of people, so fundamental that all through history, people have fought over the river valleys, over the choice sections of the earth; so important that today in the United States forty million people are engaged in gainful occupations, working for a living, because without work we cannot live; without an economic background to our life we cannot get anywhere.

I believe that those economic forces which are so fundamental have always shown themselves in society, in struggles between the possessors and the dispossessed. Whoever possesses the resources and the economic opportunities controls the means of life.

In the early years of American life, where every man practically had a farm, or an opportunity to get one, economic opportunity was widely distributed and resources were free. You could go out to the border, to the edge of civilization, out to the frontier world and take a farm or take a piece of land.

About 1890 the resources in this country were exhausted. There were no more free resources: all the important timber, all the important minerals, all the important parts of the earth, practically, were taken up; and from that time until this, we have seen a gradual widening chasm between those who possess the necessities and those who do not.

When the Constitution of the United States was drafted, Madison, Jefferson and other men, saw the danger, and they tried to provide against it. They were not successful. At the present time the ownership of most of the United States is in the hands of a tiny percentage of people. And here in the City of New York where the land alone is worth five thousand millions of dollars, the improvements three billions more, where we have over four billions of dollars in our banks, savings banks and others, four billion five hundred millions of bank deposits in this City, and the Board of Education and the United States Food Administration report 280,000 children in the schools inadequately nourished to such an extent that their health is injured: twenty-one and one-half out of every hundred children in the City of New York are seriously underfed. In this same City we have people with incomes of five hundred thousand and a million dollars a year; people who could live on five thousand or ten thousand dollars, and have all the comforts and luxuries,—the simple luxuries of life.

Here we have on one hand a quarter of a million hungry children, and on the other hand, half a billion wealth in the hands of the few.

Lincoln, in speaking against Judge Douglas in 1858 on the slavery issue, said that no order of society can last, in which one man can say to another man, "You work and toil and earn bread, and I will eat it." Now that is the society that we have established: one man works for his living, another man owns property and from the rent and interest and dividends which he gains out of his property ownership, he lives without work, if he desires.

And another man creates the shoes and the clothes and the food and the other good things that he uses, and he has those things, possesses them, enjoys them, without himself ever raising a finger to toil.

At the present time there are people at Palm Beach who have never worked for their living. They are down there living extravagantly and enjoying the soft breezes, getting strength and health.

There are men and women here in New York who have worked all their lives, been honest and sober and tried to bring up families and today they cannot pay the landlord and the grocer and the butcher and keep their children healthy under this capitalistic system although they are sober, earnest and honest, industrious people, and all of it due to the fact of the economic system under which they are living because the wages that they get are not sufficient to buy the necessaries of life, as I tried to point out on the stand in my discussion of the wages problem.

On the other hand there are people—these people who live in ease, comfort and luxury, who have never raised a finger to produce one solitary article of food, clothing or shelter, or luxury or any comforts, and this is so all the time and my studies have taught me that these conditions exist. You know them. No one who has read or thought about the conditions in the United States but knows that those conditions are true, and I say to you gentlemen that as long as those things are true, just so long will it be impossible for us to have stable peace and order in our society.

No person is more anxious than I to have an ordered, well conducted society, but I do not believe that it is possible to maintain order in society where one man or one group of men living without labor, luxuriously, and another man, or group of men, in spite of their most earnest efforts, are unable to provide their families with the necessaries of life.

In the past this same question has been raised and in the past men have come to the decision—and I agree with that decision—that the only way in which we can have justice in the world is to have economic justice. An economic justice is only possible where the majority and not the minority, controls the necessaries of life.

If democracy means anything, it means that the majority of people control the conditions of their own life. In the United States, a tiny minority controls economic affairs. And so long as one small group of men own the jobs, own the products, and own the surpluses of industry, so long will the majority be unable to secure justice. And that is why I believe that the majority of people must control in industry and economic affairs as they are controlling in the political affairs. That is why I believe that we must have industrial democracy as well as political democracy.

Now I say this, that all of these years I have been studying such problems, and I have reached those conclusions. My say-so on that is of no importance. The existence in New York and other American cities of starving children side by side with fabulous wealth, and idle people, is the thing that should be of profound concern to every person who lives, or rather to the future of the society in which we live.

At various times, as we pointed out, I have written down my conclusions in books. We had here the other day a set of those books. Some of them are purely statistical, full of tables and figures. Some of them are text books, some are pamphlets like this "Great Madness."

Whenever I collected together a great body of information which seemed to me to be important, I embodied it into a book, published it, and in some cases I published it at my own expense. Statistical books are extremely expensive, and if you sell one thousand copies of a statistical book you are doing very well. Publishers won't take them, and authors have to pay the bill.

I published those books because I felt that as a teacher, I had a certain obligation to the community that paid my salary. I was working in the State, or a semi-State University. I was working at a comparatively easy job. I had three months' vacation in the Summer time. I had leisure during the year, and I employed that leisure in working over social problems.

I believe that whenever any person gets anything that might be of value to the other people in the community, that it is his obligation to turn that thing over to the community: whether he is a scientist in physical science, or a bacteriologist, a chemist or a scientist in social science, and economics, or sociology, when a man discovers a method of separating milk, or for destroying the bacteria, harmful bacteria in milk, or when he discovers a method of checking influenza, or over-coming tuberculosis, and gives it to the world, the world acclaims the gift, and its giver.

And so when a man discovers, or so-called science discovers a method that will make people happier, give them more opportunity, a greater liberty to enjoy more social justice, I believe he has got exactly the same obligation to state what he has found. If they agree with him, well and good, if they don't agree with him, he goes on to his own scientific problems.

I said there on the witness stand that five of these books dealt with distribution: A book on wages, a book on the standard of living, a book on the cost of living, a book on income and a book on anthracite industry.

When I published those books I knew that no man could take a stand that I took in those books, and hold a job in an American University; and I published them because I wanted the American people to know the truth about the most fundamental economic questions before them to-day: the question of the distribution of wealth.

We have learned how to produce wealth in large quantities, but we haven't yet learned how to distribute it, and I wanted the American people to know the results of my studies and researches regarding the distribution of wealth.

I published those books, and as we mutually agreed, and I said in the course of my direct examination on the stand, the university and I parted company. I then went out to Toledo. After I had been there a year and a half the question of preparedness came up. I regarded the question of preparedness as a question of fundamental importance to society. I knew who was behind the preparedness campaign. I knew that no man could hold a job in the American universities and take the stand that I took on the preparedness issue. I wrote the "Germs of War" and went all over the United States, speaking on preparedness, and speaking against preparedness. I spoke in favor of a movement of preparedness that I believed will alone safeguard business and justice among men.

The Toledo University and I parted company. Then we entered the war, and I saw what I believed to be a great menace to the liberties of the American people, namely: the growing power of the plutocracy, the growing power which it was gaining through the war, and so I wrote this book on the "Great Madness" in order to try to point out to the American people exactly what was happening.

If you will notice, the book is not a denunciation of our society, it is not a denunciation of our Government, it is an exposition of certain events in terms of their economic significance. I tried to show how the economic control of the country, of the resources, and of American life is manifesting itself all through the social structure. I published that book, and here we are.

For fifteen years I have been speaking and writing and stating my views on public questions. I have stated it openly, I have stated it as honestly as I could state it; I stated it to the University of Pennsylvania, and I stated it at the University of Toledo, and I have stated it since I left the University of Toledo.

If I intended to obstruct recruiting or enlistments, if I had intended to interfere with the prosecution and carrying on of the administrative policies of the navy and army, either by creating insubordination and mutiny, or otherwise, I should have said so; I should not have written a fifty-page pamphlet and sold it for ten cents each; I should have gone out and told the soldiers so, and I should have told the prospective soldier so. Never in my life have I gone out and done anything indirectly. If I have wanted to say a thing, I have said it; if I have wanted to present a matter I have presented it, and taken the consequences. If I had wished in this case to obstruct or to interfere, I should have obstructed and interfered and taken the consequences.

The District Attorney was at considerable pains to prove to you that I am a Socialist. He asked me questions about the St. Louis Platform. He asked me questions about the Socialist Party Platform; many questions, in order to prove that I am a Socialist. I am a Socialist.

I want to tell you something about what that means: in the first place, I am an internationalist; that is, I believe in the brotherhood of all men. In the language of the Declaration of Independence, I believe that all men are created equal, that they have certain rights to life, liberty and the pursuit of happiness. That holds true of the man that lives next door to me, and it holds true of the man that lives in South Africa, and the man that lives way over in Asia. I believe in the Brotherhood of Man.

I believe that ultimately the whole world will be federated together, just as these United States are federated together. There was a time in the United States when a man that lived in Georgia or Virginia, or New York, was perfectly willing to quarrel with a man who lived in Pennsylvania or Massachusetts or in New Hampshire. If you asked a man a hundred and fifty years ago where he was from, he said, I am from Virginia; I am from Pennsylvania. He now states, I am from the United States, not, I am from the American Colonies. He was a Virginian first and an American second. But that time has passed.

Today America is kept first, and Pennsylvania second. And the time will come when the man from North America and the man from Europe and the man from Africa will say, I am a member of the human race; and the human race has certain common interests, certain common obligations, and first among them is the recognition of the fact of the universal brotherhood of all men.

I am from the United States? Yes. I am from New York? Yes. I am from Buffalo? Yes. I have a home in Buffalo? Yes. I am loyal to my home? Yes. To Buffalo? Yes. To New York? Yes. To the United States? Yes. And I am also loyal to my fellow brother man.

In other words, we Socialists look forward to a time, and certainly we are not alone in looking that way,—there are others who are not Socialists who agree with us in this,—we look forward to the time when the peoples of all the world will join hands in common brotherhood. And when we say we are internationalists, that is what we mean. A man, yes, outside the boundaries of certain nations, but within the greater boundaries of the world, he is within the boundaries of the whole world, and he is a member of the human race. And we are internationalists, in the sense that we believe in our obligations to our human brothers, and that they are the supreme obligations of the world.

That does not make us any less loyal to our homes or to our cities or our nations, but it does give us a larger and a more comprehensive loyalty.

In the second place, believing that, I believe that we can do the things that are necessary to bring human brotherhood into reality.

What are the facts of international life: education internationalizes, science internationalizes, commerce internationalizes, industry internationalizes the processes and the methods of ideas, arts and letters and life, all internationalize. What then stands in the way of human brotherhood? Why, the thing that stands in the way is that fragment of nationalism, that still remains, that fragment is capitalism.

And every nation, as I tried to point out in my testimony, in every
nation there is a little coterie of men or interests who find it to their
profit to keep national animosities alive. The peoples of the world have
no animosities one against the other, but the rulers of the world fan
those animosities into flame: religious hatred, class antagonism, national feeling, are all kept boiling and stirring in men's souls.

You go to the restaurant, or you go to the shop or you go out on the
street, and you will sit down together, and you will work together with
Irish and Austrian, Italian and Slovak, side by side, elbow to elbow.
The peoples of the world have nothing against one another, the people
of the world have more in common than they have in opposition. It is
the economic barrier, it is the economic division lines that create the
difficulty.

And we Socialists, or I, rather, am interested—and that is the reason
I am a Socialist—in destroying those economic division lines. How can
that be done? I believe there is only one way. I believe that is the only
way to destroy these economic barriers and make international life a
reality, and that is, to give to those who work the full product of their
labor; instead of having a man work for a part of what he creates,
turning the other part over in the form of interest, rent and dividends to
the owner of the job, I believe that the worker, the man or woman who
was rendering a socially useful service should get the full value of his
product. Then there would not be any surplus to invest in foreign
markets, and in foreign opportunities. Then there would not be any
surplus to be used by private individuals in the development of Mexico
or China or Argentina.

You say then that those countries would develop more slowly. Perhaps. But when they did develop that country it would come from
within those countries and it would be for the benefit of those countries
and not for the benefit of some foreign capitalist.

I believe we will never solve our international differences successfully until we have taken out of the hands of individuals the right to
invest surplus, the right to utilize vast quantities of wealth in the way
that will create friction and ultimately international dissension and war
between the different groups of peoples. Therefore I am in favor of
having the workers own their own jobs. There is only one way to do that
now.

In early America, when there was no great aggregation of wealth,
when each man could own his farm, he could own his job. At present
the telephone system is a system. The railroad system is a system. The
banking system is a system. The United States Steel Corporation system
is a system. No one man can own his own job. You cannot own a rail,
you cannot own a link, you cannot own a piece of a system because if

you take out that piece, your system is cut. If you take out a telephone exchange, you break down the integrity of the telephone organization.

Therefore the only way in which one man can own his job is to own it collectively, that is, the whole system. So that we believe that all the people who work should own the tools with which they work, just as all the people of the United States own the harbor of New York. I believe that all of the people of the United States should own the railroads and the banking system and every great social product in its entirety, just as they own the post office, just as they own several great irrigation plants, and the Panama Canal, and some other similar developments.

I believe the only solution, the only possible solution is that the people, all of the people, that they may have free economic life, is that they control the political life.

One hundred and fifty years ago they would have laughed at the idea of having a political democracy.

Napoleon said a republic of twenty-six million souls were folly. He sneered at the concept that people could govern themselves politically. Today we are beginning to wonder whether it will not be possible for people to govern themselves economically, and today, as I hold, there are many who see here the coming principle, the great proletariat control of economic affairs, and who regard it as a ridiculously absurd thing, an impossible thing, but as I say, democracy means control by the people, and I believe in democracy, and I believe therefore in the control by the people of the machinery of production. Just as I believe they should control the city government, just so I believe they should control the other branches of life. Just as they control the political returns, just so they should control the economic returns.

And so it seems to me there is no solution in any other way than similarly to control economic problems as we control political problems. They have both national and international systems.

Some of you have noticed recently that the war is over, but yet there is turmoil all over the earth: turmoil in Britain, turmoil in the United States; strikes, disturbances, and we are having very many problems yet which have not been solved even though the war be over. The solution of every problem depends on its being settled right, nothing ever is settled until it is settled right, that is, until it is settled to the best of our belief, it is not settled; and I believe that the Socialist philosophy presents to us the best avenue along which to approach the settlement of these stupendous problems of our economic life.

I do not say that the socialists have the entire solution. I do not say that the socialists when they come into power, as they surely will come into power, will dispose of all the problems of the world. By no means, as there will always be problems; but this we believe, going forward step by step through mechanics, and through chemistry, through applied science, we are solving the problems of production and are able to turn the resources of nature into food and clothing and shelter, and the other necessaries of life, so I believe society must solve the problem of distribution.

Facing all of these problems, equitably, and in the light of past experience, we believe that the only solution is to turn these things over, that is, operate and turn them over to the people who own them.

As I said the other day when I was on the witness stand, that soap is made and it should be made to keep people clean, and that if shoes are made they should be made to protect people's feet. If food is produced it should be produced to nourish the human body. But as it is today, we are making soap for profit, we are making shoes for profit, we are making food for profit. The profiteering has become, and justly so, a word of contempt and opprobrium, and profiteering lies at the heart of the capitalistic system.

The present system was organized, that is, the present system of industry was organized for profit and not for the service of mankind; and I am one of those who believe that you can never have an exact solution of any social problem until you have the machinery organized for the benefit not of the very few, but for the benefit or for the service of the great masses of the people. In other words, as they said in the eighteenth century, the greatest good to the greatest number. That holds true of economic as well as political questions.

The District Attorney also asked me a number of questions concerning my attitude towards the war. I wish he had put the Bible in evidence and asked me what I thought about the phrase, "Thou shalt not kill"; and about that other phrase, "Overcome evil with good." But he didn't do that. I would have said that I agreed with those phrases as I agreed with many others.

I told him that I believed this war was a capitalists' war, that is, that I believed that it was a war between capitalist nations. When the war broke out there were no other kind of nations on earth than that kind— so that there could not be anything else but a war between capitalist nations. By the capitalist nation we mean a nation that is dependent upon a capitalist system of production, production by means of machinery—capital.

All the great nations of the world were capitalist nations at the time the war broke out. The war was necessarily a capitalists' war. A war between capitalist nations, and as we all know now, or think we know, it was primarily a war over the trade routes to Persia and Syria, or over the "Berlin to Bagdad Railroad" if you like, to put it that way; a war open to commercial and financial rights.

I read you the other day a number of statements from the Navy League, and you will remember it is an ultra-capitalist, an ultra-conservative organization, in which they said exactly that thing which economists have stated for so long a time; students of history have said it for a long time; the Navy League comes forward and says the same thing; Mr. Wilson has repeatedly stated, and I believe it was a war between the capitalist nations and I believe it had as its chief business certain benefits for small groups of capitalists. That does not mean that I believe the people who entered the war, entered it for capitalist reasons. Obviously they could not because they had no capitalist interests. The masses of people in all the countries involved have no capitalist interest; they were being exploited, they were being worked; theirs was the loss, to their prejudice in all of the capitalist countries of the world. They entered the war for what they called patriotic reasons; they were loyal to their country; they believed that they were defending their country, their homes and their firesides and their liberties, from invasion; they entered it with enthusiasm, and they entered it honestly and sincerely, with no capitalistic motives whatever; they entered it honestly and sincerely, just as the nations entered it honestly and sincerely with capitalistic motives. And I honestly and sincerely believe that they sincerely and honestly and patriotically and altruistically entered the contest, that is, these people. So I say I believe it was a capitalists' war, a war between capitalist nations over financial and economic issues: coal, iron, trade, investments, opportunities, and the Navy League backs me up, and a lot of other authorities from that side of the fence back me up.

I told the District Attorney on the stand that I was opposed to all wars. I regard war as a social disease, something that afflicts society, that curses people. I do not suppose three people in a hundred like war. I do not suppose that three people in a hundred want war. There are some people who are pugnacious, and who love to fight, for the sake of a fight, and they might like war, but I do not believe there are three people in a hundred, certainly not five in a hundred, that do.

I believe the great majority of people agree with me that war is a curse, an unmitigated curse. All the things that come out of war come out in spite of war and not because of it.

The democracy that has come into Europe, whatever it is called, has come in spite of the war and not because of it. That would have come out in any case, and we would have had it without the expenditure of twenty million lives and a hundred and eighty billions of wealth.

I regard war as a social disease, a social curse, and I believe that we should stamp war out. To my mind the great curse of war is not that people are killed and injured, not that property is destroyed. That happens every day in peace times as well as in war times. To my mind the great curse of war is that it is built on fear and hate.

Now fear and hate are primitive passions; the savages in the woods are intimidated by fear and hate. They do not belong in civilized society. In civilized society, for fear and hate we substitute constructive purposes and love. It is their positive virtues. When we fear things, we draw back from them. When we hate things, we want to destroy them.

In civilized society, instead of drawing away from things, and wanting to destroy them, we want to pull things together and build them up. Fear and hate are negatives. Peace and love are positives, and form the forces upon which civilization is built. And where we have collectively fear and hate, it is a means of menace to the order of the world.

Furthermore, during war, we ask people to go out and deliberately injure their fellows. We ask a man to go out and maim or kill another man against whom he has not a solitary thing in the world,—a man who may be a good farmer, a good husband, a good son, and a good worker, and a good citizen. Another man comes out and shoots him down; that is, he goes out and raises his hand against his neighbor to do his neighbor damage. That is the way society is destroyed. Whenever you go out to pull things to pieces, whenever you go out to injure anybody, you are going out to destroy society. Society can never be built up unless you go out to help your neighbors.

The principle, "each for all and all for each," is the fundamental social principle. People must work together if they are going to get anywhere. War teaches people to go out and destroy other people and to destroy other people's property.

And when Sherman said that war was hell, I believe that he meant, or at least to me that means, that war creates a hell inside of a man who goes to war. He is going to work himself up into a passion of hatred against somebody else, and that is hell.

The destruction of life and property is incidental. The destructive forces that that puts into a man's soul are fundamental. That is why I am opposed to all wars, just as I am opposed to all violence. I don't believe in any man having the right to go out and use violence against another man. That is not the right of one human being to have against the other, that is not the way you get brotherhood. That is the reason I told the District Attorney on the stand that I was against all wars. I am against duelling; I am against all violence of man against man, and war is one of those methods of violence.

I believe war is barbaric, I believe it is primitive, I believe it is a relic of a bygone age; I believe that society will be destroyed if built up that way. That is, I believe that they that take the sword must perish by the sword; just as they that set out to assist their neighbors are bound to build up a strong, cohesive united society. That is the field over which I went in my direct testimony and in the cross-examination.

I have been a student of public affairs. I am a Socialist. I am a pacifist. But I am not charged with any of these things as offenses. On the other hand I believe that as an American citizen I have a right to discuss public questions. I think the Judge will charge you so. I have a right to oppose the passage of a law. I think the Judge will charge you so. I have a right under the law, after the law is passed, to agitate for a development of public sentiment that will result in a repeal of that law. I think the Judge will charge you so.

In other words, as I said in the beginning, in a democracy, if we are to have a democracy, as a student of public affairs and as a Socialist and as a pacifist, I have a right to express my opinions. I may be wrong, utterly wrong, and nobody listen to me, nobody pay any attention to me. I have a right to express my opinions.

Gentlemen, I have been throughout my life as consistent as I could be. I have spoken and written for years, honestly and frankly. I went on the stand and I spoke to you as honestly as I knew how. I answered the District Attorney's questions as honestly and as frankly as I could. I stand before you today as an advocate of economic justice and world brotherhood, and peace among all men. And I wrote this pamphlet in the attempt to further those ends.

I desire to say just one more thing: this is America in which I am on trial, and America's proudest tradition is her tradition of liberty. For three hundred years people have been coming to America: Puritans, Pilgrims, Huguenots, Quakers, came over and formed the Colonies.

Later, the Irish, the Scotch, the Germans, the Russians, the Italians, the Syrians came here, not because of the hills and valleys, not because of the climate, not because of the language, but because of the liberty of America; and the men who came here and the women who came here in 1914, came here just as sincerely in search of that liberty as the men and women who came here in 1620.

For three hundred years the world has been looking to America, and coming to America for liberty. That is the choicest and the greatest heritage, that which Americans love. What was it that these people sought to escape in Europe? They sought to escape hunger, hardship, misery, suffering, and poverty. They came over here because they thought that the resources of America would yield enough food and clothing and shelter to feed and clothe and house every human being decently and comfortably.

They came over from Europe to escape ignorance and escape the darkness in which Europe had been kept by these rulers. They came over here for enlightenment—opportunity. Many of them came over here because it gave them the only chance that the world offered to express the truth, as they saw it. They left Europe because they wanted to escape prejudice, bigotry, class antagonism and race hatred. They came over here because they thought that here they would find brotherhood among men, because they thought that here all peoples were welcome to sit down together and enjoy the opportunities that America offered. They left Europe because of its military service, its wars, and the fear and hatred of war, that is, that war engendered. They thought to come over here and find peace and plenty. They left Europe because of tyranny and despotism; the tyranny of the landlord, the despotism of aristocracy and the owners of the sources of life.

They came over here because they thought that here they would find that every man had equal opportunity for life, liberty and the pursuit of happiness. They came here seeking that liberty of the body, the liberty of the mind and the liberty of their heart and soul, and Socialist liberty. That is the background of the country in which we are living.

That is the thing of which America is proud and for which America has stood; that is the thing for which I believe America will stand today. There is nothing unique in our wealth. Other nations have wealth. There is nothing unique in our material possessions. Other nations have material possessions. But there was something unique in our liberty.

As I said to you on the witness stand, I am an American, my ancestors have been Americans for more than two hundred years. As an American I have certain rights and certain duties. Among my rights under the first amendment to the Constitution are the rights of free speech and the free press; the right to speak and print the convictions that I have. It was for those rights that our ancestors left Europe and came here. It is for those rights that some of us are contending today.

I care not for the prosperity of this country if we are going to have gag laws. I care not for the wealth of this country if we are going to be forbidden to have free speech, and an opportunity for expressing our minds and expressing our opinions and discussing the great issues that are before us.

In the old times of the Czar, we did not protest against Russia because she lacked wealth; we protested against her because she lacked liberty. What was it that we found was lacking, or what was it that we found against the Kaiser in Germany? Was it that he was not a good business man? He was an excellent business man. Was it because he was not a good organizer? He was an excellent organizer. What we had against this man was the fact that he was a tyrant, that he trampled on the rights of other people.

They had wealth in Russia, they had prosperity in Germany. In America we want liberty. And I believe that as an American citizen, that is the dearest possession for which I can contend. That is my right constitutionally and legally. But if there were no constitution and no law, it would be my right as a member of a democratic society.

Furthermore, as a citizen, I have certain duties. Citizenship involves duties as well as rights. If I saw that your house were on fire, it would be my duty to warn you and to try to put it out, that is, put out the fire, and if I could not put out the fire, to save as much of your goods and such of your family as I could save. That would be my duty as a neighbor.

I have been a student of public affairs in this country for many years. I believe this country is in danger, in dire peril. On the one hand I see imperialism, militarism and war ahead of us. In our policy toward Mexico, in the policy that we are developing under the direction of preparedness advocates about which I spoke last Friday, I see ahead of us imperialism and militarism and war.

This is not the last war, there is another war, and it will be a war between this nation and the nation that succeeds in the present contention in Europe.

On the other hand, I see ahead of us in our industrial life, exploitation, widespread, by the masters of those who work for them. I see that exercised with increasing tyranny, and I see ahead of us revolt. In other words, to my mind, the outlook in America is not bright, and I am upheld in that view by Senators, by business men, by labor leaders, by all of the responsible authorities who are speaking today for America's future.

There are clouds on the horizon. I believe America is in peril and I believe that she is in peril from internal disturbances; I believe that the danger lurks within. And I believe it rests primarily in our unfair and unjust system of distribution of wealth, and the income of the country.

As I said a moment ago, that if your house were on fire, it would be my duty as a neighbor to warn you and to try to help you save your property. I say to you now, that when I believe this nation is in danger, when I believe that our country is in danger, our common life and our common liberties are in peril, then it is my duty to warn you, it is my duty to speak out and to continue to speak out as long as I have an opportunity to do so.

You will say, if you went into my house and saved my goods, you might burn your hands, you might injure your clothes. True. It would still be my duty to risk my clothing and my hands in your service.

You will say if you speak out today against these perils in the land, you may lose your job, you may lose your liberty. And I answer you again that as a citizen it is my sole obligation to speak out when I see peril ahead, and stand the loss of position or of liberty or any other loss that may be entailed in issuing the necessary warning.

Gentlemen, I want to say to you that I want to see America free. I want to see liberty, opportunity and democracy here, as well as in every other country on earth. As long as America is not free, you are not free and I am not free. As long as any of us are in chains in this land, we are all in chains. As long as any are in ignorance in the land, we are in ignorance to that extent. As long as anybody starves in the land, we starve. As long as anybody suffers from despotism and tyranny, we are all suffering from despotism and tyranny. We belong to the body of this citizenship, and we suffer in common with it, and we benefit in common with it.

As I said a moment ago, the only principle upon which society can ever be built is the principle of each for all, and all for each. The principle of union, the principle of joint co-operative action for the benefit and the service of all.

I believe that that action is the action of the people, the action of the masses, of mankind, and that sooner or later they will insist upon their rights.

As Lincoln said, "You can fool some of the people all of the time and all of the people some of the time, but you cannot fool all of the people all of the time."

The peoples all over the world are coming into their own, they are going to come into their own more and more as the years go by. They are going to come into their own in the United States, and what happens to one of us is incidental to the great question of what happens to all of us.

I have expressed my hopes, my ideals, my ambitions for liberty in America, and for brotherhood and peace among all people of the world. I have done what I could, and for the time being the matter is in your hands.

10 DEBATE: CAPITALISM VERSUS SOCIALISM (1921)

Affirmative: E.R.A. Seligman
Negative: Scott Nearing

O N JANUARY 23, 1921, NEARING and Seligman, head of the economics department at Columbia University, debated in the Lexington Theatre in New York City. Oswald Garrison Villard, editor of *The Nation,* acted as moderator and introduced Nearing by saying:

> Every American, whatever his economic beliefs, owes a debt of gratitude to the next speaker. He was one of those Americans who insisted even in war time upon that freedom of conscience and liberty to speak and write which are guaranteed by the Constitution of the United States [great applause]. The foolish and blind law officers of a new utterly discredited administration sought to deprive him and use of the right for which he stood, and Mr. Scott Nearing went into the Court and unlike some others placed in the same position abated not one jot from the position which he had taken [great applause]. And with true intellectual heroism convinced a jury of American citizens that he was within his rights and that this was still in some respects a free country [laughter]. I have the pleasure of presenting Scott Nearing [prolonged applause].

In his rebuttal, Nearing answered Seligman's assault on Russian socialism by describing American blockades of the newly formed government, saying:

For three years we denied them medicine. For three years we
denied them food. For three years we starved their women
and children while we supported insurrection at home and
made war on them abroad—for three years after they had
already had three years of war! And now Professor Seligman
wants to know whether that is a fair example of what socialism can do [thunderous and prolonged applause].

Later that year inflation ran rampant in Germany and
Hitler's thugs terrorized opposing political parties. Political
assassinations of prime ministers and high government executives occurred in Germany, Spain, Portugal, and Japan.
In the United States the Ku Klux Klan renewed domestic
terrorism against life and property in the South.

Professor Seligman has given us what I consider two very satisfactory
definitions of the issue before us this afternoon. He has defined capitalism as that form of industrial organization where the means of production, primarily the machines, are in the control of private individuals.
He has defined socialism as the control of capital in the hands of the
group and under it there shall be no room for private rent, interest or
profit. Beginning as he does with these two definitions, I reach a somewhat dissimilar conclusion [laughter]. I do not see capitalism in so rosy
a light as does Professor Seligman and I want to try to explain to you in
the brief time that I have why not, and what the socialists propose to put
in its place, and I want to explain them under three headings: first, the
ownership of the machinery of production, second, the control arising
out of such ownership, third the direction resulting from such control.
And I want to try to demonstrate to you that under capitalism the worker
has to accept, first, intermittent starvation, second, slavery and third,
war [applause].

Professor Seligman says that capitalism is progressive. So are some
diseases [hearty laughter and applause]. Under the present system of
society, a little group of people own resources, machines, capital, all of
the machinery upon which forty million workers depend for their living.
That is, the capitalist owns the job. The capitalist owns the job without
which the worker dies of starvation. The worker therefore must go to the
capitalist and ask for permission to work. To what extent has this
ownership been concentrated in the United States? I wish that I could
answer that intelligently, but the best that I can do is to cite you the 1918
income tax returns. In that year, 1918, you remember that prices were
about what they are now. In that year, $200. a week was not a fortune
by any means. $200. a week was not much wealth in 1918. But there

were only 160,000 people in this whole United States who reported incomes of as much as $200. a week. That is, 14 persons in every thousand of the population, four persons for every thousand, gainfully employed, one family for every five hundred families in the land, with incomes of $10,000. a year, $200.00 a week. They tell us that Rome and Assyria and Babylon and those old countries reached a point of concentration where 1% of the people owned the wealth of the Empires. I say to you in America, 1918, four in every thousand of those gainfully employed earned $200. a week. I wish I could give you the figures of ownership but I could not collect them. Senator Pettigrew in 1890 had the census take an estimate of wealth and since 1890 every census has specifically excluded any estimate of wealth ownership in the United States. Be that as it may, I need not stress the point. The facts speak for themselves. We have in America a little handful of people owning the railroads, the banks, manufactories, mining and other establishments and to them go tens of millions of men and women asking for jobs, for the right to make a living. But the master, the owner replies "in order to have a job, you must produce—produce something for yourself and something for me and the interest, dividends, profits, returns, for which I do not labor." Said Abraham Lincoln in 1858: " 'A slave society is one in which one class says to another class, you work and toil and earn bread and we will eat it'." These owners of American capital, these stock and bond holders say to the American worker "you work and toil and earn bread and we will eat it." How much do they get of the bread produced by the workers? Get a copy of Senate Document 259. You can't get a copy because they were not distributed. Get a copy of that document of profiteering and find out how much they made in 1917— hundreds, thousands of percent. of profit in a single year—in America, the richest of rich countries! In America, the center of the greatest empire on earth, we report 26% of our school children underfed in the schools. We reported that before the present economic unpleasantness began [applause and laughter]. We reported that while we were still urging the worker to produce and while he was turning out not only enough for his own daily sustenance but in addition enough to provide the capitalist with a surplus and that surplus went to the front and we burned it in Europe and then the War was over and we burned a bit of it here at home and the burning got too expensive. The worker received less in wages than he had created in product. He could not buy back the volume that he had produced. The capitalist, the owner of the shop did not need to use what had been produced and given to him as surplus. He wanted to dispose of it. The War gave him a chance. Exports gave him some chance but then that chance was ended and the capitalist said to the worker last April, last May, last June, the capitalist said to the worker, "There will be no more work." And in textiles, boots and shoes, automobiles and now later in steel and other industries, they are laying them off. I got a report from the New York State Industrial Commission this week: 643,000 men and women out of work in New York State. What have they done? Why, they cannot have work. But what have they done? Why, they have produced too much. They have created too great a surplus. They must wait to produce more until this surplus is consumed. Can they consume it? No! Because they did not receive enough wages to buy it back [applause]. And so in this country today, three million people are out of work. You do not see these figures stated in the newspapers.

In the first six months of 1920, the average number of commercial failures per month was 500; in July 598; August 633; September 661; October 802; November 892; December 1,854; the first three weeks of January 1,482, and so the number mounts. Professor Seligman has already referred to this. I have a book here called "A History of Panics in the United States" written by a Frenchman, translated by an American business man, and this book gives a record of the panics that we have had under capitalism: "1814, 1818, 1826, 1837, 1848, 1857, 1864, 1873, 1884, 1893, 1897, 1903, 1907, 1913"—and 1921 [laughter]. That book contains one of the most damning indictments that has ever been written on capitalism. "Capitalism," says the author, "consists of three phases: prosperity, panic and liquidation" [laughter]. Prosperity is the period when the dinner pail is full and the hopes are high, when the little man drops his tools and leaves his bench, borrows his capital, buys a machine and goes into business. Panic is the period when the little fellows get the tools and the machines shaken out of their hands and start back for the bench and liquidation is the period when the big fellows pick up what is around loose, put it in their pockets and go off richer than they were before [hearty laughter and applause]. "Progressive" says Seligman. I say "No! Successive." And as long as capitalism lasts, so long will men and women by the millions walk the streets looking for work and so long will their gas bills be paid and their children starve—successive starvation, successive periods of physical misery and death from lack of physical means in the center of the greatest wealth that the world knows. That is what capitalism has to offer the world [applause].

What do we Socialists want? Why, we want to own these things ourselves [laughter]. As we own the Harbor of New York, so we want to own the coal mines, the railroads, the factories in order that no surplus may be produced, in order that the value of product shall be represented by the value paid to a consumer [applause]. So that he who creates can buy back the value that he creates [applause]. Quite simple and quite inevitable in the long run.

But I don't stress that point. It is not essential. It is my second point about which I wish to talk—about slavery. "Whenever a man says to another man, 'You go and work and earn bread and I will eat it,' said Lincoln, "it is slavery." That is capitalism and that is my chief charge against capitalism and that is the thing that we Socialists set up as our highest hope in Socialism, not that it will give us more bread, but that it will give us steadier bread, more regular bread, more bread, and not that we will get more to eat out of Socialism but that we will get more liberty. That is where we place our hope and I want to explain the contrast because it is fundamental. The United States I said was owned by capitalists—worse than that owned by capitalist corporations, owned impersonally, not by individuals who have made their pile and bought their machinery—owned by Trusts, owned by great organizations with their stocks and their bonds and their big business mechanisms. I wish I had time to read you this last report of the National City Bank to show you how that ownership works out. Here is a list of the Board of Directors.This is the biggest bank in North America. Here is a list of Board of Directors: Percy A. Rockefeller, William Rockefeller, J. Ogden Armour, Nicholas F. Brady of the New York Edison Company, Cleveland H. Dodge, Philip A. S. Franklin, etc. What is the National City Bank? Why, it is the center of a great web of economic power. Here is the report issued by the Pujo Committee. At the center of the spider's web, they put a great banking concern, J. P. Morgan & Company and around that banking concern, they group railroads, public utilities, industries, mines and other forms of industrial enterprise. At the center of the power lies the strength and the weakness of the system, lies the banker. I have not time to dwell on that further than to call your attention to this fact that the Federal Reserve System with its 30,000 banks and its Board of Directors, sitting in one place around the table, has more power than any single Institution on the face of the civilized earth, and that Federal Reserve System is in private hands. It is privately owned practically. It is under government supervision, yes, but the Federal Reserve System is the nerve center, the center of authority, the center of power and what are they going to do with this control that they exercise through their banking machine? I want to read you a paragraph from a weekly letter sent by one business house to its clients. "The War taught employing classes in America the secret and power of wide-spread propaganda. Now, when we have anything to sell to the American people, we know how to sell it. We have learned. We have the schools, we have the pulpit." The employing class owns the Press, the economic power centering in the banks, schools, pulpit, press, movie screen, all the power of wide-spread propaganda now. "When we have something to sell to the American people, we know how to sell it." Slavery—going to the boss and asking for the privilege of a job;— slavery—sending your child to school and having him pumped full of virulent propaganda in favor of the present system [great applause]. Slavery in every phase of life all tied up under this one banker's control. Is it true that no man is good enough to rule another man without that man's consent? Is that still true in America or in the world? If that be true, every worker in the shop shall have the right to say who shall exercise authority over him in the shop. Every worker in an industry has the right to pick these or help these members as Board of Directors. Do you suppose the workers in the National City Bank elected William Rockefeller and Percy Rockefeller and J. Ogden Armour? [laughter]. In the United States, a worker goes to work on a machine owned by the boss. He works on materials owned by the boss. He turns out a product owned by the boss. He lives in a country where the organized power of the boss concentrated in the banking system is supreme over every phase of life. He is a slave—industrial slave—because he cannot call one economic right his own and we Socialists want to have industry not only owned by those who participate in it but we want to have those who participate in industry direct the industry in which they participate. Industrial self-control, self-government in industry as Mr. Cole has put it—that is all—simple ideas—ownership by the worker of his own job, the control by a man of his own economic life.

And third, I spoke about the direction of industry. I read you the report of the last annual meeting of the United States Steel Corporation. At this meeting, according to the New York *Times,* here was voted two million and one-quarter shares of common and one and one-half million shares of preferred stock. Stockholders who attended the meeting represented 340 shares of preferred and 4,000 shares of common and the rest were voted by proxy—so many million shares on this side, so many million shares on this side, and the policy of the United States Steel Corporation is formed and unionism is crushed out and this or that line of industrial policy is pursued by a little handful of men and women who have nothing better to do with their leisure time than to go and sit through a meeting of the United States Steel Corporation stockholders—that is the biggest corporation in America—direction not only by absentee ownership but direction by little cliques of lawyers holding proxies in their hands, by executives of great industries speaking in the name of stockholders. And what did they do? Last year, in the United States, that is in 1919, they floated twelve thousand millions of new capital stock and bonds; 1920 they floated fourteen thousand millions of new capital stocks and bonds. Did you have any say in that? Does the worker speak when it is decided to put these twenty-five billions into new capital under circumstances when it is almost certain that it cannot function? Did the workers speak? No, it was done by voting shares. They go out into Thrace. They support General Wrangel. They go down into Mexico. They follow into Hayti. And then what happens? Other stockholders in other countries, Royal Dutch Shell Stockholders, British Stockholders, voting policy against Standard Oil; Standard Oil Stockholders if they ever vote, voting policy against Royal Dutch Shell; and you hear the echoes of the conflict over the markets of France and you hear the echoes of their conflict for the rights in Central Europe. What is going to be the result? When will it be necessary to put the war paint on the battleships? When will it be necessary again to call out the batallions and send them? In 1914 Great Britain had a highway to the sea. Germany wanted it. A pistol shot sounds in Central Europe and ten million men go to their graves to decide that Great Britain shall hold Bagdad and that Germany shall pay what she can [applause].

In 1914, there was not a Socialist State in Europe—capitalist Germany, capitalist France, capitalist Russia, capitalist Italy, capitalist Britain—all the great group of capitalist Empires grabbing the world to rob it and fighting one another to the death to determine who should have the right to do the plundering. They produced a surplus as I said. They could not spend it at home. They took it abroad and in the course of taking it abroad they had to make War—capitalist War—and working men went and fought and died in that capitalistic war which they told us through their propaganda machinery was a War for democracy [applause]. What does the worker want? Why he wants to keep the strings of economic life himself. Capitalism offers him intermittent starvation, industrial slavery, recurring War. Socialism offers him subsistence, economic self-government, a basis for peace.

And I would like to ask Professor Seligman if he and I were miners up in Panther Creek, in the Philadelphia Reading Coal and Iron Company, whether he would be an ardent supporter of the present economic system [great applause]. And I want to ask him this further question, whether under those circumstances, he would put any obstacle in the way of the coming of some such system as I have described to you [great and prolonged applause].

11 DEBATE: CAN THE CHURCH BE RADICAL? (1922)

Affirmative: John Haynes Holmes
Negative: Scott Nearing

T HE SUBJECT OF THIS DEBATE addressed Nearing's long-standing contention that the church was unable to apply its ideals to eradicate widespread social maladies. He maintained that the church as an institution produced no economic goods to generate income and therefore must of necessity be conservative to attract the rich of the establishment for its economic viability. The church might be liberal to tinker with the social establishment and its defects but not radical to change the root causes of these defects.

Rabbi Judah L. Magnes introduced the speakers (Holmes was minister of the Community Church in New York) and acted as chairman. The debate was held February 12, 1922, in the Lexington Theatre in New York City.

Nearing: Anybody who can close as many avenues of approach in 35 minutes as Mr. Holmes has done should have been a debater and not a preacher. But there are one or two admissions that he made in the opening enthusiasm of his speech which I think are quite damaging. In the first place, let me say a word about this universal negative. I don't know much about the technique of dialectics, but Mr. Holmes told you that he could prove that a woman could have sixteen children by finding a woman who had sixteen children, and that he could prove that a cow could have a two-headed calf by finding P. T. Barnum's two-headed calf. But unfortunately, this topic is not "Can Nature Be Radical?" but

"Can the Church Be Radical?" And on looking up the definition of church in the New Standard Dictionary I find that the word church means, "The Christian community and its ecclesiastical organization," so that universal negative might apply with reason to sixteen children and two-headed calves, but not to this subject.

Now, there is another point that Mr. Holmes made, which seemed to me rather unfortunate from his point of view. He said that we are not dealing with the church in the past, and not dealing with the church of the present. He said we are dealing simply with the possibility of the future. Then, to bolster up his argument, he cited to you three church leaders, two of whom are dead. He also cited to you a number of pronouncements from Harry Ward's book, utterances of what the church said. Now, we have analyzed most of the words in this topic, but there is one we have not talked about and that is, Can **the** church speak radically? Without any question, although the latest utterance from the Federal Council of Churches of Christ in America on the subject of disarmament began with the statement that "We believe in a sweeping reduction in armaments"—that is, they are willing to slaughter their fellow humans with eight-inch, not with sixteen-inch guns—so that all of their pronouncements are not radical.

But, even though all of their pronouncements are radical, what happens in the case of a strike? What happens in the case of any labor crisis? Is the church radical—what does it do? Not what does it say? Now, I am willing to accept my opponents's case as he states it, with those two or three little and rather minor modifications, and argue with him on his position. Can the church—Can *the* Church *Be* Radical in the Future? Can *the* Church *Be* Radical? I conceive the problem a little differently from the way in which he conceives it, although I will accept his argument on its basis. As I see the issue, it is as follows: There are in the world millions of men and women who want to be radical; that is, who have gone through the experience of poverty, and exploitation, and war, and who are convinced that the present system cannot be painted, or soldered, or tinkered into an effective working scheme. They believe that the thing has got to be changed throughout, has got to be revolutionized, that there must be radical, root, complete, thoroughgoing modifications in the present social order. I say there are millions of men and women who have been led to that faith and who believe and who desire radical modifications in the world. These people are looking for something to tie to. They would like to belong to an organization. They would like to pay dues somewhere. They would like to pass out circulars for something. They would like to shout for some machine which would save the world for them. That, of course, is typically American; perhaps I might go further and say typically human, just as a child likes to go to the confectioner's and get a penny's worth of candy. It is much easier to do that than to make the candy. So people like to put in five dollars' worth of radicalism. They want something to function radically. And my opponent says that if you drop your five dollars in the collection basket of the church, that in the future you will get five dollars' worth of radicalism, or maybe more, out of it.

That is the issue, do you see? For these eager, seeking, yearning millions who have been convinced by bitter experience that the present machine is not a satisfactory workable machine, for those millions here is the open question: "Can the Church Be Radical?" Mr. Holmes says "Yes," and I want to examine the question for 30 minutes. We are agreed that the church is not radical. We are agreed that the church— **the** church—is not radical. We are agreed that the church has not been radical. Mr. Holmes spoke of the long, the melancholy and the tragic story of the delinquencies of the church in the past. I need not add any arguments to that brilliant statement of the church's position, long, melancholy, tragic; it has stood with the vested interests against the rights and liberties of the people. It stood thus on slavery. It stood thus on feudalism. It stands thus today on capitalism. It has organized and maintained inquisition, and the Protestant churches have organized and still maintain their attacks on science. It has burned its thinkers and persecuted those who dared to differ with it.

Now, Mr. Holmes knew I was going to say all of that. He told you so in advance. In these respects the church is exactly like any other social institution. It places a premium on conformity. It emphasizes going along, and it smites those who refuse to go along like any other social institution.

Now, I am talking to the millions, who want some institution to be radical, who want to drop a five dollar bill in a collection plate somewhere and have some institution reorganize the world for them. The church is a social institution, and its record, long, melancholy, tragic, is a record of the things that it has done to thwart progress and protect privilege. Well, now, let us see, can the church be radical? It is not. It has not been. Can it **be** radical? I answer, "No," and for the following reasons: In the first place, because the church has a creed, and the creed is drawn up by a convention, and a convention cannot be radical. The convention is composed of lefts, and rights, and centers, and the decisions of a convention are centrist decisions. And, therefore, taking by and large the convention of a great group of humans, you can pretty safely figure that a church creed, even if it were made today, would not represent a left position, it would represent a center position. It is in the nature of creeds to be centers, and so, as Emerson points out, when you go to hear a Presbyterian minister talk about Presbyterianism, you know in advance what he is going to say, because if he said anything else he would lose his job.

The utterances of the church are limited by their creeds, their constitutions. We have a Constitution in the United States. When you do anything, or try to enact any legislation that does not suit those in authority, you are unconstitutional. Well, now, in the church you are a heretic. You are against the creed. And the church as a church has a creed. Now, the worst thing about the creed is that it is a creed. The next worse thing about it is that it was made, as a rule, a long time ago, the longer the worse, because the farther it is from the actualities of the present and the possibilities of the future. The church as an institution is hemmed in by something that conventions and conclaves and diets did in past years or past centuries, and therefore it is prevented from acting in a thoroughgoing fundamental manner on the principles and issues of the future.

In the second place, the church cannot be radical because it is an economically unproductive, social unit, requiring large economic support, and it is therefore tethered to the source of its support. Mr. Holmes told you I was going to attribute the shortcomings of the church to capitalism. Not for a moment. What I have to say about the church would be equally true under communism. The church is non-productive. It does not make shoes. It does not make carpets. It does not make wagon tires. It does not make any economic goods. It has pipe organs and rocks and stone walls and other expensive accessories. And these things must be paid for. In 1916,—that is the latest report of the Census Bureau—the church in the United States spent $328,809,999. That is a third of a billion dollars. That is about one-third of what the Federal Government spent at the same time. Where did they get it? When the church wants money, when anybody wants money, he goes not to the good, but to the rich, because it is the rich that have the money. That is why we call them rich. Now, one peculiarity of rich people is that they are not radical. And so the church, a non-productive unit, is compelled to go to the conservative elements of the community for its support. Why the conservative elements? Because those who own the property and have a vested interest in the system are those who are asked to contribute to the church.

When the Inter-Church World Movement was organized, they had an executive committee with John D. Rockefeller at the head of it. Now, they did not pick Mr. Rockefeller, I assume, because of his spiritual qualities, nor because of his executive ability. They picked him because he was Mr. Rockefeller; they picked him because of his financial position. And that is generally the method of financing any non-productive social unit. If you want to run a charity society, you pick rich people to help you. If you want to run an orphanage, you do likewise. If you want to run a church, you get rich people interested in the church, because unless they contribute the church cannot function.

Now Mr. Holmes might tell you that there are churches out in the country towns without a single rich man in the congregation. I know that. But my answer to the proposition is a general one, not a specific one. I say the church, as a church, to raise that third of a billion dollars, has got to go to the people who have the third of a billion dollars, and among them are many of the richest people in the United States. They are the supporters, the beneficiaries of the present order. And the church must trim its sails to suit the breath from their nostrils before it can open the strings of their pocketbooks. The church has a creed, a constitution, a bill of rights that is has to live up to. That is a tether that holds it in. The church has an income that it must raise. That is a tether that holds it in.

In the third place, the church as an institution, represents a great vested interest. Notice, in this same census volume there are the reports from 227,000 churches. That is a quarter of a million jobs, positions, professional opportunities—jobs. You have a quarter of a million people who are interested, as all people are, in holding jobs. That has always been the core of any institution. The heart of any institution is the mechanism of those who make up the man-power of the institution, those who do the work of the institution, those who hold the jobs, the positions in the institutions—a quarter of a million of them.

Now, to go on; in these churches there are 1,952,000 Sunday school superintendents, teachers and other minor church officials, volunteers, yes, but they also hold jobs; that is, they have prerogatives. They are Sunday school superintendents! And when they go down the street, the people say, "There goes the superintendent of the Sunday school." Two million of them in the churches! They don't make money. They have prestige, position, a little brief authority, because of their official connection with the church. And then, that is not the worst of it. In these same churches there are 41,926,000 members—42,000,000 members! Now, let me ask my friend, Mr. Holmes, if he has read over the election returns for 1920. There were 16,000,000 votes for Harding. How many of those 16,000,000 do you suppose came out of the churches? There were 9,000,000 votes for Cox. How many of those 9,000,000 votes do you suppose came out of the churches? There were a million votes for Debs and Christensen. How many of those votes do you suppose came out of the churches? I don't know, but I know that all of the 42,000,000 did not vote for Debs and Christensen. They got only a million votes, and there were 25,000,000 votes cast, and these were the people that voted for Harding and Cox, the membership of the church, 42,000,000 conservatives.

Mr. Holmes spoke about American labor. Has anybody here accused American labor of being radical? Not at all! These 42,000,000 are the heart of American bourgeois conservatism. They believe in the present order. They vote for it. They talk for it. They support it. They pay for it.

And when war comes, they fight for it. And they make up the great body of the church, 42,000,000 of them! Can they be radical? In 1916, the value of the church property was $1,676,000,000. They say the only thing more cowardly than $100,000,000 is $200,000,000. Well, there is eight times one million dollars worth of conservatism right there in the churches. Can an institution like that be radical? A quarter of a million place holders, two million unpaid place holders, 42 million members, nearly two billions in investments! Does radicalism come from such sources? As Mr. Holmes says, grapes do not grow on thorns or figs on thistles. The church is one of the great, powerful, rich, institutions of the present order, untaxed by the present order, with places and property to defend in the present order. Will the church turn against the present order?

I think it says somewhere that no house divided itself shall stand. Is that correct? Mr. Holmes says the words are not quite correct, but the thought is there. No house divided against itself shall stand. The church as a part of the present order must support the present order if the present order is to continue. Was the church conservative? It was. Is the church conservative? It is. Has it been one of the most conservative institutions in the community? It has. Why? Because of its creeds, because of its organization as an institution, because it is a part of the mechanism of established society, with places of wealth and power which it has always been to the interests of the church to maintain.

Can the church be beautiful? It can. Can it be charitable? Yes. Can it prove a source of inspiration? It—may. Can it be liberal? Perhaps. Can it be radical? [cry of "no"] It is as hard for the church to be radical as it is for water to be dry. Conservatism is the very essence of its life, the fibre of its organization, the marrow of its bones. And out of such an organization comes no radicalism.

Now, let me just take the last five minutes that I have at my disposal, to sum up the position that that leads us to. Does this analysis lead to blackness and despair because the church cannot be radical? Can nothing be radical? Not at all. This is not pessimism, just social analysis. You who believe that there is hope, have only one source, and that is yourselves. Every man must be his own radical. You remember old Captain John Smith who said, "If a man would have a thing well done, he must do it himself." Now, that may not be true regarding the transportation of milk, or the operation of subways, but if you want to be radical, you have got to do it yourselves.

You dare not commit the functions of radicalism to any institution, church or otherwise, because the moment you do, the moment you have a hired representative, a creed and bricks and mortar, you have fastened the shackles of conservatism permanently on that institution, and never while the stones remain upon one another, never while the creed lasts, never while the paid representative continues to represent, will your institution be a radical institution. It will stand by the present order, and I care not whether your institution be a church, an educational system, a political party, or a trade union. No matter what the nature of your organization, you dare not trust an institution to be radical. Why? I have tried to point out why.

The essence of an institution is a compromised, centrist position, neither to the right nor to the left, but somewhere in between the extremes of doctrine. Radicalism means thoroughgoing, going to the root, going to the bottom of things, and you millions who would like a radical change in the world had better keep your five dollar bills in your pockets, and spend them for sandwiches and coffee or other things to maintain life, not institutions. Institutions may be very beautiful, institutions may be very useful, institutions may serve many purposes, but institutions are not radical. And you who believe, we who believe, in the fundamental reorganization of the present social life, have one course and only one to pursue, and that is to study and to think and to observe and to draw our conclusions and to hold our faith high and clear and keep our ideals uncontaminated, and when the time comes act—*we,* not the church, not an institution, but *we* must act.

You can get 20 miles of transportation in New York City for a nickel, and for a few nickels you can have somebody tend your furnace and sweep your front doorstep when it snows, and so you get into that frame of mind which is summed up by the phrase, "Let George Do It." Let the church be radical for me! I will pay to have it done. No! You will pay, yes, but you won't pay for radicalism. You will pay for conservatism, for the preservation of the institution into which pours your wealth.

Does that mean that we shall have no institutions? I make no such assertion. The present organization of society is built upon institutions. Will these institutions be conservative? They will. Will you who hope for radical changes have any opportunity for radicalism through institutions? In all probability you will not, and particularly not in an institution like the church which is vested and sewed in and tied down with the mechanism of an established order of society.

Every man his own radical, every man his own thinker, every man his own ideals, every man his own understudy and his own actor when the time for action comes—that is the only basis for radicalism. That is the only basis on which the present order of society will be changed.

12   THE NEXT STEP (1922)

NEARING'S FIRST WIFE, Nellie Seeds, was the publisher of this book from their home in Ridgewood, New Jersey. The book "is dedicated to the task of emancipating the human race from economic servitude."

Taking the example of his beloved teacher Simon Patten, Nearing steadied his view of life on a grand scheme for the long-term future. His abiding passion to rid the world of devastating war and the miseries of billions of common workers prompted him to formulate a federation of all nations. Seeing the turmoil of his age, he proposed that the basis for world peace must rest upon an economic, not political, federation.

After pointing out the inadequacies of the League of Nations, he built an economic structure beginning with nearly-autonomous local producers of goods and services and ending with a world parliament. His aim was to eliminate the superiority of ownership over labor, which he felt inevitably led to class distinction and conflict.

His postscript to the book is characteristic of his sense of dialectic and teaching: "No reader should accept the statements made in this book unless they appeal to his reason and correspond with his experience, nor should he reject them merely because they run counter to his prejudices or his convictions."

With economic life established on a world scale, it is inevitable that the range of men's thoughts and the lines of their social groupings should assume the same general scope. The late war made it quite apparent that war means world war, and that a real peace is impossible unless it is a world peace. The post-war experience has shown with equal clearness, that prosperity means world prosperity, and that it is impossible to destroy the economic well-being of an integral part of the world without destroying the well-being of the whole world. These things were suspected before the war, when they formed the themes of moral dissertations and scholarly essays, of syndicalist pamphlets, socialist programs and revolutionary appeals. But it required the hard knocks of the past eight years to lift them so far out of the realm of theory into that of reality, that any thinking human being who faces the facts must admit their truth.

The economics of the modern world make it inevitable that thinkers on public questions, particularly on economic questions, should frame their thoughts in world terms, and that the practical plans for the organization and direction of human affairs should be built around an idea which includes these three elements:

1. Any workable plan for the organization of the world must have an economic foundation.
2. Such a plan must include all of the economically essential portions of the world. It will be ineffective if it is confined to any one nation, to any one group of nations, or to any one continent.
3. Such a plan must rely, for its fulfillment, on world thinking and world organization.

These propositions do not imply that economic forces and world organization must become the centers of exclusive attention. There are potent forces, other than economic ones, and there are forms of local organization that must be developed or perpetuated as a matter of course. But for the moment the economic forces and the world phases of organization have assumed a position of primary importance.

The principal scheme recently advanced as a means of co-ordinating the life of the world—the League of Nations Covenant—violates all three of these essential principles. In the first place, the League Covenant, with certain minor exceptions, is a political and not an economic document, devoting its attention to territorial integrity and the preservation of sovereignty, and passing over such economic problems as resource control, and the competition for raw materials, markets and investment opportunities as though they were non-existent. In the second place instead of concerning itself with all of the integral parts of the world, it treats nations other than the "big five" (Britain, France, Italy, Japan and the United States) as though they were of second or of third rate importance. China, India, Germany, Russia and Latin America, with considerably more than half of the world's population, and with at least half of the world's essential resources, were slighted or ignored. In the third place, the League Covenant is not based on world thinking. On the contrary, it was designed to set up one part of the world, the victorious Allies, against four other parts of the world: the enemy countries, Soviet Russia, the undeveloped (unexploited) countries, and the small and powerless countries. Political, sectional and provincial in its point of view, the League, as a means of world organization, was destined, from its inception, to pathetic failure. World economic life is an established fact of such moment that it must be reckoned with in any scheme for social rebuilding.

A capacity for organization and for conscious improvement distinguishes man from most of the animals. In the past, men have organized the army, the church, the city, the nation, the school. The events surrounding the industrial revolution have placed a new task on their shoulders—the task of organizing world economic life.

Without doubt this is the largest and the most intricate problem in organization that the human race has ever faced. On the other hand, the interdependence of economic life invites co-ordination, while the advances in organization methods, particularly among the masses of the people, render the transition from local to world organization quite logical and relatively easy—far easier, certainly, than the first hesitating steps that the race took in the direction of co-operative activities. Even if the task were far more difficult than it is, the race must perform it or pay an immense price in hardship, suffering and decimation.

The work is already begun. Private capitalists have built world systems of trade, transport and banking. Soviet Russia has made an heroic attempt to organize one portion of the earth's surface along economic lines. For the most part, however, the task of co-ordinating the world's economic life awaits the courage and the genius of a generation that shall add this triumph to the achievements of the race.

Certain well-defined and widely understood principles, that might almost be called axioms of social procedure, are to be reckoned with in any effort at world economic reorganization. For convenience of discussion, they may be summarized thus:

1. *The wheels of industry must be kept turning smoothly, regularly and efficiently.*

A country like Russia, consisting, for the most part of agricultural villages, can survive, even though machine industries practically cease to function, while such countries as Germany and Britain, built of Bremens, Hamburgs, Essens, Glasgows and Manchesters are dependent for their food supply as well as for their supply of raw materials upon the continued production and transport of commodities. The State of

Rhode Island, with its 97.5 per cent of city and town dwellers, typifies this dependence. Given such concentrated populations engaged in specialized industries, and the cessation of production means speedy starvation for those that cannot migrate.

2. *Provision must be made for improvements and betterments.*

The increase of population and the normal advances in science and industry both demand a volume of product adequate to cover the necessary increases in equipment.

3. *The people who do the work must dispose of the products they turn out.*

They may consume them all, or they may reserve a portion of them for new roads, for additional rolling stock, for the advancement of art and learning. Whatever the character of the decision, the right and power to make it rests with those who produce the goods of which a disposition is being made.

4. *Justice and fair dealing must be embodied in the scheme of production and distribution.*

This does not mean absolute justice, but as much justice as the collective intelligence and will of the community are able to put into force. For the attainment of such a result, the forms of social life must be constantly altered to keep pace with economic change.

5. *The foregoing principles must apply, not to one man, or class, or people, but to all men, all classes and all peoples.*

Recent events have shown that an injury to one is an injury to all. Reasoning, foresight and experience will convince the people of the world that a benefit to one is a benefit to all. While men continue to live together, their livelihood problems must be thought about collectively, and the solutions that are determined upon must be applied to all, without discrimination.

How shall such results be obtained? By what means is it possible to lead men to a world vision? Who can persuade them to work toward the building of a sounder society than that with which the world is now laboring?

Of all the issues that confront the teachers of men, this is one of the most pressing and most insistent. Those who have taken upon themselves the task of seeking out and of expounding ideas have seldom faced a graver responsibility than that with which they are at the moment confronted. World facts demand world thoughts and world acts, before the human race can adopt saner, wiser and more enlightened economic policies. World thoughts and acts are impossible without world understanding. Therefore it is world understanding that is most imperatively needed in this critical hour.

The people of the world have many things in common—economic interests, science, art, ideas, ideals. Ranged against these common interests there are the traditions, prejudices, hatreds, national barriers, sectarian differences, language obstacles and racial conflicts that have proved so effective in keeping the peoples separated. The common interests are the vital means of social advancement, and it is upon them that the emphasis of constructive thinking must be laid in an effort to promote world understanding.

There is no need to apologize, then, for adding to groaning library shelves a book dealing with world economics, the purpose of which is to propose a plan that will pull together the scattered threads of world economic life. The time is so ripe for an examination of these problems that no man may consider himself informed who has not pondered them deeply, and no man may consider that he has done his duty as a member of this generation, who has not helped, at least in some degree, to unify the world's economic activities. Most particularly does this apply both to the statesmen and other public men who are striving to rejuvenate a dying order, and to the organizers and leaders of the new order that is even now pressing across the threshold of the western world.

War menace constitutes another indication of the chaos existing in modern economic society. The purpose of economic activity is to produce wealth. The purpose of war is to destroy it. The two are therefore in direct antagonism; yet the greatest war machines are maintained by the greatest industrial nations. To reply that they have the big war machines because they can afford to pay for them, is no conclusive answer. The organizing of nations for war came into present-day society with the present industrial system. Industrial leaders have engaged in a great competitive struggle from which the final appeal was always the appeal to arms. Furthermore, one of the most profitable businesses has been that of making the munitions and supplies required for the prosecution of war. Nor is there wanting evidence that modern wars have been made for profits—that they have been "commercial wars," as President Wilson put it.

There is no longer any question but that the forces behind the world war were in the main economic. The war was fought by capitalist empires, for the furtherance of capitalist enterprises. The publication of the secret treaties entered into by the Allies in 1916 gives conclusive proof of the land grabbing character of the Allies' intentions. There can scarcely be any question of the existence of similar intentions on the side of the Central Empires. The forces that constituted the war menace in 1914 were the economic forces arising out of the competitive economic régime that dominated the European world at that time.

Though its nature and its causes are little understood, there is no issue of more immediate concern to the western world than the intelligent solution of the vexing questions arising out of the production and distribution of wealth.

These five limitations: centralization, nationalism, profiteering, the handling of economic affairs in the name of property rather than in that of human welfare, and the class struggle—make it difficult or impossible for the directors of the present economic system to extend it in response to the pressing demand for expansion. Like other social systems that have prevailed in historic times, the capitalist system of economic control has its limitations, and like many another system, it seems to have reached them.

Economic function would seem to be most effectively aided by some organization of the economic units that would provide a structurally sound skeleton for the whole economic mechanism. The needs of particular localities, the requirements of larger groups within one industry, the economic relations of continental areas, and finally the world organization of industries must be provided for. In order to meet this situation, it would seem desirable to think in terms of several different grades or classes of economic units. As a working basis, four are suggested:

1. *The local unit, which would be some particular phase of the economic process that normally functions as a whole.*

This unit is now a working part of the present economic order, and whether it is a colliery in Wales, a division of the P. L. M. Railroad in France, a mill in Bombay, or a farming community in Saskatchewan, it would continue the process of turning out goods and services under the new economic régime as it does under the present one.

2. *District units composed of a number of neighboring local units in the same industry or in closely related and co-operative industries.*

The district is an aggregation of conveniently situated local units, and is organized as a ready means of increasing the efficiency of the groups concerned. It might cover the tobacco factories of Havana, the coal

mining industry of the Pennsylvania anthracite fields or the dock working activities of Belfast.

> 3. *The divisional units which would be designed to cover a conven-*
>   *ient geographic area, and to include all of the economic activities*
>   *in a particular major industry within that area.*

The boundaries of the districts would vary from one industry to
another. The boundaries of the divisions would be uniform for all industries. The whole world would therefore be partitioned into a number of
divisions, such, for example, as: North America, South America, South
Africa, the Mediterranean Basin, Northern Europe, Northern Asia,
Eastern Asia, Southern Asia and Australia. In setting the boundary lines
of these divisions, economic homogeneity, geographic unity, the distribution of the world population and the character of existing civilization would all be called into question. Under such a grouping would fall
the agricultural workers of Southern Asia, the transport workers of
North Europe, the manufacturing workers of North America.

> 4. *World industrial units, so designed as to include within their scope*
>   *all of the producers of the world classified in accordance with*
>   *their occupations.*

To-day, the outstanding method of classifying the people of the world
is to take them in relation to their political affiliations. The new grouping would arrange all of the peoples in accordance with their economic
activities. A simple form of classification would include: agriculture,
the extractive industries, manufacturing, transport, trade, housekeep-
ing, and general (miscellaneous) trades. The classification might be
made far more elaborate, but for clarity of discussion a simple
classification is of great assistance. Every person in the world who
performed a useful service would belong to one of these great industrial
or occupational groups, and the aggregate of the membership of the
groups would equal the aggregate of all the producers of the world.

Under this plan, therefore, each individual would have a series of
economic affiliations. He might, for example, be a docker on the
French Line at Le Havre (local affiliation); a dock worker in the Le
Havre district (district affiliation); a transport worker of North Europe
(divisional affiliation); a worker in the transport industries of the world
(industrial affiliation).

Since each of the producers in the world would have this series of
relations, all of the producers would be grouped together in local, in
district, in divisional and in world industrial groups, so that the economic life of the world would present the picture of a completed economic

structure very similar to the political structure that has been evolving for
many centuries, and which has reached its highest forms of development in such new countries as Australia and the United States, where
each person is a citizen in a borough, city or town, in a county, in a state
and in the whole nation or federation of states.

While political life has been thus organized about the administration
of certain public affairs, economic life has remained disorganized, or
has been organized largely with an eye to owners' profits. The producers society will be organized in economic terms very much as the
present society is organized in political terms. Each producer will be a
participant in the life of economic units, graduated from the local economic unit to the world industry.

The most elemental of the federations would be the local producers'
federation, which would correspond, quite accurately, to the town or the
city of the present day, save that its size and character would of necessity be much better regulated than the character and size of the present-
day town or city. The modern city has been built as a profiteer's para-
dise. From the construction of houses to the erection of office buildings,
the one foremost question: "What per cent will it yield?" has been the
guiding principle behind city construction. The local industrial federation will have, as its chief task, the provision of a living and working
place for people, hence the character of the industrial community will
be determined with a view to the well-being of the inhabitants rather
than to the profit of landlords.

The local federation would be under the control of a local council, the
members of which would be elected by the producing units or groups
composing the local federation, very much as the modern city is managed by a council elected by wards or aldermanic districts. Except for
the choice of representatives on the council by occupational groups,
rather than by geographic divisions, the local federation would closely
resemble the municipal government of the present day. In addition to its
present functions, however, it would assume the task of dealing with
issues arising between two or more of the local producing groups. That
is, it would have economic as well as political functions, although it
would not necessarily carry on more productive enterprises (gas, water,
house-construction, abbatoirs) than do municipalities at the present
time.

The local producers' federation would be responsible for two chief
lines of activity. On the one hand, it would seek to maintain working
relations between the various local economic groups by adjudicating
those local questions that affected two or more of the groups. On the
other hand, it would take charge of, and administer, those matters of

common concern, such as the water supply, the local educational institutions, and so on. This second group of functions would be similar to those now performed by the city council, the board of health, the board of education.

There would be a local producers' federation wherever a number of local industrial units agreed to function together. Counties, cities, boroughs, and school districts are, at the present time, organized very much in that way.

The local producers' federation would therefore differ little from the existing local groups, such as towns and cities, save that its constituent elements would be occupational groups rather than geographic divisions, and that it would be functioning in the economic as well as in the political field.

The second series of federations might be called the producers' district federations. They would include all district industrial groups within a given economic field. Such a district federation would correspond, roughly, to the present state as it exists in Mexico or Australia, or to the provinces in Canada.

The district federation would function in three ways. First, there would be the issues arising between the industrial organizations that composed the district federation; second, there would be the issues arising between local federations within the district, and third, there would be those common matters, like health, education, highways and so on.

The third series of federations would be the divisional producers federations, which would correspond, roughly, to such aggregations of states as the Commonwealth of Australia or the United States of America. The boundaries of such a federation would follow the boundaries of the principal land areas and the chief population centers. North America, South America, South Africa, the Mediterranean Basin, Northern Europe, Northern Asia, Eastern Asia, Southern Asia and Australia would furnish a working basis for separating the world into such geographical divisions. Each of these divisional federations would function along the same general lines as the local and district groups.

The fourth, in the series of federations, would be the world producers' federation, which would be an organization composed of all of the major industrial groups. These groups, each of which would be organized on a world-wide basis, would unite in the world producers' federation in order to further those interests that were of consequence to two or more of them, as well as those common interests that were of concern to all alike. The world producers' federation would be built on the same principle as the local producers' federation, but unlike this latter federation, the world federation has no prototype existing at the present time.

The world producers' federation would be a world authority, linking up those interests of world consequence that are now waving about like cobwebs in the wind.

Throughout its entire course this outline has been designed in such a way as to separate sharply the producing units and the administrative groups (federations). The local, district, divisional and world industrial units are the back-bone of the public machinery in a producers' society. For the purposes of facilitating the work of administration, these producers' groups are brought together, at various points, in local, district, divisional and in a world producers' federation, all of which federations derive their power directly from the industrial producers' groups. The world producers' federation therefore has no direct relations with the local producers' federation, any more than the government of a county, in a modern state, has with the central federal authority. The authority of the world producers' federation, like that of the local, district and divisional producers' federations, is derived from its constituent industrial member groups, and is confined to the questions that are of immediate concern to a number of them, or that are the common concern of all.

This arrangement will make difficult the production of a state of present type which has drifted far away from some of the most pressing necessities of the common life, and into the hands of politicians,—a situation that permits tyranny on the one hand, and that makes any adequate check on the activities of these political rings difficult or impossible. This danger would be considerably reduced by delegating administrative power to the federations, holding each within its prescribed range, and keeping the real power in the hands of the local, district, divisional and world industrial groups.

The decision of the world producers' federation would therefore be binding on the industrial groups, and not upon the local, district and divisional producers' federations, except in so far as the industrial groups compelled these federations to follow the policy of the world producers' federation.

It is probable that an exception would have to be made in the case of issues arising between two divisional producers' federations. The burden of settling such an issue should rest, however, on the industrial groups rather than on the world producers' federation.

This with-holding of authority from the federations in general, and from the world producers' federation in particular may be open to criticism, but it has several strong points in its favor. Through its control of resources, transport and the like, the world producers' federation will wield an immense power. Its constituent members, having aided in its decisions of policy, may follow a similar course of action in the divisional and the district producers' federations. Again, the alternative to the organization of a series of disconnected federations is a centralized bureaucracy of such magnitude, and holding such vast power, that it would be both unwieldy and dangerous, beside violating that very essential rule of local authority in local affairs.

The structural organization of the world producers' federation would be similar to that of the United States of America or that of the Russian Federated Soviet Republic. The constituent groups would be economic and occupational rather than political or geographic, but the principle of federated autonomous groups would be the same. Each of the major industrial groups that belonged to the world producers' federation would have sovereign power over those matters which affected that group alone. The federation, on the other hand, would have jurisdiction over matters affecting two or more of the world industrial groups, as well as over those matters which were of common concern to all of the member groups.

The general lines of organization for the world producers' federation would be somewhat as follows:

1. The workers in each of the major industrial groups would vote in June of each year for the members of a world parliament which would be the central authority in the world producers' federation.
2. The world parliament would consist of from 800 to 1000 delegates, elected in each of the major industrial groups by the producers in that group.
   a. Each industrial group would be entitled to at least 50 members in the world parliament, and to one additional member for each 50,000 workers over two and one half millions. But no group would be entitled to more than 150 members in the world parliament.
   b. The members of the world parliament would be elected by popular vote in each of the major industrial groups, the franchise being extended to all producers, including those who had been producers and were rendered incapable of activity through age or infirmity.
   c. Each industrial division would be entitled to at least five members of the parliamentary delegation from that particular industrial group, but the details of representation from each of the major industrial groups would be left in the hands of the group.
3. The world parliament would be elected in June and would meet in July of each year. Since the world congresses of each of the major industrial groups would meet in the preceding January, they would have six months to thresh out their individual problems, before

they were called upon to consider the general problems confronting all of the groups.

4. The world parliament would select, from its own membership, an executive committee equal in size to ten per cent of the total membership of the parliament.

   a. On this executive committee each of the world industrial groups would be entitled to at least five members.

   b. The executive committee would be the steering committee of the world parliament, and when the world parliament was not in session, the executive committee would be the responsible body.

   c. The executive committee would meet once in four months, or oftener at its discretion.

5. The executive committee would select, from its membership, a number of administrative boards, at the same time naming the chairman of each board. Each of these administrative boards would be charged with the responsibility of handling a unit problem, such as the control of resources, the control of transport, and the like.

6. The chairmen of the various administrative boards would constitute the executive heads of the world producers' federation. They might be called the world producers' federation board of managers. This board of managers would be responsible to the world parliament executive committee.

   a. If, at any time, the board of managers failed to secure a vote of confidence from the world parliament executive committee, on any matter involving a question of general policy, the board of managers would be automatically dissolved, and the executive committee would proceed at once to select a new board that would replace the old one.

   b. If the executive committee failed to select a board of managers that could secure a vote of confidence, the world parliament would be automatically summoned to meet one month from the day on which this failure to elect occurred.

   c. As soon as it convened, the world parliament would proceed, as a first order of business, to the election of an executive committee which would function.

   d. If the parliament failed to elect an executive committee capable of functioning, the parliament would be automatically dissolved, a special election would be held within ten days, a new parliament would be selected, and would assemble thirty days from the date of this special election.

   e. By these means, the whole machinery of the world producers' federation would be rendered immediately responsive at all times to the sentiment of its constituency, and the board of managers would be compelled to function in line with the policy of the executive committee and of the world parliament, or turn the work over to another group.

7. The world parliament would exercise, directly, or by delegated authority, all legislative, executive and judicial functions that pertained to its activities. It would therefore create the departments or subdivisions necessary to the carrying out of these various functions. The members of the world parliament would be elected for one year, subject to recall at any time by the constituency that elected them. The parliament would decide on the qualifications of its own members.

A world government has no virtue in itself, and may as easily degenerate into a scramble for office as may any other phase of group relationship. Its success would only be possible where its power was strictly limited to the control of those matters that had reached a plane of world importance. Even then success would be impossible unless those responsible for making essential decisions saw the world problems as wholes rather than as localized and separable problems.

There are a number of problems that have passed beyond the control of any single nation, and that should therefore be made the subject of world administration. Among them are: (1) the control of resources and raw materials, (2) transport, (3) exchange, credit and investment, (4) the world economic budget, and (5) adjudication of world disputes. Under a world producers' federation, the administration of these five problems would be in the hands of five administrative boards selected by the executive committee of the world parliament.

The administrative board would thus be a group primarily of experts, charged with the specific task of handling some problem of world moment, and responsible to the board of managers of the world producers' federation for the success of its activities.

Social disaster is not the only path to social knowledge. It is not necessary for a generation to suffer from typhus or to be ruined by war in order to be convinced that these dread diseases are menaces. The desire to prevent famine is felt by millions who have never come any nearer to it than the stories in the papers. Society learns, indirectly, through education—slowly of course, but none the less surely.

The average man is convinced of the desirability of trying to avoid disease, hunger and the other ills that affect him personally and immediately. He is not yet convinced of the efficacy of a similar attitude toward war, revolution and other disasters which inevitably destroy some portion of society, and which in the end will prove as preventable as disease and famine. Social disaster seems more inevitable because it strikes more people at one time, while individual disaster has been more carefully studied, is better understood and is more localized.

Grave dangers menace present-day society. Economic breakdown, war and social dissolution with their terrible scourges—pestilence and famine—have already overtaken millions. It is plain that some new course of social action must be planned; that some social experiment must be inaugurated that will ward off the impending disasters.

Social experiments should be made, as chemical and electrical experiments are made, after all of the available facts have been carefully considered and digested. The results of such wisely planned experiments in the social field may be just as dramatic as the results of similarly planned experiments in the field of natural science.

13 OIL AND THE GERMS
OF WAR (1923)

N EARING WAS 40 YEARS OLD when he wrote this monograph and his first wife, Nellie Seeds, published it from
Ridgewood, New Jersey. He was entering several years of
intellectual and emotional distress. The previous year he
had resigned from the Socialist Party because of the bicker-
ing factions, particularly Norman Thomas's criticism of the
new Soviet government. The following year he and Nellie
Seeds separated; two years later after much soul-searching
he joined the Communist Party.

In the meantime, he returned home one day, sat down,
and declared himself a vegetarian. He put a wooden bowl
on the table and took up chopsticks. The doilies and knick-
nacks of middle-class life that had accumulated in his
household stood against his work. He could not write and
speak against the shamefulness of unfettered corporate profits and horrendous wars that devastated the common people
if he were not more among them.

A revealing inscription on a private copy of this book
reads: "Mother, Christmas 1923. Love & greetings, Scott
Nearing."

John D. Rockefeller and a number of his associates set up one of the
most important landmarks in the economic history of the United States
when they organized the Standard Oil Company in 1870. The business
atmosphere of the time was dominated by the idea of competition—the
common assumption being that competition was not only inevitable, but
that it was "the life of trade."

Mr. Rockefeller held a different view. His ideal was a large, well organized, efficiently managed industrial unit, based on the principle of co-operation rather than of competition, and from his first investment in an oil refinery in 1862, through the organization of the Standard Oil Company, and during the succeeding years, Mr. Rockefeller did his best to get his potential competitors to come inside and share the benefits of joint effort. He never insisted on playing a lone hand, but surrounded himself with such men as William Rockefeller, S. V. Harkness, and H. M. Flagler. For the motto: "Producers compete!" Mr. Rockefeller substituted: "Producers unite!" and acting on this principle, within ten years he had under Standard Oil control more than nine tenths of the oil refining business of the country. This was the first great demonstration, in the American business world, of the precept: "In union there is strength."

The position of the Standard Oil Co. was rendered still more secure by its control of the pipe lines through which the oil was transported, by its rebate contracts with the railroads, by its ruthless wars on stubborn competitors, and by the very efficient way in which its business affairs were conducted.

Standard Oil profits were large from the outset. A number of government investigations show that between 1882 and 1906 the total of cash dividends paid by the company was $551 millions, which was an average of 24 per cent. per year on the outstanding stock. In addition to the dividends, there were surpluses that made the total profit account for the period about $714 millions.

Here was a fateful combination: a valuable and very limited natural resource; the principle of industrial co-operation; enormous profits on a rapid turn-over, heaped up in great surplus funds. The result was inevitable. Standard Oil quickly became one of the masters of American public life, and those who questioned its sway or crossed its path made a quick exit from public office. Public investigations followed attacks by private "muck-rakers," and so insistent was the public demand for action that on May 11, 1911, the United States Supreme Court handed down a decree declaring the Standard Oil Co. a trust in restraint of trade, and ordering its dissolution into a number of constituent companies, such as the Standard of New Jersey, the Standard of Indiana, and the like.

The Standard of New Jersey is only one of the Standard Oil Properties, and the Standard Oil Properties is only one of the many oil empires that have been built in the United States and in Europe during the brief period in which oil has mounted to a position of such supreme industrial and diplomatic importance. But this was only the commercial side of the oil revolution. The new fuel modified the whole method of warfare.

The four new and decisively important transport factors developed during the late war were the submarine, the airplane, the tank and the motor transport service. The country which had only coal could use no one of these devices, but was confined to the steam-engine and the horse on land, and the coal-burning ship at sea. The oil-rich nation could make war in the air; could transport its armies in motor cars, which are much more mobile than steam engines; could fight with land battleships and, because of the less weight of oil fuel, could mount heavier naval guns than its coal-using rival.

The Germans had coal in abundance, but little oil. German armies moved in trains or walked. The Allies had an abundance of oil. Their armies were more mobile; their air fleets were better supplied with fuel; their submarines had an abundance of motive power, and their battle fleets were being rapidly transformed to the oil-burning basis.

The multitude ascribed the triumph to the soldiers. The more experienced statesmen, who were on the inside of the national councils, understood that the triumph of the Allies was the triumph of superior air-fleets, naval units, and of superior army mobility due to the use of motor cars. The men in the trenches fought equally well on both sides, as anyone who was at the front over a long period of time is ready to admit.

The World War was thus an oil-won war, proving conclusively that the national supremacy of the future rested on oil as a source of military and naval power.

No Great War was necessary to show thinking people the direction in which the economic wind was blowing. As far back as 1910 the responsible statesmen and business men of Great Britain had seen what was coming.

The modern British Empire was built upon coal. As one writer has very effectively put it: Imperial Britain owes her supremacy, not to the number and tonnage of her ships alone, but also to her monopoly of fuel.

Meanwhile the Standard Oil Company had invaded France. The French Government was about to turn the control of petroleum back into private hands, and the Standard, through the organization of several subsidiaries prepared to take care of the business. This accounts for the fact that the Standard of New Jersey has more subsidiaries in France than in any other country of Europe.

Such was the ostensible motive behind the move of Standard Oil into France. But this was mere camouflage. In Mesopotamia and Persia there were oil reserves estimated to equal the total oil reserves of the United States. These reserves were largely in British controlled territory, but under the San Remo agreement, there was a chance for French interests to share in their development. Besides, the French government was the only real rival that the British Government had left in Europe and the Near East, and as the competition between the two was very intense, there seemed nothing more logical than for the Standard Oil interests to use the French Government to secure a share of Near East oil concessions.

What a picture this Near East scramble presents! What a sight for the gods! Greek farmer boys and artisans lay aside their tools, and, in the name of Jesus, don uniforms and sail away to fight against the heathen Turk, while Turk farmer boys and artisans lay aside their tools and arm themselves to destroy the unbelievers. On either side the soldiers pass in bold array. Public men harangue and flatter them, priests exort them, newspapers extol them, crows applaud them. They reach the front; camp in over-crowded, disease-ridden, waterless places; march through the baking heat, ragged, half-starved; they ravish the country-side, trampling crops, sacking farms, destroying olive groves, burning villages; they meet in battle, sweat, bleed, suffer, agonize, die. For them it is a war to vindicate a faith, and to save their hearth-stones from dishonor. But behind them, in London, Paris and New York, sit old, cynical, scheming men, laying the plans for the next campaign, and wondering whether the result of a given battle will be an extra dividend for Shell Transport or for Standard Oil.

What of the future? The countries about the Caribbean are "independent" nations, but, alas! when the independence of a weak nation is weighed against important oil reserves, it is mere dust in the balance. The great imperial countries must have oil, and in order to obtain it, they must go where oil is to be found. As each oil field is discovered, and its richness is proved, it will be the object of a fierce rivalry—of a life and death struggle between those who are contending for the economic and political supremacy of the world.

Must there be war? Yes, there must be war so long as men are bent on taking their livelihood from others instead of producing it for themselves. War is a business. Like any other business, it is not conducted on the sidewalk. Behind the lines there are the general staffs, the experts in strategy, the technicians, the military schools. In the army and navy departments there are men whose sole duty it is to map out the campaigns far in advance of their execution; to design and to build guns, forts and ships; to experiment with explosives and poisonous gases; to construct air-planes, tanks and submarines; to arrange the detail of army operation and equipment—to what purpose? They are working toward the goal of all military science—the destruction of life and property.

Strictly speaking, war is organized destruction. There is nothing impetuous, emotional, or accidental about a war as there is about a street fight. On the contrary, it is just as carefully worked out as the most methodical business in the world.

Modern states spend more money on war than on any other single government activity. Since the purpose of war is destruction, modern states devote their chief energies to wiping out the wealth and the life that have been accumulating through the centuries.

War is more than hell. It is a disease that breaks out among peoples at intervals, doing unmeasurable damage. The last war, for example, resulted in the destruction of some ten millions of lives on the battle-fronts; in the death of some 25 millions of civilians from exposure, famine and plague, and in the destruction of perhaps 275,000 millions of dollars worth of wealth, not to mention a demoralization of the economic life of Europe that is more acute five years after the war than it was in 1918.

Among all of the diseases that have fastened themselves on the body social, war is the most dramatically disastrous. Hence the conquest of war would give renewed hope to all of those who are striving for a better world.

How can war be conquered? Only by discovering and removing the causes that lead to war. A war to end war is as grotesque as a cholera epidemic to end cholera. War will be conquered when men have discovered and destroyed the germs that make war inevitable.

Social diseases—like diseases of the physical body, arise from certain causes. Those causes must be clearly understood before any successful remedy can be applied.

It is all well enough to call in a doctor after the patient has developed typhoid fever, but the really important thing is to be sure that no one else gets the disease from the same source. When a public health expert is detailed to fight an epidemic of typhoid, his first question is directed to the source of the difficulty. "Where does this thing come from?" he demands. Until he has found the answer, the community cannot feel safe from the spread of trouble.

The same truth holds for every problem that confronts society. "Where does this difficulty have its origin?" is the first question that statesmen must ask of poverty or ignorance or war.

Oil qualifies as a germ of war under any possible classification. The struggle for oil is typical of the conflicts that have been occurring during the past half century, with the essential resources as their objectives. Industries are organized within the political boundaries of a country, but there is no country that contains all of the resources necessary for its survival, and therefore the industries of each must reach outside of the country for the missing raw materials. In the case of great countries like Britain, France and Germany not only oil, but copper, rubber, cotton, hides, fats, wool and numerous other essentials must be imported.

Here, then, is the germ of modern wars. The great, driving, unceasing pressure for the control of economic resources is the largest single fact in the conflict between political groups, and unless this conflict can be eliminated or modified, men must continue in the future, as they have in the past to slaughter one another periodically in the interest of economic advantage.

How can this problem be met? Here is the germ of modern wars. Can it be destroyed? One or two conclusions suggest themselves:

1. The present economic system, based on the profit motive and organized in national units cannot even attempt the task.
2. There is only one sound method of approach to the problem, and that lies through a recognition of the following facts:
   a. The people of the world, irrespective of race or nationality, have two common objectives—to go on living and to live better.
   b. The resources upon which better living depends—fertile land, coal, water-power, oil—are not the product of human energy. On the contrary, they were formed irrespective of the human race.
   c. These resources are therefore the common property of those who inhabit the globe, and the people of the United States have no more claim to copper because it happens to be in Michigan than has the Girard Estate to anthracite coal because it happens to own the lands under which the coal lies.
3. The resources of the earth must therefore be used to enable the people of the earth to go on living and to improve the conditions of their lives.

There has been one oil war. Suppose there is a second and a third and a fourth. Suppose that in the course of these wars one great nation survives the struggle and secures a monopoly of all of the oil resources of the world. This nation will be in a position to levy a tax on every human being who uses oil in any of its forms. What then? Will the conqueror survive his conquest? History says: No! Will the payers of tribute gain in happiness? Again, the answer of experience is in the negative.

The people of the world need oil. How are they to get it on an equitable basis? How have they used the seas? The seas are not nationalized. They are open highways to be used by those who wish to carry on commercial activities. Oil is not national. Baku petroleum has not changed its character since the Russian Revolution, any more than the oil of Mexico is modified by being transferred from Standard Oil ownership to Mexican Government ownership.

The important resources—oil, coal, iron, copper, water-power—are a part of the mother earth upon which lives the human race. Humanity is dependent for its existence upon the use of these resources, and that without reference to race or nationality. Under these circumstances, it seems inevitable that some plan must be perfected under which the essential resources go to those who need them, and in proportion to the need.

The revenues of the United States Government are distributed among the various government departments and among the different sections of the country in proportion to the needs of the various departments or sections, just as the coal and iron-ore of the United States Steel Corporation are divided among its constituent companies in proportion to their needs. If there is a shortage in either case, the quotas are scaled down until the total available supply is distributed among the applicants for it.

Politically, therefore, the question resolves itself into a discussion as to how an authority can be set up, which will be wide-spread enough to have jurisdiction over the essential economic advantages and resources of the world, and which will, at the same time, be sufficiently representative so that all of the claimants for the use of any economic advantage or resource shall have a voice in deciding as to its disposition.

Many people believe that the League of Nations will provide the answer, but to those who have studied the origin and development of the modern nation, the League of Nations seems as inadequate to meet the need as is an Indian canoe to transport iron ore from Duluth to Buffalo, or a prairie schooner to haul farm machinery from Illinois to Dakota. The canoe and the prairie schooner both had their uses, and in their day they were wonderful assets in the struggle of the human race for control of the continent, but they have been superceded by the steamboat and the locomotive. So it is with the modern nation. It played its part while the life of men was isolated and local, but with the coming of world life, a league of nations is as ineffective as a fleet of canoes or a convoy of prairie schooners.

The economic organization of the world must be undertaken by those who are immediately concerned with the economic activity—the men and women whose energy makes the wheels and keeps them turning. The new world organization must be a producers' organization, built along the lines of modern productive activity.

With the transport workers, the construction workers, the miners, the agricultural workers, the manufacturing workers of the world organized, each in their respective occupational groups, the foundation would be laid for a world producers' federation that could handle the problems of resources and raw materials, of transport, of finance, and of other world economic problems in a unified and scientific manner.

The race depends today on the engineer,—on the individual who understands how to make nature's resources into things that men need. By sad chance, the world has fallen into the hands of profiteers, whose aim it is to maintain the largest possible margin between cost and selling price. The profiteer (owner) challenges the engineer (worker). The profiteers' goal is "grab and keep." The engineer's goal is "produce and distribute." It is the slogan of the engineer on which the foundations of the new world must be laid. It is the carrying out of this slogan on a world basis that will make war unnecessary and impossible.

Scott with his sister Mary in 1905.

The house Scott built in Arden, Delaware, was part of a single-tax community based on Henry George's principles. Scott stands while his first wife, Nellie Seeds, sits besides Professor Frank Watson of the University of Pennsylvania. Scott coauthored his first book, *Economics*, with Watson.

Scott became staff instructor at the Rand School for Social Science in 1917.

Scott in 1926.

Scott is ushered away from speaking in public when a Communist Party meeting was locked out of a hall in Boston in 1928. He was released after quoting the First Amendment to the U.S. Constitution.

Helen's first visit to the Soviet Union in 1931 was Scott's fourth.

Scott on one of his hundreds of lecture and debating platforms.

Scott in the early 1950s.

Scott in Colombo, Ceylon, in 1968.

A peace rally at the University of Maine in Orono in the sixties featured Scott as a speaker against U.S. participation in the Vietnam War.

Scott in the late sixties.

Scott and Helen with a visitor in their first home in Harborside, Maine, where they lived since 1951.

Lunchtime with young helpers at the Nearing home in Harborside, Maine.

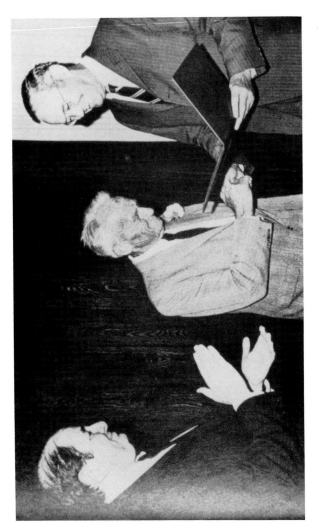

In 1973 Scott received his Honorary Emeritus Professor of Economics degree from the University of Pennsylvania, which had fired him 58 years earlier for work against child labor.

Scott showing young people around the farm (1979).

Scott and Helen in 1978. *Photo credit Lotte Jacobi.*

Scott and Helen in 1978 in their new stone house overlooking Penobscot Bay. Scott was in his nineties, Helen in her seventies.

Helen shucking garden peas at the stone house in 1984.

14 DEBATE: THE SOVIET POLITY AND WESTERN CIVILIZATION (1924)

Affirmative: Scott Nearing
Negative: Bertrand Russell

D URING THIS TIME, public lectures, panels, and debates were exciting popular forums of education and entertainment. One of the sponsors of such debates was The League for Public Discussion in New York City, which sponsored this meeting between Nearing and Russell. An aim of the league was to present the luminaries of the day, such as George Bernard Shaw, H.G. Wells, Havelock Ellis, Anatole France, Romain Rolland, Winston Churchill. Its program for this debate stated that it strove to arrange meetings and lectures "with participants such as Rev. Stickney Grant, Margaret Sanger, Rev. John Haynes Holmes, William Jennings Bryan, Heywood Broun, Scott Nearing, Bertrand Russell and others of similar calibre."

A curious juxtaposition occurred that year: Lenin, the founder of the U.S.S.R., died, and Calvin Coolidge was elected U.S. president. General debate across the nation about the Soviet experiment could still be held in public, although the intellectual atmosphere of "The Red Scare" was thickening. At the same time, Coolidge would be remembered as the president who said, "The business of America is business," a sentiment that to Nearing meant the continuation of worker hardship.

In this debate Nearing warns his audience of the approaching 10 years that will bring an extremely severe depressed state of the economy, rocking the nation to its core.

Is the Soviet form of Government applicable to Western civilization? By Western civilization I presume that we mean Western Europe, Canada, the United States and those other portions of the world which have during the last century or two directly adopted the economic and social forms of European civilization.

In maintaining the affirmative of this question, I desire to present at this time three points. First, what is it that makes a particular form of Government applicable? Second, what is the Soviet form of Government? Third, why do I believe that it will fit Western civilization? And if I succeed in answering or in explaining those three points adequately, I will have succeeded in building up an affirmative of this question— Will the Soviet form of Government prove applicable to Western Civilization?

First, then, what is it that makes a form of Government applicable to a particular situation? Forms of Government correspond with certain stages in social evolution. Europe furnishes an excellent example of this general proposition. For example, if you go back a thousand years in the history of Europe, practically the entire continent was under the domination of a form of Government which has since been described as the feudal system or the feudal state.

The feudal system was a system of landlordism under which one part of the population owned the land which was worked upon by another part of the population. The part of the population which owned the land—that is, the landlord element or landlord class—ran the political Government because it ran the economic system.

At that time throughout Europe this feudal form of Government was applicable to European civilization. It was based economically on agriculture. It was based socially on a class division, primarily into a class of land owners and a class of peasants. I therefore suggest that at this stage of the development of European Government the character of the occupation of the people, the agricultural character of industry, was the primary determinant of the form of Government.

In this form of government or in this form of society including this form of Government, there was the beginning of another form of Government. One by one there sprang up what were known as the free cities. These were centers first of commerce and later of handcraft industry.

Into these centers there came people from all parts of Europe and Asia, settled down, took up various branches of commercial and industrial life, and formed the second type of Government that Europe has produced in the last ten centuries—a form of Government built on commerce and on the beginnings of modern specialized industry.

And one by one these cities grew up, not alone in one part of Europe but all over Europe, from east to west and from north to south. The free city Government grew up where industry and commerce grew up. And in this second form of Government we have a second example of the general proposition that forms of Government correspond to stages in social evolution.

The free city, that is, the center of commerce and industry, expanded. Britain became a commercial and industrial country—Belgium, Holland, France, Germany, Northern Italy and so on following. And as this change occurred in the form of production, in the form of life, as agriculture was pushed more and more into the background and commerce and industry took its place, a third form of Government arose which we call the bourgeoise state.

In one case, in England, it took the form of a limited monarchy. In another case, in France, it took the form of a Republic. But essentially the basis of the state remained the same. It was organized in the interests of certain commercial and business classes. It performed their work and did their bidding. Hence, we have a third illustration of the general proposition that the forms of Government follow the lines of social evolution.

As I said at the outset, these forms have appeared in all parts of Europe—not at the same time, because feudalism lasted in some parts of Europe longer than it lasted in others. But when feudalism gave place to industry and commerce the feudal state merged into or evolved into the modern capitalist state.

I take these illustrations and make this detailed statement because I wish to found my whole argument on this major proposition: that the forms of Government correspond to the stages in social development. They do not correspond to ethnic qualities. They do not correspond to linguistic units.They do not correspond to any of the racial or religious differences that are ordinarily alleged as the lines of demarkation between nationalist groups. The forms of Government do correspond to certain forms of economic and social evolution. The stage at which Europe now is is this stage of the capitalist state. We ordinarily call it nation.

Why did the Soviet form of Government then appear in Russia? These things do not happen. They correspond with certain stages in social evolution.

Parenthetically, let me say here that forms of society sometimes die, break down, disintegrate, disappear. Feudalism disintegrated and disappeared thus in France toward the end of the eighteenth century. Forms of society break down and disappear. And various causes induce this breakdown. Sometimes they break down through internal decay. Sometimes they break down through the impact of external forces. The breakdown of the old Roman system was due to both forces, decay from within and attack from without.

Russia, a country which is still eighty-five per cent agricultural, retained the essential elements of feudalism into the twentieth century. And therefore into the present century there came the old feudal bureaucracy of Russia—a group of landlords running a country stretching over eight millions of square miles and a vast population of one hundred and thirty millions, most of them peasants, and all of them under the thumb of this little landlord bureaucracy.

Those of you who have read Russian literature, Gogol, for example, or any of the other satirists of Russian life, or those of you who are familiar with Russian history, know that the Russian bureaucracy was not efficient. It was centuries old and it had failed to develop with the evolution of the rest of Europe. It had held Russia back, keeping it agricultural, keeping it feudal, fending off the evolution that had gone on in Germany, in Belgium and England and in other capitalist countries.

But with the beginning of the present century there began in Russia the new business life. And the revolution of 1905 was essentially a movement of the Russian businessmen to shake themselves loose from the millstone of bureaucratic inefficiency that was hanging about their necks. They, too, wanted a chance to use the coal and the iron and the oil and the timber of Russia as the businessmen in other countries had done. And since the Czar and his ineffective ministers tied them up with red tape, they were anxious to get the Czar put in a position where he couldn't interfere with legitimate business enterprise.

So that Russia in the opening years of the twentieth century was partly feudal—the Czar was a feudatory monarch—and partly adolescent capitalist. The Russian business life had just begun to show its head, just begun to feel the rising tide of its power. Russia was thus between eras neither feudal nor capitalist.

And when the war struck Russia, it destroyed both feudalism and capitalism. The bolsheviks did not destroy the Russian ruling classes. The Russian ruling classes destroyed themselves between 1914 and 1917 through their inability to mobilize and to handle their military and internal life. The people of Russia starved. They lacked clothing. They lacked machinery. The railroads broke down. Fuel was scarce. The whole life of Russia from 1915 to 1917 was in chaos. And, finally, when early in 1917 the Russian armies began to quit and go home, it was because the Russian people were convinced that the whole business wasn't worth going on with. And they were convinced of that because they were hungry and cold and sick and war-weary.

That is what happened in Russia. The old order—partly feudal, partly capitalist—crumbled under the blows of the war. And when Kerensky came into power in March, 1917, he came into power in a bankrupt country with the transport and industry wrecked and the army everywhere in full retreat.

Russia in 1917 had lost more heavily than any other belligerent country because of its inefficiency, because of its incompetence. And the break-down of Russia was the break-down of an established social order under the crushing weight of two and a half years of war.

Therefore, when the old order broke down, since there were 130,000,000 people who had to go on living, they rustled around and found a new order. The Soviet form of Government is the first expression of that new social order. And it came in Russia because the old social order broke down first there. If the old social order had broken down first in Germany, the new social order would have come first in Germany. If it had broken down first in England, it would have come first in England. The old social order ceased to work in Russia, and the hundred and thirty millions of people there had to have something. And they adopted a new form, and that form we call the Soviet form of Government.

What is the Soviet form of Government? That is the second question I want to present. I have tried to explain why it is there. What is it? I suppose Mr. Russell and I will not differ on this point. We can hardly do so at this stage of the game. And so I imagine that I can define it very briefly, and I shall set out with that in view.

The Soviet form of Government is a temporary or transition form to bridge over the abyss between capitalism and socialism. The Soviet form of Government is not a socialist or communist Government. The Soviet form of Government is a transition Government. It is a bridge over an abyss, working toward communism and away from capitalism.

It is highly centralized, therefore. It is in the form of a dictatorship. This dictatorship is exercised by the delegates of peasants and workers—originally of soldiers, peasants and workers; now of peasants and workers—and is dominated by the communist party, which consists of about 600,000 men and women who have in view something which they describe as economic emancipation of the producing classes.

That means the elimination of all exploitation, that people shall own their own jobs and control their own product and decide what policy industry shall follow, just as we are entitled to decide what policy politics shall follow. I am not saying, understand, that they have this in

Russia. I am saying that this is the goal or objective of the communist party: To establish communism. No communist asserts that they have communism in Russia. All of the leading communists are on record as saying that they have not communism, particularly under the new economic policy.

Russia, the Russian form, the Soviet form is a dictatorship under the control of the industrial workers, primarily—not of the peasants, although the peasants participate—a dictatorship dominated by the communist party aiming at economic emancipation.

Three outstanding characteristics differentiate the Soviet form from our form of Government. First, local constituencies are economic and not geographical. The Soviet of Moscow is elected by street car workers, school teachers, steel workers, building trades workers—not by residents of the first, second, third and fourth assembly districts as in New York [laughter].

The basis of representation is economic or occupational and not geographic or regional as under our system. I believe that constitutes one of the great contributions of the Russian system, because life today is divided most sharply along occupational and not most sharply along geographic or regional lines.

The second outstanding characteristic of the Soviet Government is its proposition to organize economic life as we have organized political life. In the Middle Ages, political life was in the hands of little princelings and dukes and one kind of ruler and another. We have taken that chaotic localized political form and unified it under a federal, state, city, county, borough, village, system of administration.

Our political life in England and Germany and the United States and Canada and Australia is scientifically worked out, planned, blueprinted. The Russians propose to work out, plan and blue-print economic life. We still let little bankers, manufacturers and other private profiteers and enterprises carry on their private bucketeering activities in economic life. The Russians propose to eliminate profiteering in economics as we have eliminated profiteering in politics. That is their second great contribution—to scientifically organize the economic life of Russia.

Their third essential contribution is contained in the phrase which they quote in their constitution: "He that will not work, neither shall he eat." Under our system of society the biggest owner gets the biggest return, though he may make no contribution to society. But because he owns property, he has great income.

Under the Soviet form, their fundamental law, their constitution asserts that such a man can't even vote or hold office, but that the rights of the country are restricted, the political rights, to those who perform productive and useful service.

Those, in my judgment, are the three characteristics that differentiate the Soviet form from our form. First, economic occupational constituencies. Second, the scientific organization of economic life. Third, the necessity of every able bodied adult to render some service to the community.

This form is the product of seven years of war, civil war, famine, disease and hardship. The Russians have beaten this form out of the very flesh and marrow of their lives. They have put into it millions of lives and tens of millions of living units of suffering agony, while we have been going to the movies and living on the fat of the land. The Russians have hammered this thing out of their necessities.

When will it fit Western civilization? Not now. When did it fit Russia? It fitted Russia when the old order broke down. It will fit Western civilization when the old order breaks down. If peace and prosperity and progress are the outstanding characteristics of Western civilization, the Soviet form of Government will never fit Western civilization. If peace and prosperity and progress can be maintained in England and France and Belgium and the United States, the Soviet form of Government will never fit. If, on the other hand, international war and class war and hard times break down the fabric of Western society, then the Soviet form will be inevitable.

And my whole argument centers around this proposition: that the Soviet form of Government is a transition form of Government between capitalist society and socialist society, and that when capitalist society breaks down we will have the Soviet form of Government.

What are the chances that capitalist society will break down? I suggest that you read Mr. Bertrand Russell's latest book, *The Prospects of Industrial Civilization* [laughter and applause]. If you are still unconvinced, fellow countrymen of his, Sidney Webb and Beatrice Webb, these two have prepared a book called, *The Decay of Capitalist Civilization*. And if you are still unconvinced, Signor Nitti, Ex-Premier of Italy, has written a book, *The Decadence of Europe*.

Any one of the three books, I think, is sufficient to convince any intelligent man or woman of the inevitableness of the presence of decay in European society, and all three together I think will be intellectually convincing to any person who is still capable of developing new lines of thought. And if, perchance, you are not yet convinced, I suggest that you read the Dawes Report. It is only 14,000 words long and not bad reading. And in the Dawes Report there are the germs of enough future wars, international and class wars, to destroy any civilization that ever existed, let alone the civilization of Europe [applause]. We are getting ready for the next international war now. On every envelope that you get out of the Post Office, it says, "Let's go, Citizens Military Training Camps."

International war, class war, civil war and hard times are the three battering rams that are destroying your civilization. And although you happen to live in the richest country in the world and although you happen to live on the easy side of life and although things seem to be going well with you now—the Germans felt the same way in 1913. And that is only ten years away. And ten years hence a lot of you will be singing a different tune, if that is the tune that you follow at the present time.

So I say all over Western Europe when capitalism breaks down, as it must, there will be the dictatorship of a group of industrial workers under a highly organized and sternly disciplined party like the communist party in Russia, and they will build a society based on economic constituencies and they will organize under engineering scientific direction the economic life of the world, and we will have a new social order which we might call communism or socialism, but the transition stage to that new social order will be characterized by the essential characteristics of the Soviet form of Government [applause].

Mr. Russell started out with the promise of cheering you up. When he left you, he had you hunting mountain lions with bows and arrows [laughter].

Like a good philosopher, Mr. Russell divides life into categories. I never mentioned Karl Marx, but what I said he labeled Marxian and then he proceeded to hammer Karl Marx. Well, now, I have no objection to having what I said called Marxian. But I didn't say it because Marx said it. I said it because I believe it was true. When I asserted that the form of Government corresponds with the stage of social revolution, I proved it not by quoting Marx but by quoting history. And if Mr. Russell wants to disprove it, he must disprove it not by quoting Marx nor arguing with Marx but by arguing with my history.

Mr. Russell should distinguish between two very important elements in the bolshevik situation. When I described them I described them in two categories. I described the aspects of power under the communist party, the dictatorship, and I also described the economic forms which the Soviet Government was realizing, namely, economic constituencies, the scientific organization of economic life and the demand that everyone should be rewarded in proportion to his service, not in proportion to his property.

The parallel between Cromwell and Russia holds as to the dictatorship. So does the parallel between Russia and Italy hold as to the dictatorship. You can take the Fascist movement in Italy and parallel it step by step with the Cromwellian or the Russian dictatorship. But neither Cromwell nor Mussolini has proposed any form of economic reorganization [applause].

Now, says Mr. Russell, because Russia is still agricultural and the West is industrial, we can expect the forms to be different. I think so. The Russian leaders got their training in Germany and England and the United States and Switzerland and France, which are all industrial. And then they went back and tried to apply their theories of communism to an agricultural country, and they didn't fit exactly therefore the necessity of the new economic policy. When those same policies are applied to an industrial country they will not fit without the new economic policy [applause].

But that is not the difference between Mr. Russell and me. He says when you have a population able to read and write you cannot proceed in the bolshevik way, you must find another way. I will drag into the debate, with apologies, a quotation from an article which Mr. Russell wrote in the *New Republic* on the 17th of November, 1920: "While admitting the necessity and even utility of bolshevism in Russia, I do not wish to see it spread or even to encourage the adoption of its philosophy by advanced parties in the Western world." And in another article in the same periodical on the 3rd of November: "I am compelled to reject bolshevism for two reasons: First, because the price mankind must pay to achieve communism by bolshevik methods is too terrible and, second, because even after paying the price I am not sure that they will have what they went after."

Mr. Russell doesn't like bolshevism; neither do I. Mr. Russell doesn't like war; neither do I. Mr. Russell doesn't like dictatorship; neither do I. If Mr. Russell was going on a picnic on Decoration Day he wouldn't like a rain; neither would I—and yet it might rain [laughter and applause].

Now this is the question that I want to ask Mr. Russell: When the crisis does come, which you admit and which I believe will come, when the crisis does come and when the British capitalist system breaks down, for example, what will be the form of the transition society? I don't insist that Mr. Russell produce a form, but I ask that he suggest a form.

And I'd like in that connection to call your attention to a remark of Mr. Ramsay McDonald—Mr. McDonald, whose present job is to prove that there is another form, and who hasn't yet proved it. Mr. McDonald wrote a book in 1920 called *Parliament or Revolution*. And in that book he says: "So far as this country is concerned we have reached a stage when the socialist process, when the socialist program is a matter of political fighting. A parliamentary election will give us all the power that Lenin had to get by a revolution."

Now, note: "Of course," says Mr. McDonald in the same paragraph, "if it came to be that we had a bankrupt country, a demoralized and disorganized people, and anarchy from one end of a ruined country to another, a committee of public safety might well step into Whitehall and make up its mind to impose a new order upon an old chaos" [applause].

Now that is exactly what happened in Russia in 1917, and that is exactly what happened when Cromwell took the reins of power in England in the seventeenth century. In other words, when one social system breaks down and another one has to be rebuilt, there is a transition stage during which a committee of public safety steps in and takes control and imposes a new order upon an old chaos. And that is what happened in Russia, in the first instance, and that is what will happen in England after Mr. McDonald gets through with his present experiment [applause].

Now I am not arguing, as Mr. Russell seemed to imagine, that we can meet the aristocracy of the United States today, known as the Rotary Club and the Chamber of Commerce [laughter]. I realize quite well that the American plutocracy not only has its fingers on American economic life but that they have the political and the propaganda machinery of the country wholly within their grasp. My argument did not concern that stage in social evolution. I argued that the present system would break down and that when it did break down—that is, when the ruling class can no longer deliver the goods—then the change that I have suggested must come, not by act of Parliament but by the appointment of a committee of public safety.

Now that is the issue between Mr. Russell and me. It is up to Mr. Russell to show that when a breakdown does come there is another way out. I wish there was another way out. I wish that Mr. McDonald's way was the way. I wish that people were intelligent enough in America to make economic and social changes by act of Parliament. But I also wish that we wouldn't pass espionage acts and lynch negroes in America— and yet they do it [applause]. You can wish all you like, you have got to face the realities of life as we have them.

Now, says Mr. Russell, the alternative is bows and arrows and barbarism. It is—provided that there is nothing to replace this miserable economic fiasco called capitalism when it breaks down. And if Mr. Russell's counsel prevails when the capitalist system breaks down, you will get a stick and a knife and make yourself a bow and an arrow.

That isn't my idea of the way to handle that particular job. I believe that right now, before the capitalist system breaks down, when certain of us can see the breakdown coming, it is up to us, first, to say so and then to gather together as many other people as can see it and then to get together and work out a practical working program to meet the breakdown and to put something else in the place of the old chaos, namely, a new order.

Mr. Russell has no objection to find with the communist philosophy. He has no objection to find with the socialist state. He only says it can't be done. Well, my answer to that is this: That nothing has ever been done till it was tried [applause]. And everything that has ever been done has been tried many times before it was done right. And if the Russians haven't found the right way, it is up to Mr. Russell and me to help Americans find the right way [applause]. All of this talk about bows and arrows and barbarism is merely a waste of valuable time. What we want is a practical statesmanlike way out of that tremendous difficulty.

Let me sum the thing up in this fashion: We agree substantially as to the form of the Soviet Government. Will it fit the Western world? Well, first, will capitalist society break down in the Western world under the earthquake shocks of war and class strife and economic hard times? Mr. Russell thinks so, and so do I. That is our first point together. We believe that the capitalist system will fail. We believe it is failing now.

Second, what will take place of the capitalist state, of the capitalist order. We both believe that it should be—and I believe that it will be—a socialist or producers state. And we go along somewhat together on that point.

Third, when the breakdown comes, will a highly centralized committee of action be necessary? I believe it will. Must it be under the direction of producers rather than of property owners? I believe it must. Must it be dominated by a highly organized and sternly disciplined party? I believe it must. Must it aim at economic emancipation? I think it must. And I think that it will have to do that by socializing the social machinery of production, resources, utilities, industries, merchandising and the like, by socializing and organizing industry, by establishing self-governing units organized on a basis of occupational representation, and that the first law must be: "He that will not help produce, neither shall he share in the products of industry" [applause].

Those are the transition steps, those are the economic forms which Soviet Russia is now trying to take. And I believe that those are the transition steps and those the economic forms which England and Germany and France and the United States will be compelled to take when the time comes.

In other words, all of these questions that I have just presented to you I answer in the affirmative. Mr. Russell answers some of them in the negative. Now I revert to my question. When the crisis does come—not whether we can fit the aristocracy now, not what Karl Marx said, not human frailty and incapacity—when the crisis does come to the hundred and ten millions in America and to the forty-five millions in Britain and the sixty-five millions in Germany and the thirty-five millions in France, when the crisis does come what will be the form of the transition society, if it isn't the Soviet form? [applause]

15   GLIMPSES OF THE SOVIET REPUBLIC (1926)

NEARING'S LOVE OF TEACHING AND EDUCATION led to a study of the school system in the Soviet Union. He spent two months there in 1925 and published a 159-page book on education in the U.S.S.R., a book that he believed to be the first such extensive study in English.

At the same time, he wrote this 32-page monograph as a personal report of his visit to Russia. It is one of the few writings in which he uses the first person. While most other writers concentrated at the time on political and diplomatic abstractions, Nearing focused on the workers and what the revolution was attempting to do for them.

The Soviet Republic covers about eight million square miles,—more than twice the area of continental United States. Within this vast domain there are 140 millions of people, speaking many dialects and languages, and engaged in every form of occupation from hunting and fishing, to railroading, mining and factory production. These people are recovering from international and civil war, from disease and famine. They are trying to work out new ways of carrying on their economic and social life. Every day changes are made in some part of the Republic, and the changes in one place differ from the changes elsewhere.

During two months I traveled in this immense country, among these tens of millions, making observations and inquiries along a thin line stretching from Northern and Central European Russia through the Ukraine and across the Caucasus. I did not get so much as a glimpse of Siberia. The country, the customs and the language all were foreign to me, and although I was patiently listened to and hospitably treated everywhere, it does not require a great deal of imagination to realize that in the course of these sixty days I saw very few Russians and very little of the Soviet Republic.

During my stay in the Soviet Union I tried to distinguish between: (1) What I saw. (2) What I heard. (3) What I thought. Here I desire to tell only some of the things that I saw,—to give a partial photograph of life in the Soviet Union as it looks to an interested and sympathetic outsider.

Many careful studies must be made and many volumes must be written before even a fraction of what is going on in the Soviet Union can be adequately told. This is a brief pen-picture; it is neither inclusive nor exhaustive. Perhaps it is not even typical. Like any other visitor in a big, complex, changing country, I describe, not the Soviet Union, but only a part of what I saw there.

Here I have merely tried to picture the Soviet Union as a going concern, without indicating where it is going. I have done this deliberately, because any understanding of the situation in the Soviet Republic must begin with a realization that the social order existing there is just as concrete as the social order existing in Illinois. The working class is the ruling class in the Soviet Union in the same sense that the capitalist class is the ruling class in Illinois. But in the Soviet Union, as in Illinois, there is an established functioning social order.

American newspapers have succeeded in making many of their readers believe that the Soviet Union is a welter of chaos. I traveled through the Union, by day and night, for two months. I talked with all kinds of people and visited many different institutions. Here is a record of some of the things that I saw. My hope is that Americans who read these pages will realize that most of the press stories about the Soviet Republic are, to say the least, ill-informed and inaccurate.

Responsible American statesmen have persistently refused even to consider recognition of the Soviet Union, on the ground that "there is nothing to recognize." If these men would spend three weeks in the industrial centres of the Republic, visiting the social and economic institutions that I saw during my stay, they could hardly fail to realize the absurdity of their position. Many foreigners have had such an experience in the Soviet Union. I do not for a moment suggest that recognition would follow such a visit. I merely wish to point out that the Soviet Union has an established, stable government and an established, stable economic system. Intelligent Americans should know these facts even though the State Department is unable to recognize the Soviet Republic.

My way into the Soviet Republic lay through Poland. During three days I traveled in this Treaty State, with its population of 28 millions and its army of 600,000. Poland is a child of British diplomacy and French capitalism. It has not had a Soviet government. It is as imperialistic as the most ardent empire in Europe. I never expect to see a more striking contrast than that between the Polish side and the Soviet side of the Polish border.

Poland, as I saw it, symbolized human wretchedness. It was late in the fall when I went through the country. Potato harvesting was at its height. Women were doing most of the digging. Some used a short mattock. Most, however, dug with short, straight-handled shovels. Every woman that I saw working in the potato fields of Eastern Poland was barefoot. Eight or nine hours of the work-day they bent over this exacting toil for a beggarly wage. Peasant women walked barefoot through the mud of Warsaw's streets. Peasant men, in rags and barefoot, followed their carts to the Warsaw markets. Early in the morning barefoot, ragged children shivered beside the cattle and goats that they were tending.

Only the soldiers and the business and professional men were warmly dressed. The officers were everywhere, with their gaudy plumes, their gay uniforms, their epaulettes, spurs, swords and automatics. Privates had good clothes and good boots, swords, guns and automatics.

The countryside was miserably cultivated. The roads were bad. Scores of families were living in dug-outs built of rail-road ties, windowless, half covered with earth.

As we approached the frontier the signs of military activity grew more numerous. Armed Polish sentries were posted at short intervals along the railroad; barbed wire entanglements stretched back from the track on both sides as far as the eye could see; great piles of barbed wire lay ready for use along the right of way.

On the train that took us across the border there were seven passengers. At least a dozen armed Polish soldiers watched over us as though we had been a band of criminals. At the line of the frontier the train stopped and these Polish soldiers, at a word of command, jumped from our train and boarded another that was carrying Chicherin and his aides on their trip into Poland and Germany. Then we crossed into the Soviet Republic.

On the Soviet side of the frontier there was an outpost with half a dozen men in uniform standing about. There was not an arm in sight, nor any suggestion of military preparation. Two soldiers of the Red Army boarded our train. Both were peasant lads, and so far as one could see, neither carried weapons.

"How is it," I asked one of them, "that you carry no weapons? The Polish soldiers who came with us to the border all had swords and guns." He laughed good-humoredly. "We do not want to cut throats," said he. "We want to join hands with the workers of the whole world." Then he pointed out of the window to some peasants who were ploughing. "That is our country—my country—horses, ploughs and wheatfields. That is the new Russia. All have land and all work."

I pondered. Was this the propaganda about which I had heard so much, or was it the real feeling of a peasant-boy for the countryside? During the next few weeks I talked with scores of soldiers and officers. Almost without exception they said the same thing. They were organized into an army because they believed that was the only way to protect the world revolution. It was production that interested most of them, however, and not military operations.

Our train was pulling away from the border through pine and spruce timber, with only a little cleared land here and there. Suddenly we emerged from the woodland and came abreast of a saw-mill and lumber-yard.

There is probably no single economic unit that can be as disorderly as a saw-mill and lumber-yard. In the course of a day a big saw turns out hundreds of pieces of different shapes and sizes. Unless they are well handled they soon accumulate into an impossible tangle. Ever after they are sorted, the pieces of lumber are quite frequently piled irregularly, and as a consequence they dry crooked. I had seen a number of such third-rate lumber-yards in Poland. This was the first one I had observed in the Soviet Republic. It was immaculate. The lumber was all sorted, was well arranged, and piled with the greatest exactitude. The fire-wood was all cut to length and well stacked. I grew up in the lumber woods of Northern Pennsylvania. I have seen many saw-mills with their lumber and wood-piles. In all of my experience I have never seen a more professional job than the arrangement of this lumber-yard just across the Soviet border from the Polish town of Stolpce.

A few minutes later we reached a freight yard and a little collection of houses on Soviet territory. Here our baggage was examined, and we waited for the Minsk train. Three things impressed me at this little junction point: (1) The workers that I saw all had on good shoes or leather boots (usually boots) and excellent over-coats. Many of these coats were also of leather, well lined and water-proofed. (2) Food was abundant; it was cheaper than it had been across the border in Poland, and all of the working men and women that I saw seemed to be well-fed and vigorous. (3) The freight house was well organized; the freight-cars were newly painted; the yards were in excellent order; the engines all seemed to be in good repair; the shifting engines were handling their work efficiently. While we were waiting for our train a freight pulled in with a number of car loads of Czecho-Slovakian-made agricultural machinery. The work here was apparently as efficient as it would be at any small junction point on an American railroad.

I went over to the freight agent—a man of perhaps 22, alert, pleasant, obliging. Several railroad men were gathered around him, talking. "Tell me," I asked, "are working people better off here than they were before the Revolution?" All looked at me in surprise. Then they burst out laughing. They thought it was a joke. The freight agent sobered up and answered for the rest: "Look for yourself," said he. "Look at our clothes. They are warm and water-proof. Go over to that restaurant where we eat and try the food. It is cheap and good. We work an eight-hour day. Our wages give us a good living. You see this freight yard? That, too, is ours, and we treat it accordingly. We are organized. We have our clubs, our reading-rooms and our meeting halls. You know what Russia was before the Revolution. Does that answer your question?"

That was my first glimpse of the economic life of the Soviet Republic,—workers well-fed, well-clothed, and working an eight-hour day; a local lumber-yard in excellent condition; a well-kept freight yard; rolling-stock in good repair. And all of this was on a hostile border, far removed from the important centres of economic and political activity.

Do not get a false impression. The Soviet Union is terribly poor. Its economic life is badly organized. It has barely begun the struggle to put its house in order. Years must elapse before the unification of its economic machinery approaches a point where it can produce a supply of goods adequate to meet the needs of its people. But now, less than three years after the end of the Civil War and the famine, in comparison with Poland it is a Happy Hunting Ground.

The tedious round of passport permits and visas is completed. The train leaves Moscow at eleven-thirty. Another day and I shall be in Riga—back in the West.

The train crosses the great open stretches of snow-covered plain, traverses the forest and reaches the frontier. There, baggage is carefully examined and we enter Latvia. Russian newspapers and books are taken away from us. As people return to civilization they are compelled to leave behind all traces of Bolshevism.

Latvia, Lithuania, East Prussia and Poland have all been crossed. In the course of about 800 miles we have run the gauntlet of twelve passport examinations. That is the Sanitary Cordon, built around Russia by the Treaty of Versailles to keep Bolshevism out of Western Europe. It is harder to penetrate than the police lines at a big fire.

Now we are in Berlin—the centre of German political life. But the labor-leader-politicians with whom one talks evidently have not read economics since 1913. There are music and art and drama on all sides, but it is the music and art of the eighteenth and nineteenth centuries, mixed with a few American and English plays and some jazz. Shop windows are filled with gay clothes and trinkets. The chief business of Berlin shop-keepers is to sell unnecessary things to folks who are not anxious to buy. The city is over-run with profiteers. Rich limousines hurry along the streets and well-dressed, comfortable people enter and leave the theatres and the fine restaurants.

But in the working-class quarters thousands of families are trying to live on twenty, twenty-five and thirty marks a week (30 marks are $7.50) and the unemployment increases daily. Meanwhile the German Parliament votes to endorse the Locarno Pact and thus ties the mass of the workers to the wheels of imperialism.

I spent a week in Berlin talking with people and not understanding their reactions. I felt queer and out of place. Then one day a German asked me how it seemed to get back from Russia, and I answered that it was like going from a bright spring day into a cellar. He was offended, and I was sorry. But I shall not repeat the offense. Little by little I am shaking off the atmosphere of the Workers' Republic. Soon I shall again behave like a civilized being.

16 WHITHER CHINA? (1927)

A FTER MUCH DELIBERATION by both Nearing and the Communist Party (it was ambivalent about his membership), he joined the party in 1927. Independently of this, he was asked by a former student, now a government worker in the Chinese Republic, to be economic advisor to the Chinese Railway Administration, requiring a tour of several years in China. He left by ship but en route extensive violence broke out in China. The People's Party had split and Mao Tse-tung and his followers were forced to the Northeast to establish their peasant stronghold (and would not govern all China until 1949).

When Nearing arrived in Shanghai, a bloodbath was occurring in the country as Chiang Kai-shek's forces, the other major split in the People's Party, were attacking leftists. Later in Peking, Nearing spoke in an auditorium to rebellious students—completely in the silent eerie dark so that no one, not even the speaker, could identify another.

Nearing remained three months in China; his position with the administration was out of the question. In Russia Stalin had convened Friends of the Soviet Union as a sign of international solidarity, and Nearing was asked by the U.S. Communist Party to represent the United States. He traveled the Trans-Siberian Express to Moscow to attend the conference before returning home.

Since the imperialists were superior and the Chinese were inferior, it followed that the Chinese were excluded from participation in social activity on an equal basis with the imperialists. The imperialists were compelled to emphasize this line of cleavage in order to protect their privileges. The Chinese were forced to recognize it, and crossed it at their peril.

The cleavage between the two groups was reflected in the unequal treaties; in the special economic privileges enjoyed by the foreigners; in the open and frequent violation of Chinese sovereignty; in the policing of China by imperial soldiers and warships. It appeared no less openly and far more intimately in the ordinary social relationships.

Chinese are excluded by the foreigners from public places in China, simply because they are Chinese. Colonel Malone, as lately as May, 1926, took a picture of the notice-board at the entrance to the Shanghai Municipal Gardens, excluding bicycles, dogs and Chinese. The most offensive phrases have since been modified, but in effect bicycles, dogs and Chinese are still excluded. In September, 1927, an elevator in a big office building at 4 Avenue Edward VII, Shanghai, carried a notice which read: "Chinese clerks employed in the building will kindly avail themselves of western entrance and lifts. No coolies or messengers, except Post Office Messengers, are permitted to use this lift." Instances of a similar sort might be multiplied. The Chinese, in their own country, are pushed into the background by foreigners.

The facts of this discrimination are less emphasized than its manner. The foreigners in China treat the Chinese workers with whom they come into contact in the most peremptory fashion. "Here, boy," to the servant, "get my hat." "That is enough," to the ricksha coolie, "now get out!" "No," said a Chinese servant, "I prefer to work in a mission-ary family, even though the wages are smaller. In the missionary family I am never kicked like a dog." Colonel Malone wrote: "During the recent troubles in Hankow, a British 'China-hand,' who had lived for many years in China, informed us, through the medium of the British press that the Hankow coolies . . . are humanly little more than domes-ticated animals." A few thousand foreigners in China, living on the fat of the land, are exploiting the Chinese masses and deliberately forcing them into a position of inferiority in order that they may the more readily accept the vassal status which they now occupy. The imperial-ists in China treat the Chinese workers as imperialists always must treat exploited masses.

Imperialists in China are exploiting more than the workers, however. They are exploiting the whole Chinese people. They must therefore extend their discrimination to all classes of the Chinese population. In the foreign settlements of the principal Chinese cities, Chinese are excluded from the hotels and clubs with the same ruthlessness that servants and coolies are cursed and cuffed.

Take Shanghai, the principal port of China, as an illustration. Chinese and foreigners have been doing business together and meeting each other daily for generations, yet the social lines between the imperialists and the natives are sharply drawn. "Shanghai is a club city. Every nationality, practically, has its club and some have two. The leading business men's club is the Shanghai Club, with its famous longest bar in the world. This was organized by Englishmen years ago and probably has a membership of 1,500, all foreigners. . . . The citizens of the U.S.A., about ten years ago, started their American Club, which now has approximately a thousand members, occupies its million dollar building, and excludes Chinese. Both Americans and British have their 'country' or recreation clubs, which bar the Chinese from membership. The French have recently opened a palatial club, but here again no Chinese are ever proposed for membership. The Japanese likewise have a business men's club, which excludes Chinese from membership, but which permits Japanese members to entertain Chinese friends as 'visitors.'"

Harry F. Ward, who was in China at the time of the Shanghai Massacre, in May, 1925, was greatly impressed by this attitude of foreign arrogance. The only use certain foreigners have for the Chinese is "to make money out of them, and while they are doing it they curse them with contempt, and cuff and kick them when they dare. One of their spokesmen offers the opinion that there are slave races in the world and that the Chinese are one of them, and unfortunately this attitude is too liberally represented in the English-speaking press out here. The day after the shooting in Shanghai the Chinese press was restrained in its editorial comment. Then came some editorials in the English press taking the position that the superior race could do no wrong, laying all the blame on the Chinese with strong language."

While (imperialist) superiority in China has a root that is obviously economic, missionaries, teachers, doctors and business men who come from the imperial countries live on a scale of economic superiority. They have big houses. They employ many servants. Their food rations far exceed those of the average Chinaman. They are much better clothed. They import foreign delicacies for their tables and foreign luxuries for their houses.

In the case of the business man this high scale of living should occasion no surprise. Does he not enjoy an equal standard of conspicuous consumption in his native land? But, strange though it may appear, the average missionary and teacher in China also takes it for granted that he should enjoy a scale of living far above that of the Chinese with whom he works. Men and women who, in the United States, would never dream of having a servant, in China have maids and valets in addition to a kitchen staff.

When this question is raised, the missionary answers: (a) That the Chinese people come and beg for work, and that the eight or ten dollars a month which they receive will keep a whole Chinese family, although it is only a trifle to a foreigner. (b) That the Chinese do not respect a foreigner who does his own work. (c) That no white man could live on the pitifully low standard of the Chinese workers. Grant the truth of all these contentions, and it nevertheless remains true that the foreigner who goes to help the Chinaman begins by helping himself to a standard of comfort that only the very rich in China can afford.

Thus, to the concessions, settlements, compounds, and other forms of economic advantage which the imperialists enjoy in China, there must be added this unfailing indication of his superior position: he is able to live on a standard that is manifestly above that of the ordinary native. This is as true of schools and missions as it is of business houses. It extends throughout the whole field of imperial occupation. In many cases the same force—the army and navy—that is called in to protect the imperial merchant and banker is also called in to protect the missionary and the school teacher from the same imperial country. The life of the foreigners in China is lived apart from the life of the Chinese— how, otherwise, could one group continue to exploit the other?

Race superiority enters into the most commonplace as well as the most weighty of affairs. The good things of life are for the foreigners, who have the Chinese at their mercy, with social standards, with dollars, if need be, with guns.

China is saddled and bridled. The imperialists and their fellow-countrymen are booted and spurred and riding madly. Tolstoi wrote that the rich are willing to do anything for the poor except get off their backs. He might have added that the moment the rich get off the backs of the poor, they cease to be rich, and must struggle for their living side by side with the rest. The same is true of imperialist exploiters: imperialism consists in riding subject peoples. If the imperialists got down, they would no longer be imperialists but just ordinary humans like those they are now exploiting.

War demand had spurred native business. The process of industrialization had been pushed forward with unprecedented speed, and a generation of Chinese business men had been called into existence whose interests lay, very clearly, in an economically independent China.

The same industrializing process had established a wage-earning population of from two to four millions, subject to the pressure of rapidly rising prices, and working under extreme conditions of exploitation.

Thus the forces were gathering out of which arose the second cycle of the Chinese Revolution. Briefly, these forces may be outlined in the following way:

1. Imperial aggression from 1912 to 1919, centering in the Twenty-one Demands made by Japan and in the Peace Conference decision that Japan should hold Shantung.

2. Beginnings of mass agitation and revolt.
   a. The student revolt of 1919, actively supported by important elements of the Chinese merchant class. The boycott of Japanese goods.
   b. The labor revolt, beginning with the Hongkong Seamen's Strike of 1922.
   c. Reorganization of the Kuomintang (1924) on the basis of mass support.
3. The new imperial offensive. The Shanghai massacre. The bombardment of Wanhsien. The mobilization of an army and navy in China.
4. Extension of the mass movement.
   a. The seventeen months' boycott of British goods, centering in Canton.
   b. The epidemic of strikes throughout China, 1925–26.
   c. Organization of the Communist Party of China. Soviet advisers. Principle of the class struggle.
   d. The peasant movement in Kwangtung and Hunan, 1926–27.
   e. The Northern Expedition, 1926–27.
5. The counter-revolution, beginning in April, 1927, organized by Chinese business elements, to check the rising mass movement of 1926–27.

It is impossible, at this time, to present an adequate picture of the period of the Chinese Revolution from 1919 to 1927. The materials are not yet available. An examination of the data that is at hand, however, cannot fail to convince the observer of Chinese events that the years 1926–27 witnessed the beginnings of a mass movement in China that has not been paralleled anywhere in the world since the Russian Revolution of 1917.

If China can shake off the grip of Western imperialism, avoid the worst abuses of private capitalism, and establish the foundations of a new social order, freed from economic competition and war, this whole Asiatic area may be able to follow suit. Since the Asiatic area includes two-thirds of the world's population, such a development would carry in its train unprecedented advantages for the human race. No culture movement in history has ever included so vast a portion of mankind. No culture movement has ever struck so suddenly or so deeply into the traditional life of the world's masses. Literally, therefore, in vastness, at least, this Asiatic revolution is without historic parallel.

The Chinese movement, looked at in this light, becomes one of the most significant in history. The Chinese movement is not only a movement away from imperialism—it is a movement toward a new social order in a portion of the world hitherto largely untouched by modern economic and social developments.

Imperialism has been checked in Asia—checked by the Asiatic revolt, centering for the time being in China. Is it possible to estimate the extent of this revolt or the rôle which China has played in stimulating it? During the last three or four years the subject has attracted much attention among students of Asiatic affairs who have tried to answer these questions from a background of first-hand observations, but without any general analysis of economic forces.

Asia, for convenience in this discussion, may be divided into:

1. Former Chinese territory that has been lopped off by the great empires during the past few decades. In this category would fall Korea, Formosa, Annam, Siam, Burma, Thibet. Broadly speaking, this territory is or has been a part of the Chinese Empire. It is all geographically contiguous.
2. Imperial possessions in Asia outside of China, such as the East Indies, the Philippines. These territories have never been under Chinese control but all are near China.
3. Independent Asiatic States that have never been subject to China, Turkey, Persia, Afghanistan. These states have been oppressed by imperialism, but never by China.
4. Finally, there is the great Eastern empire, Japan; industrialized; pressed by an excessive population; reaching for raw materials and markets on the Continent of Asia, and troubled at home by her own radical and labor movements.

Korea is a good example of territory, formerly belonging to China, that has recently been seized by imperialists. Korea had long been looked upon as a tributary to China, but following certain attacks on foreigners by Koreans in 1866, Japan ignored China and made a treaty directly with Korea. This treaty served as a stop-gap until the Sino-Japanese War of 1894–95. At the close of this war Japan stipulated, as one of the terms of the treaty, the "independence" of Korea. Within a decade the peninsula was under the complete control of Japan.

Japan and Tsarist Russia had been competing for control in both Manchuria and Korea. The defeat of Russia by Japan in 1905 gave the latter a free hand in Korea, which was seized by Japan with the full knowledge of the great powers, including the United States. The Treaty of Protectorate was dated November 17, 1905.

During the next five years Japanese imperialists exploited Korea intensively. By a second forcible treaty (1907) Japan acquired military, judicial and administrative rights in Korea and disbanded the remnants of the Korean army. The Oriental Development Company was organized in Japan to take over Korean land and other enterprises. Japanese goods were dumped into the Korean market at ruinously low prices. Korean workers, hired on Japanese enterprises, were roughly handled. The press was muzzled. Coercion was widespread; wholesale arrests were made.

Korea, with its 20,000,000 of people, was officially annexed to Japan August 29, 1910. From that date until the end of the World War, Korea was in turmoil. F. A. McKenzie gives a first hand account of those terrible years in *Korea's Fight for Freedom* (New York, 1920). The result of the reign of Japanese frightfulness was a mass movement that culminated in the Declaration of Korean Independence of March 1, 1919. On that day in Seoul, 100,000 people met in Pagoda Park and solemnly declared Korea an independent nation.

Economic power has already shifted its center from Europe to the U.S.A. As industrialism grows in Asia, three great units emerge, to dominate the world life of the years that lie immediately ahead: the United States, China, Russia. All front on the Pacific, with the United States the spokesman for the Americas, and China the ultimate spokesman for a United Asia.

No sooner will the United States have settled her account with John Bull, by crushing the British Empire, as it must inevitably do in the next general war, than it will find itself facing a new and more dangerous rivalry—a rivalry of races and cultures as well as of economic interests. A Eurasian bloc, inspired by the Soviet Union, headed by an organized, armed China and with Japan as a subordinate, but powerful member, two-thirds of the world's population and a vast portion of its wealth, committed to principles of economic coöperation, but willing and eager to defend itself against the arrogance and predatory ruthlessness of the last two of the Great Empires.

This is the inescapable conclusion from the stated premise. Europe has already been reduced to vassalage. Her annual tribute to the United States is in the neighborhood of three-quarters of a billion dollars. The War of 1914 shattered her economic structure irrecoverably. Half her territory and a third of her population left capitalism behind in 1917 and went Soviet. The next war for which she is so busily preparing will still further reduce the relative economic power of Western European imperialism, while central and southern Europe will probably join the Union of Socialist Soviet Republics at an early stage in the struggle. As capitalist Europe dies, Soviet Europe will be born, and it is now probable that the movement will spread from the East, among the peoples who are in contact with the Soviet Union toward the West of Europe.

The Soviet Union will continue to be the spiritual father of the new social order. But the Chinese will be its business manager.

17 BLACK AMERICA (1929)

F OR THE PRESIDENTIAL ELECTION of 1928, Nearing campaigned for the Communist Party on the Pacific Coast
and through the Deep South. He was shocked by the race
separation in the South—the poverty, despair, and human
waste. He called it the Slave Belt and took hundreds of photographs of the living conditions of black workers and the
widespread signs of economic depression and segregation.

Then he wrote *Black America* about the status of black
men and women in the United States, basing the book on an
economic rather than political basis. He included 159 of his
photographs.

Northern textile mills had moved into the South for the
low wages and long work hours, sometimes 72 hours a
week. Ferment was growing. Across the nation, the standard of living was declining, especially among farm families. A study revealed that 60 percent of the general population was living below the poverty level of $2,000.

On Tuesday, October 29, the New York Stock Exchange
on Wall Street plunged into a sellers' panic. Stock price
losses for the next two years totaled an estimated $50 bil-
lion. Life for millions of Americans turned into complete
misery, and families were destroyed. The signs and fore-
casts of economic ruin that Nearing had been writing and
speaking about for years became desperate realities.

Among modern empires none is more devoted to abstract principles
of freedom and self-determination than the United States. "All men are
born equal," declared the founders of the Republic on July 4, 1776;
"Government of the people, by the people, for the people," promised

Abraham Lincoln; American school children sing: "My country 'tis of thee, sweet land of liberty!" If declarations and professions could give liberty and self-determination, the United States would be a free country.

But the policy of empires is not made by moral precepts. Economic necessity is the compass by which the owners of land and productive tools steer the imperial ship of state.

Among the great modern empires only one contains a subject race within the homeland. The British Empire has subject races in Egypt and India; the Dutch Empire has a subject race in Java; the French, Belgian and Italian Empires have subject races in Africa; the Japanese Empire has a subject race in Korea. The American Empire, in addition to its subject races in the Philippines and in the Caribbean, has within its own national boundaries a subject race of more than twelve million American Negroes.

The matter is little discussed from this point of view, even in the United States. Almost nothing is known about it abroad. Yet the Negroes, who make up a tenth of the total population of the United States, have been, for more than three hundred years, the slaves, peons, vassals, servants, tenants and wage-workers of white American landlords and capitalists. Today they are the largest single American reserve of mass labor power.

Throughout the English colonies in America, particularly in the South, there was a severe labor shortage. Land was free. The passage from Europe was long and hazardous. Men who had sufficient energy and initiative to cross the ocean were not willing to remain as wage workers when they could have farms or businesses of their own.

Tobacco, rice and cotton plantations were expanding in the South. Ship-building and lumbering were developing in the North. Both in the South and in the North there was more work than there were workers.

The American Indians could not be enslaved. They died before they would obey a task-master. They refused to work for wages. The colonists therefore turned to compulsory labor as a means of recruiting workers.

Non-free laborers who came to the American colonies were chiefly of three classes: criminals, indentured servants, and slaves.

The supply of criminals and of indentured servants was never adequate. Then, too, there was strong objection to the transportation of criminals, for many of them were rough, dangerous men. At a very early date the American colonists turned to another source of labor supply: the African Slave Coast.

The first black slaves were brought into the American colonies in 1619. From that year until 1863 the African Slave Coast was the source of a regular supply of black labor that went into all of the American colonies and later into the southern plantation states where the large-scale growing of cotton, sugar, tobacco and rice made slavery profitable.

The Slave Coast was discovered by Portuguese navigators when they ventured down the western shores of Africa in search of a sea route to India and China. The profitable trade in slaves, gold and ivory which they developed led the traders of other European nations to begin a competition which eventually brought French, Dutch, German, Danish and English commercial interests into sharp conflict with the Portuguese.

Along the Slave Coast, which extended from Cape Verde, on the north, to Cape St. Martha on the south, lived various types of Negroes. Some of them were fierce and warlike. Others were docile. The latter were eagerly sought as slaves.

The natives of the Slave Coast had made notable cultural advances. They smelted metals, shaped pottery, wove, manufactured swords and spears of metal, built houses of stone, and produced artistic ornaments. They had developed a considerable and well organized trade with the interior. This native African culture of the seventeenth, eighteenth and early nineteenth centuries was confronted by the insatiable American demand for black slaves.

The slave trade began incidentally enough. The white traders were looking for spices, jewels, rare woods, gold, silver. They were not man-stealers. But as Negro servants became fashionable among the great folk of Europe, the slave trade grew profitable.

Ships sailing from the Slave Coast with a cargo for home ports made a practice of picking up such slaves as they could easily secure. By 1450 the number reaching Portugal each year was between 600 and 700. For this limited number of African Negroes the slave traders found a ready market.

When the whites first went to the Slave Coast there was little slavery among the African natives. Some captives taken in war; an occasional debtor, unable to meet his obligations; violators of religious rites, were held as slaves by the chief or head man of the tribe. At times such slaves were sold, but the slave trade was never established as a business until the white man organized it.

White men organized and subsidized the business of slave catching among the African natives. They provided the guns, the ammunition, the rum. They frequently formulated the plans and instigated the raids. The raids were made by Negroes—the stronger and fiercer among the African tribes.

How many Negroes were carried away from Africa between 1450 and 1863? Estimates vary. There is a general agreement, however, that during the years of greatest slave-trading prosperity at the close of the eighteenth and the beginning of the nineteenth century, the number of slaves leaving the Slave Coast must have been at least 100,000 a year.

Add to these numbers actually shipped from the Slave Coast, the Negroes who were killed in the raids, those who died in the Slave Coast camps, where mortality was very high, and the total gives some idea of the millions of blacks who were torn from their native villages in the course of three centuries to supply the American slave trade.

In 1790 slaves were held in all states except Maine, Vermont, and Massachusetts. There were 3,707 slaves in Pennsylvania; 11,423 in New Jersey; 21,193 in New York. They were concentrated, of course, in the South: North Carolina, 100,783; Maryland and District of Columbia, 103,036; South Carolina, 107,094; Virginia, 292,627. Thus more than a third of the 697,624 slaves in the United States in 1790 were in one tobacco-growing State: Virginia. Georgia at this time had only 29,264 slaves.

The cotton gin (invented in 1792) made slavery profitable over a much larger area. By 1860 slavery had been virtually eliminated in the North and West. Of the 3,953,760 Negro slaves in the United States in that year, there were:

111,115	Slaves in	Arkansas
114,931	"	" Missouri
225,483	"	" Tennessee
275,179	"	" Kentucky
331,059	"	" North Carolina
331,726	"	" Louisiana
402,406	"	" South Carolina
435,080	"	" Alabama
436,631	"	" Mississippi
462,198	"	" Georgia
490,865	"	" Virginia

(Negro Year Book, 1925–6, pp. 225–6.)

Plantation culture of cotton, tobacco, sugar and rice were confined by climatic and soil conditions to Virginia, the Carolinas, Georgia, Florida, Alabama, Mississippi, Louisiana, Kentucky, Tennessee, Arkansas, Missouri and Texas. Automatically, therefore, these states became the slave states—the center of the American Negro population.

When the United States emerged from the Civil War in 1865, 14 percent of its population was Negro. These Negroes were either African born or else they were descendants of men and women who had been kidnapped in their African homes and transported across the Atlantic to help enrich the 347,725 American families which were reported as holding slaves in 1850.

The four million Negro slaves and the half million free Negroes who made up the Negro population of the United States in 1865 are the ancestors of the twelve million Negroes who constitute present-day Black America.

Under the slave system the centers of Southern economic power lay in the cotton, tobacco, sugar and rice plantations. Under the new economic order which has arisen from the ruins of the slave system, the centers of Southern economic power lie in two directions. On the one hand there are the railroads, the industries, the mines, the banks, the public utilities, the insurance and merchandising that make up Southern business enterprise. On the other hand is the cultivation of cotton, sugar, tobacco, rice, corn and other Southern agricultural staples.

Negroes, in states such as Mississippi, Georgia and South Carolina, make up approximately half of the total population. In the other Southern States the proportion of Negroes in the population is a quarter or two-fifths. To what extent do Negroes own, control or direct the economic life in communities of which they form so large a part?

The question cannot be answered statistically, save for farm ownership. There are no adequate figures showing the distribution of stocks, bonds, mortgages and title deeds by race.

A visitor to the centers of Southern economic enterprise does not require statistics in order to realize the complete domination of the whites. It is merely necessary to pass through corporation offices; to read the names of boards of directors; to attend conventions of men in various leading business lines; to dine in business clubs. The industrialists of the South are white, almost to a man.

Southern railroad and public utilities are owned chiefly by the whites. Control is exclusively in their hands. They are the directors, the executives, the managers. They decide policy, and direct organization. Tens of thousands of Negroes are employed on Southern railroads. Most of them work as laborers in maintenance and construction crews. A few hold skilled positions. There the story ends. Negroes do not advance "from the ranks" to shape the destiny of Southern railroad enterprise. The South is a white man's country where Negroes work under white supervision.

Southern manufacturing industries are also under white domination. The iron and steel industry with its subsidiaries, the textile industry, the tobacco industry, are almost completely controlled by white enterprise. In many Southern industrial plants Negroes do not work at all, except in menial capacities. Laws, in some of the Southern States, require separate workrooms for Negroes, and thus practically exclude them from establishments in which white workers are employed. As industrialization has proceeded in the South, the whites have monopolized not only the executive posts and the skilled and highly paid trades. They have also held the run of factory jobs.

Occasionally Negro management has made attempts to enter the industrial field, raising capital among Negroes and employing Negro labor. The instances are rare enough to excite newspaper comment. Almost uniformly they have failed after a very brief existence, leaving manufacturing in the hands of the whites.

Negro business men may be found in all parts of the South—running groceries, selling vegetables, conducting restaurants, hotels, barbershops. There are Negro builders and contractors, Negro insurance men, Negro newspaper and magazine managers, Negro printers. Negroes have entered many other occupations in the fields of trade and service.

Two matters are worthy of note in this connection: first, these Negro business men are usually not engaged in any basic industry. Steel, lumber, textile, tobacco are entirely out of their field. Second, they usually serve Negroes. In many cases their patronage is exclusively Negro. Negroes have not penetrated the major industrial enterprises of the South. Even wholesale merchandising remains with the whites. The businesses in which they are active lie on the fringe of the business world.

Banking is a function of the Southern whites. That, of course, is one of the reasons why major Negro enterprises have not been more successful. The Negro has been compelled to go to white bankers for his line of credit. Southern white bankers do not manage their banks for the purpose of pushing Negroes forward along lines of major business enterprise, and there are few Negro bankers to whom Negro business men can turn. Until the World War era, Negroes had scarcely entered the banking field.

Furthermore, Southern banking and business enterprise have been directly allied with Northern banking and business enterprise. Though it is no longer true that Southern business is chiefly dependent on Northern business, the post Civil War development of the South was pushed forward and financed in large part from the North. In those days, even more than today, Northern business was exclusively in the hands of the whites.

Neither in the South nor in the North could Negro business men get adequate credit. As in every other important field, banking was a white man's world to which Negroes were only grudgingly and occasionally admitted.

Free Negroes in the South, long before the Civil War, were engaged in many lines of small scale business enterprise. Today they occupy many of the same fields. Negroes who engage in Southern business are in areas of secondary importance. They have not touched basic business enterprise. In the less strategic business fields, suffering all of the disabilities that go with membership in an inferior, subject race, Negroes enjoy meager opportunities in retail trade, in service to Negroes, in furthering Negro enterprise.

The strategic centers of Southern economic power—railroading, textile, steel, lumber, manufacturing, building, banking are occupied by Southern white men. Merchandising is also largely in their hands.

One field the Negroes have entered—the field of land ownership. The Census of 1920 reported 159,651 Negro farmers who owned their farms in full. In a few sections they actually control better land and make more profits from their land than do the competing whites. This is exceptional, however. Most of the Southern land is in the control of the white race. The Agricultural Census of 1925 reported 3,131,418 farms in the South. Of these farms 831,455 were operated by Negroes and 2,299,963 by whites. Even where Negroes have made the most progress, the Southern whites dominate the economic situation. They are the owning class.

Most Southern Negroes work on land owned and controlled by white farmers. There were 636,248 Negro tenant farmers in the South when the Agricultural Census of 1925 was taken. Practically all the land farmed by these tenants was owned by whites. The Census of 1920 reported 1,192,504 Negroes occupied as wage workers on farms. Since nine-tenths of the Negroes in the North and West live in cities, these Negro agricultural wage workers must have been employed almost entirely in the Southern States. (The Census does not make the separation by race and by states.) The great majority of these Negroes worked for white employers. Out of five Southern Negro farm operators, four are tenants. Out of ten Southern Negroes occupied in gaining a living on the land, eight or nine are directly dependent on the whites for their livelihood.

Most of the Southern blacks work on land owned by Southern whites. Sometimes they work as tenant farmers; sometimes as wage workers. In either case they are economically at the mercy of white exploiters.

Negro labor is replaced by white labor at the moment hard times begin. As a Negro employment manager stated the case, "Our people are the last to be hired and the first to be fired." In support of his contention he cited several instances in which Negro workers had been taken on during boom times and dismissed as soon as the boom had subsided.

In some cases Negroes who had worked for years with a perfectly clean record were dismissed before white workers who had been employed a comparatively short time.

Frequently it is difficult to prove that the Negro has been dismissed because he was a Negro. The employer gives no reason except that he no longer needs his man. In the spring of 1928 six colored elevator operators were working in a Chicago office building. One Friday night at 6 o'clock they were handed their pay and told that they need not come back. One of these men had been employed at the same job for 26 years; a second had worked for 16 years, a third had worked for 22 years. All six were given the finest recommendations, but the next day when the building opened, white operators were on the elevators.

Negroes must not only live by themselves in most parts of the United States, but in many sections they must travel by themselves. Laws for the separation of Negro and white in public conveyances are in force in Tennessee, Florida, Mississippi, Texas, Louisiana, Alabama, Kentucky, Arkansas, Georgia, South Carolina, North Carolina, Virginia, Maryland and Oklahoma (*Opportunity,* February 1924, p. 43). Such separate conveyances for Negroes are commonly known as "Jim Crow" cars.

The first "Jim Crow" cars were run in Massachusetts in 1841. Immediately after the Civil War the idea of the "Jim Crow" car invaded the South. Florida and Mississippi passed laws in 1865, providing that no free-man, Negro or colored, may ride in a first-class passenger car set aside for white persons, except "in the case of Negroes or Mulattoes, travelling with their masters in the capacity of nurses." This latter clause quoted from the Laws of Mississippi (1865, p. 232), tells the story of the position of the Negro as effectively as may be. Negroes accompany whites anywhere provided they go in an inferior capacity. Maryland has a segregation law, passed in 1904, under which passengers travelling within the state must be separated along race lines. Georgia passed a law in 1891 that provided for the segregation of the Negroes in street cars. Louisiana passed a similar law in 1902; Mississippi in 1904; Tennessee and Florida in 1905; Virginia, 1906; North Carolina and Oklahoma in 1907. Where separation in street cars is not provided for by state law, Southern cities pass ordinances to achieve the same result.

Negroes are not exploited and discriminated against economically because of their inferior capacity. If inferior capacity were the test, the whites would distinguish between Negroes in proportion to their capacity to perform the particular task in hand. Those Negroes who were competent to perform the task would be selected for it; those Negroes who were unable to perform the task would be rejected because of their lack of competence.

Economic discrimination against the Negro rests on no such basis.

From slave days certain Negroes have displayed unusual capacities in all of the important lines of human endeavor. There have been highly gifted Negro singers, poets, actors, logicians, scientists, organizers; but these outstanding leaders of the Negro race have been treated by the whites not as poets, scientists and organizers, but as Negroes—that is, as members of an inferior race.

Negroes in the United States are discriminated against economically because they are Negroes, irrespective of their personal capacities. This is so universally true both North and South that it is virtually axiomatic.

While the whites continue, as a race, to own the sources of economic power with which the blacks must work in order to live, a definite consciousness of whiteness will remain among members of the exploiting race and an equally definite consciousness of blackness will be forced upon members of the exploited race. The present strained race relations must continue no matter what the qualities or the fate of individual Negroes may be.

Negroes make up the largest single segregated group of American mass labor. While they remain segregated and while the ownership and control of economic opportunity remains in the hands of the whites, the Negroes must inevitably continue to be the object of white exploitation.

American Negroes are a subject race economically. Economic subjection and exploitation are reflected in political subordination.

Politically, American Negroes hold no position of importance anywhere in the United States. Negroes are not elected to important public offices even where Negroes are in the overwhelming majority.

In 1890, Mississippi began a movement to legally exclude Negroes from the franchise. Other Southern States immediately followed the lead of Mississippi. South Carolina in 1895, Louisiana in 1898, North Carolina in 1900, Alabama and Virginia in 1901 and Georgia in 1908, laid down legal restrictions under which the mass of Negroes were no longer eligible to vote. Laws or constitutional provisions which restrict Negro voting are now in force in Mississippi, South Carolina, Louisiana, North Carolina, Alabama, Virginia, Georgia and Oklahoma.

How do these laws operate?

1. *Literacy*. Voters must be able to read and write.
2. *Property*. Voters must own a certain amount of property.
3. *Poll Tax*. The voter must have paid his poll tax within the year or for a number of years.
4. *Employment*. The voter must have regular employment.
5. *Army service*. Soldiers who fought in the Civil War or in certain other wars, or the descendants of such soldiers may vote.

6. *Reputation.* Persons of good reputation, who understand the duties of a citizen may vote.
7. *Grandfather clauses.* Persons who could vote before the Negroes were enfranchised or descendants of such persons may vote.
8. *Understanding clause.* Persons may vote who understand some selected clauses of the constitution and who can explain these clauses to the satisfaction of the registration officials.

Under these provisions any Negro voter who is objectionable to the white election officials may be disfranchised.

With the economic depression of 1927–1928 and the growing hard times came unemployment and wage cuts. The Negroes, generally unorganized and largely unskilled, were among the first to feel the economic pressure. The white ruling class was using the occasion to force the Negro masses back toward their former occupational levels and their former living standards. Depression in industry offered an occasion for returning the Negroes to their farm-hand jobs and keeping them economically in their places.

The Negroes have tasted the sweets of higher income, greater privileges, larger opportunities, broader life standards. They will not be so easily cajoled or coerced into accepting the lower standards which the ruling white class has decreed for them.

Nevertheless the whites continue the downward pressure. The blacks have but one alternative: to resist.

Experience is teaching the American Negro that an imperial ruling class such as that which now dominates public policy in the United States needs subject races to work and sometimes to fight. The imperialist rulers will take any necessary steps to hold the subject race in its subordinate position. If, in a crisis, they are compelled to grant the subject race privileges, they will take the first opportunity to withdraw them and to drive the members of the subject race back into their position as inferiors and menials.

The white ruling class of the United States is engaged in building a system of exploitation for profit and power. Even if it wished to do so, it could not free Negroes from this system. Emancipation must come from the exploited, not from the exploiters.

Recent Negro migrations into Northern cities—Chicago, Detroit, Cleveland, Buffalo, Pittsburgh, Philadelphia, New York—have brought masses of Negro workers into direct competition with white workers. The Negroes are at the bottom of the economic ladder—generally unskilled, almost wholly unorganized, members of a subject race, ideal victims for exploitation. White employers are taking advantage of the Negroes—using them to force down wages, to break strikes.

White workers have not yet waked up to the situation. They still believe the ruling class propaganda about "racial inferiority." They still exclude Negroes from many of their working-class organizations.

Cheap Negro labor has been a source of profit to American exploiters for three hundred years. Today Negroes are organized to demand higher economic standards. White workers must back these demands to the limit.

Negro workers must join working-class organizations. They must help to build trade unions, cooperatives, a political party that represents working-class interests. Along no other path can the Negro masses hope for emancipation.

White workers must make every effort to bring the Negro workers into trade unions, into cooperatives, into a working-class political organization. There is no more vital task before the American workers today than that of establishing working-class solidarity across race lines.

There can be no victory for the working-class while workers are divided along race lines. Black and white workers must stand together for working-class emancipation.

Emancipation for the American Negro, as for any other subject race under the capitalist imperialist system, can come only when the Negro working masses have joined the white working masses in smashing the economic and social structure built upon individual and race exploitation, and by replacing it with a cooperative economic system under working-class control.

18   THE TWILIGHT OF EMPIRE (1930)

T HIS BOOK PROMPTED Nearing's resignation from the Communist Party. A long-term project analyzing imperialism, the manuscript was to be published by International Publishers, which published party books, and was sent dutifully to Moscow for approval. Nearing's basic thesis was that imperialism accompanied the development of civilization and therefore could be traced to ancient empires.

Moscow rejected the manuscript, basing its rationale on the official interpretation of imperialism that Lenin had lain down in his book *Imperialism*. Lenin set the precedent of 1870 as the beginning of the rise of imperialism, although Nearing pointed out that Lenin was forced to use 1870 because his exile in Switzerland restricted his research to this date. Since Nearing's research and interpretation of imperialism reached historically far beyond Lenin's, *The Twilight of Empire* was refused the imprimatur.

Party discipline required subjugation to the official doctrine; mere sympathy with worker betterment was not enough. Nearing faced the dilemma of bowing to party discipline and abandoning the manuscript or abandoning the party and publishing the book elsewhere. He chose the latter. He resigned with a public letter, but the party accepted no resignation. It expelled him, with a long announcement in the *Daily Worker* of January 8, 1930.

At the same time, Nearing resigned from active politics and all memberships, including the Garland Fund (which eventually published this book with its Vanguard Press imprint) and the Civil Liberties Union. He based his wholesale resignations on being 45 years old and urged that his replacement be under 30 so that active and passionate blood could carry on the energetic work required of leftist goals.

Meanwhile, the nation reacted to the onslaught of the Great Depression. Workers demonstrated across the country for unemployment insurance and better guarantees for a decent livelihood. Radicals took the unrest as the inevitable sign of degenerating capitalism and called for sweeping structural changes in government as a solution. In reaction, Hamilton Fish, Republican representative from New York, seeded Congress with the beginnings of the House Un-American Activities Committee.

When barbarians were victorious over their neighbors, they plundered and exterminated them. They had no permanent living place until the later period of barbarism. Like all nomads, their property could not exceed, in bulk, the amount they could carry with them when they were forced to move.

Slaves, beyond a very small minimum, were a liability. If the victors did not kill the vanquished, how should they dispose of them?

With the beginning of agriculture as an important source of livelihood, and particularly with the establishment of trade and the foundation of permanent trading centres, peoples gave up nomadism; settled in permanent places; began the acquisition of large quantities of economic goods; found profit in large-scale slave labor. At this point, instead of exterminating their rivals, after the custom of barbarians, civilized people spared their lives and put them to work. For extermination, civilization substituted slavery, which is the earliest form of mass exploitation.

The transition from barbarism to civilization was marked by these characteristics: private ownership of productive tools and of slaves; exploitation at home of the slaves and other workers; exploitation abroad of conquered territories with their peoples.

The owning class at home, because of its superior economic position, became as a matter of course the exploiting class both at home and abroad. The owning class needed slaves to perform its labor, raw materials for its industries, markets for its commodities, and a strong military force to protect its interests. These have been the outstanding characteristics of imperial states for more than five thousand years. They are, at the same time, the outstanding characteristics of civilization.

Foreign conquest and exploitation (imperialism) have been among the leading activities of all civilized peoples. During this historic period, victorious ruling classes have exploited foreign territories and alien peoples for profit. The method of exploitation has varied. The principle of exploitation and the resulting class struggles, wars and colonial revolts have remained constant.

The imperial world is divided into tribute collectors and tribute payers. The imperial business class receives the tribute of the world, spends what it must or what it will on its overhead and on its luxuries, makes additional investments in the provinces, and collects fresh stores of unearned income. Centralized ownership of the agricultural land and of natural resources, the monopoly over cash and credit, the manipulation of financial and business exploitation, drain the economic surplus of this world into this one centre.

At the imperial centre the ruling class lives at the banker level. Luxury abounds. An owing, ruling class, supported on parasitic income, fills its cup of life and enjoyment to the brim.

The day has passed when the members of the ruling class work or fight. Myriads of slaves, serfs or ill-paid wage earners do the work; provincials or mercenaries do the fighting; business managers, stewards and officials do the trading. Members of the imperial ruling class are the money-lenders; the investors; the land-owners; the idle rich; the politicians, living on the cream of a world built out of labor exploitation and oppression.

Imperialists collect, profiteer, enjoy. The empire pays the bill. The local middle classes are squeezed out. The farmers are driven from the land in order that the rich may invest in it and work it on a large scale with slave or serf labor. Taxes and tribute flow to the imperial centre from the surplus created by the labor of farm hands, herdsmen, artisans, who live humbly and work hard.

Thus the prosperity at the centre of imperial power is maintained upon the surplus produced by a very large number of workers in the provinces. It is the product of a very highly organized system of exploitation.

Whatever may have been the proportion of construction that had a productive character, the vast amount of building at Ur, Thebes, Babylon, Athens, Rome and other imperial cities stimulated both commerce and industry. Raw materials were brought from the corners of the earth. Skilled artisans were trained and employed in great numbers. Millions of slaves labored through centuries. The feeding, housing and equipping of these workers kept traders, manufacturers, contractors and officials busy.

Urbanization meant construction. Whether the building was productive or unproductive, it provided a method for concentrating surplus wealth; stimulated productive activities, both at the imperial centre and throughout the empire; enlarged and greatly enriched the professional

and business classes, and speedily became a depository of treasure that
was coveted and sought after by barbarians and by rival imperial cities.

Inevitably, urbanization involved wealth concentration. First the
wealth and income of the empire were concentrated in the imperial city:
Thebes, Babylon, Rome; second, it was concentrated in the cities as
opposed to the rural areas; third, it was concentrated in the hands of the
owning ruling class in the cities, and particularly in the imperial city.

Wealth and income flowed into the public treasury of the imperial
city and into the private pocketbooks of the rulers. Wealthy people from
other parts of the empire gravitated toward the imperial city. Extravagant homes were built. Costly food and clothing were consumed. Luxuries were in great demand. An extravagant standard of conspicuous
consumption was maintained. Rare commodities from the whole world
filled the homes of the rich, and the demands for luxuries diverted a
considerable portion of wealth into these unproductive channels.

High taxes, rents and profits, necessary to maintain the extravagant
life of the wealthy class in the cities, drove the farmers from their land
and concentrated an army of destitute, turbulent, unemployed humanity
in the slums. Dispossessed farmers; artisans, lured to the city by the
promise of high wages; and slaves made up the plebeian masses, who
were given bread and circuses, and who became a source of crying
discontent and mass revolt.

Thus there arose a centre of wealth and culture, with beautiful buildings, theatres, festivals, literature, philosophy, art, with new wants and
a greatly expanded home market. Within the walls of the culture centre,
supporting it with one hand and reaching up the other hand to threaten it
and tear it down, were the exploited masses,—the poverty that lined the
wealth and power of the rich.

Surplus wealth, concentrated through the process of commercializa-
tion and urbanization, was diverted in part to productive and in part to
unproductive uses. The ownership of this wealth, and the income from
it, centred in the imperial capital; in the cities generally; in the hands of
a small and very rich owning class that lived in extravagant and frequently idle luxury on the labor of artisan, serf and slave masses.

City life is an essential part of the imperial process. It is also one
cause of the increase of imperial overhead.

Commercial cities are small affairs in the beginning. They can be
personally handled like any small organization or business. World empires, however, involve a bureaucratic machine with a constant overhead cost made up of: (1) the cost—direct and indirect—of maintaining
parasite classes; (2) the diversion of large portions of the imperial income to the construction and maintenance of unproductive buildings;
(3) the costs of the military organization and of the bureaucratic
machine.

The parasitic classes are a constant charge on the imperial income. They exist all along the social scale. At the one extreme are the idle rich. At the other extreme are the idle poor. Between are the hordes of confidence men, speculators, operators, gamblers, promoters, prostitutes, thieves, sycophants.

The idle rich are a constantly growing charge on the imperial income. The greater the concentration of imperial wealth, the richer does this class become. Not only do the members of this class consume more than they produce, but the cost of their per person consumption is far greater than the cost of the per person consumption among the workers. In the later stages of the imperial cycle the idle rich are either owners of land, investors in business, or both, and their property entitles them to live without working on the labor of the producers. At this stage of the imperial cycle, "law and order" means, primarily, the guarantee to the idle rich of an uninterrupted flow of unearned income.

Machine industry broke in on the sequence of the imperial cycle. It also added greatly to power of the imperial ruling classes by developing industry, transport, merchandising and trade at the expense of agriculture, and by greatly enriching the business class as compared with the agricultural class.

Until the development of machine industry, it required an agricultural population of at least four thousand persons to maintain a trading centre of one thousand persons. In the middle ages the disproportion was far greater. Even in the opening years of the twentieth century in Russia and the Balkans, more than four-fifths of the population was centred in the agricultural villages and less than a fifth in the trading centres. Even after the business class had wrested control of policy from the hands of the landed aristocracy, the great majority of the people were still in agricultural villages.

Machine industry reversed this situation. The development of agricultural machinery made it possible for a nation like the United States to feed itself with less than one-fourth of its gainfully occupied population engaged in agriculture. Other imperial nuclei, like Great Britain, practically eliminated agriculture and relied largely on the importation of agricultural products.

Machine industry reduced agricultural production from a position of numerical major importance to one of numerical minor importance. At the same time it added to the wealth of the business class the immense profits of the new system of mass production.

Even when the great mass of the population was engaged in agriculture, the business class made large enough profits to place the balance of economic surplus in its hands. As machine production drew more and

more producers from the farms to the industrial centres, the economic
balance was weighted more and more strongly in favor of the business
class.

Machine production not only centred economic power in the hands
of the established business class in the old imperial countries by adding
to their economic surpluses, but it gave them new tools and weapons for
conquest and exploitation and enabled them to penetrate the undeveloped countries and call into being similarly equipped imperial
classes.

No productive system known to history has yielded such large economic surpluses as the machine-industry system, ushered in by the
Industrial Revolution. The machine age is, therefore, on its face, the
age of the most intense foreign conquest and exploitation.

Such is indeed the case. The past fifty years have seen the growth of
unimagined quantities of economic surplus. They have also witnessed
an expansion of the Western empires over the entire planet, and exploitation by them of populations in every corner of the globe.

World empire, on the widest scale ever known, has resulted directly
from the growth of surplus under the system of machine-age production. The same force, however, was rapidly building beyond the individual empires a world-wide economy.

Thus, in the course of its history, the system of business for profit has
evolved from the local trading centre to the world market; the civil state,
built upon trade, has evolved from the tiny city state to the world
empire; the tools of exploitation have evolved from hand tools to world
trusts and banking syndicates; the volume of surplus has grown from a
few domesticated animals in the possession of the herdsman, a few tools
and utensils in the house of the land worker, a few bits of metal in the
pack of the merchant to the vast capital equipment of factory and railroad; the immense stores of unconsumed materials to the billions that
pass back and forth in the modern imperial credit transactions and
settlements.

After the Industrial Revolution, the new machine industry gradually
separated owners and workers. The former became the controlling element in social and political affairs, setting up the bourgeois state and the
system of bourgeois culture as bulwarks against any possible enrichment of the wage-earning masses that were subject to their exploitation.

Economic developments intensified this class struggle. Mass production meant massed labor. Larger ships were built. Immense factories
were opened. Mining became a great industry. Rail systems employed
thousands. The pressure, under this new system of work, was intense.
Labor power was bought, on the open market, by the highest bidder.

Living costs rose. The workers were caught and crushed between two faces of a vice. They were exploited by the job-owners, robbed by the landlord, and starved by the trader until they literally could not live. But they could organize and they could fight. The result was the labor movement.

During the War of 1914 and the years immediately following it, the small shopkeepers, the professional class (the "liberals" and "intellectuals") took sides almost to a man with the imperialists. While the war was on they helped to win it. After the war was over they helped to bolster up the crushed structure of capitalist imperialism and to prepare it for its next slaughter fest.

The Social Democrats and the labor bureaucrats joined hands with the petit bourgeoisie in their effort to rehabilitate capitalism. The left wing of the labor movement, led by the Communists, actively continued the class struggle, pointing out the impossibility of capitalist stabilization; the inevitability of further wars; the immense and growing success of the workers' and farmers' Soviet society.

It was these revolutionary elements, organized after 1922 in 56 countries, that became the ideological leaders of the militant world labor movement,—carrying on a campaign against capitalist imperialism and its war preparations on the one hand and against reaction in the labor movement on the other.

The post-war period saw the lines of world struggle re-forming. The persistence of the Soviet Union gave a rallying point for the militant labor forces. The success of Soviet economy heartened the class-conscious masses everywhere. If the workers and farmers could achieve such results in Russia, why not in other parts of the world?

In the Soviet Union, where, alone, the proletarian revolution had gained and held power, a new economic and social system began to take form,—first under war communism; then under the New Economic Policy, adopted in 1921–1922, and later under the Five-Year Plan of 1928–1933.

This new Soviet economy was an alternative to capitalist imperialism. It included:

1. A scientific economic plan that replaced the economic chaos of capitalist industry by a planned economy under a central directing agency.
2. The contemplated establishment of a world economy and a world administration of producers in place of a multitude of competing capitalist states and empires.
3. Citizenship in terms of occupation rather than of birth-place or dwelling-place.

4. The social ownership and control of resources and production goods: land, timber, coal, iron, oil, railroads, factories, grain-elevators.

5. Production for use: the conversion of wheat into bread; of cotton into cloth; of lumber into houses; for the purpose of feeding, clothing and housing people, and not for the profit of an owning ruling class.

6. Guaranteed livelihood: a share of the product for each producer, so that as long as a person takes part in production, he need never fear poverty, except such poverty as all other members of the group must suffer.

7. Socialized leisure: the short workday; the limited work week; yearly vacations with pay; the opening of libraries, museums, concerts, operas, dramatic performances to the masses. A chance for all to share in whatever cultural opportunities society may have to offer.

8. A non-exploiting, classless society, in which no one person or group of people can live without productive activity upon the wealth produced by others,—a society in which the working class and leisure class of capitalism are replaced by a system under which all able-bodied adults take part in production and all share in leisure.

In terms of social history, such a social system is beyond civilization. Its production form is new, and on its new production form men are building a social order that will be as different from civilization as civilization is different from barbarism. Thus the proletarian revolution, a child of the industrial revolution, is a part of the transition process from capitalist-imperialist economy and social organization to a new economy and a new social order.

19 WAR (1931)

NEARING CONSIDERED the subtitle of this book (*Orga-nized Destruction and Mass Murder by Civilized Na-tions*) the most telling description of war that he could mus-ter. While other writers described war as an instrument of national policy, an inevitable periodic expression of the essential combative nature of human beings, or a welcome reinfusion of energy into the social body, Nearing viewed war through its brutal battlefield effects on society and the individuals who suffered it.

Of all his books, this was the one he was most proud of. In it he discusses how war ravages the masses of peoples, destroys the wealth they created, allows the ruling class tighter management of a country, diminishes freedom through the calculated propaganda used to rouse the popu-lace to fear, hate, patriotism, and fighting forces. He calls for the abolition of war just as society abolished slavery and yellow fever. In the end he prescribes a program for a warless world in which the profit of war is eliminated by constructing a planned world economy, a league of indus-tries to disseminate the needs of everyone and eliminate want, poverty, and misery. This should not be utopian dreaming, he writes, any more than the idea of eliminating slavery was utopian and therefore considered impossible.

Curiously, the book was published the same year that Herbert Hoover signed the law making "The Star-Spangled Banner" the national anthem, a war song of bombs bursting and the rocket's red glare.

The directors of military activity are usually concerned, not with preparations to defeat a particular enemy, but with preparations that will enable them to defeat any possible enemy or combination of enemies. Thus, war-making is a science, the purpose of which is to enable one group of war-makers to hold its own in a world of war-makers.

Plainly, therefore, war is not the result of some fleeting impulse or passion. Popular feelings are aroused and utilized to "help win the war", but the technique of war-making is as carefully worked out as the technique of any other science. Military engineers devote their lives to war-making and take it for granted, just as chemists or civil engineers devote their lives to the oil industry or the railroad industry and take them for granted.

War is a trade as well as a science. Even during peace years millions of people, in the principal civilized nations, secure their living directly from war-making. During periods of fighting the numbers who live by war are greatly augmented.

Foremost among those whose living comes directly from war-making are the officers of the armies and navies; the technicians and specialists who devote their energies to designing military equipment, improving weapons, directing the construction of defenses; and the teachers of military strategy and tactics. With these men, war-making is a profession, a life work. They study for it as they would study for any other profession and spend their best energies and most fruitful years learning, practicing, and teaching the principles of war.

Millions have a direct income-stake in the war machine. Millions more, by providing for army and naval maintenance, have an indirect income-stake in war-making. But these millions, for the most part, receive a wage or salary barely sufficient to keep them above the poverty line. The money pay of soldiers, for example, is pathetically small. Many workers in arsenals and munition plants receive less than a living wage. Beside these millions, there are a few owners and directors of business enterprises who build their fortunes on war.

The names of Krupp, Schneider, Vickers and Du Pont are known throughout the world. All four fortunes have been built upon the production of war materials. The Rothschilds, the Readings, and the Morgans have piled up fortunes in war financing.

War is an emergency. Weapons, munitions, and supplies must be had at any cost. Those who control the supplies reap huge profits by boosting prices and taking all that the traffic will bear. War profiteers make fortunes both from military preparations and from the actual conduct of war.

War is an important ruling-class pre-occupation in each of the principal nations. Members of the ruling class hire war technicians by the thousands. They recruit and conscript the rank and file of their armies and navies by the millions. The actual direction of war is given into the hands of the most trusted members of the ruling class.

Whether they rely upon mercenaries, conscripts or volunteers, the business classes organize war with the same professional care that they organize any other phase of their activities.

The question: "What is war?" can be answered in one sentence: War is destruction and mass murder, premeditated, planned, and organized by the ruling class of a nation and directed against the enemy.

West Point and Annapolis train men for the life purpose of war-making. There are no other colleges or universities maintained by the United States Government or by any state government in which food, clothing, lodging, and tuition are provided free for all students. More inducements are thus offered for a military education than for any other form of higher public instruction in the United States.

Reserve officers' training corps in American colleges and citizens' military training camps give technical military education to a much larger number than can be accommodated at West Point and Annapolis. Again, those who submit themselves for training receive railroad fare, instruction, board, and lodging.

Finally, there is the mass military training given in the army, in the national guard, and in other military or semi-military organizations. In most of the principal European countries this includes compulsory military training for all men at certain ages.

Propaganda is one of the most important aspects of the war machine. War on a nation-wide scale, involving widespread suffering and repeated, heart-breaking losses, can be successfully carried on only if it can be popularized. Consequently, propaganda is an essential of war-making. Through this propaganda the ruling class will sell war to the masses.

Propaganda must be sufficiently effective to insure the following: adequate appropriations for the army, the navy, and other branches of military service; willingness of the populace to endure compulsory military service or to enlist in case of a war emergency; the subordination of all other interests to military necessity; unquestioning loyalty and patriotism, the support of the fatherland, "right or wrong".

Propaganda is carried on by means of the school, the press, the church, advertising, the radio, the movies and other agencies that divert, amuse, arouse, and excite. Through these means, habit patterns may be shaped, and food for thought may be provided in accordance with the wishes of those who control the propaganda machinery.

School, press, church, movie, radio—these are the major channels through which the ruling class in each industrial country reaches the mass with its military propaganda. So thoroughly are these propaganda institutions organized, and so widespread is the network of power that they have built up, that almost every family in a modern industrial society can be supplied almost every day with the materials that will determine its feeling and its thinking.

The political unit of industrial society is the nation. National loyalty or patriotism is elevated into a public faith. The national flag is made a symbol of this loyalty, and children are trained from infancy in the tradition of national honor and the defense of the fatherland and the flag.

The agencies of war propaganda must first create a devil—the enemy. In certain cases of long standing competitive struggle like that between France and Germany or France and England, there is a hereditary enemy, and this part of the task is easy. When former friends, such as Germany and the United States, go to war against each other, the task of instilling fear and hate in the masses is more difficult.

The preaching to the masses of fear, hate, and patriotism is one of the chief tasks in all civilized countries. In peace-times the emphasis is laid upon patriotism. In war-time it is based on fear and hate. During the years preceding the War of 1914, nationalism and patriotism were stressed in every great civilized country. The motive of fear was played upon only occasionally. With the coming of the war, however, the preaching of fear and hate became the principal function of the propaganda machine in each of the civilized empires.

Until recent times civilized nations relied upon religious institutions to stir up war-lust in the masses. During the nineteenth century, however, the school and the press supplanted the church as the chief means of building a war psychology. With the coming of the twentieth century, the movies and the radio were added to this secular arm of war propaganda. When the twentieth century ruling class decides to prepare the masses for war, it has at its disposal church, school, press, radio, and movie.

During peace-times the propaganda machinery justifies war in principle. When hostilities break out the particular war is heralded, applauded, and sanctioned.

The returns from war may be classified into three categories: economic, political, and social. While it is impossible to separate sharply these three classes of war income, the division provides a convenient basis for study.

The economic advantages of war-making are the most tangible. They include: (1) direct economic war gains; (2) opportunities to trade and exploit; (3) the destruction of economic surplus; (4) war profits; (5) profits of neutrals; (6) the business aspects of war; (7) population control through war.

Direct economic gains from war may be grouped under four heads: booty, land, indemnities, and tribute.

The economic advantages of war are enjoyed chiefly by members of the ruling exploiting class. The booty, land, indemnities, and tribute secured through war go primarily to the members of the ruling class, or to the organizations in which the members of the ruling class are interested. Opportunities to trade and exploit are necessarily advantageous, in the first instance, to members of the trading and exploiting class. The destruction of economic surplus, and the stimulation of demand which result from war, make good business for exploiters. They also provide steady work for those who are not drafted for duty in the military machine. War profits go, in the first instance, to war profiteers. The experience of the War of 1914 showed that the advantages derived by workers in the form of high wages were offset by the rising cost of living.

Who benefits through the political advantages of war? The centralization of power obviously benefits the ruling class. The extension of political boundaries and the destruction or crippling of dangerous rivals are likewise of primary ruling class advantage. Although it may be argued that victory in war protects the masses in the victorious country against the slavery or degradation that might be endured as a result of defeat, the fact remains that the outcome of the Franco-Prussian War, of the Russo-Japanese War, or of the War of 1914 did not indicate that any important political advantage was derived by the workers in the victorious countries. Indeed, the principal mass gains were registered in the revolutionary situations created in the defeated countries.

The masses pay the costs of war. They pay, no matter whether a war is won or lost. Ruling classes frequently gain by war. If they win decisive victories they secure wealth and enlarged territory. If they are consistently victorious, as were the Romans and the British, they may win the right to rule and exploit the whole known world.

The masses have no such chances. Before the war they are the "factory fodder"; during the war they are the "cannon fodder"; after the war they help to rebuild the shaken power of their masters.

The masses pay in speed-up; in lowered standards of living; in blood; in anguish. They pay in the increased dictatorial power assumed by the ruling class during a war, and later relinquished only as the masses rise and struggle against the bureaucracy.

The income and outgo items involved in war may be set down side by side:

War income	*War cost*
booty	injures health
land	curtails well-being

indemnities	blots out life
tribute	breaks up social relations
trade	destroys wealth
exploiting power	consumes current income
destruction of surplus	piles up debt
war profits	destroys productive power
centralization of power	civil rights denied
extension of boundaries	popular institutions abandoned
crippling of rivals	society blotted out
unification of society	leads to bankruptcy
mixing people	loss of liquid capital
breaking cake of custom	lowered standard of living
purging of nations	dismembered society
creation of revolutionary	spreads fear and hate
situation	destroys the best

The gains of war are, in the main, ruling class gains. The losses of war, are in the main, mass losses. There are exceptions but this generalization is true on the whole.

The science of war, like other sciences, has been created by the ruling class. The art of war, like the other arts, has been fostered by the ruling class. War, as an institution, has been organized and aggrandized by the ruling class. In earlier times, war was its greatest game. In modern times it is its supreme adventure. The ruling class builds and uses the war machine, and the balance sheet of war stands in its favor.

Examine the historic record, beginning with a single recent war, like that of 1914–1918. The publication of the Secret Treaties and the drafting of the Treaty of Versailles; the Conferences at Genoa and Lausanne; the Dawes and Young Plans; the treatment accorded to India, Egypt, Mexico, China leave no possible room for doubt as to the chief driving forces that animated the principal participants in the war. German interests desired a railroad from Berlin to Bagdad. French interests wanted Lorraine iron and Saar coal. British interests had their eyes on Mesopotamian oil. Japanese interests were looking for a free hand in Manchuria. Russian interests sought a seaport in a moderate climate. American interests were protecting their enormous investments with the Allies.

"Of course it was a commercial war!" exclaimed President Wilson, in his St. Louis speech, after he had come into first-hand contact with the European war-makers. How could an intelligent man, possessed of the facts, reach any other conclusion?

The masses of people may not have known that the war was commercial. They may have been inspired with the loftiest emotions when they gave their lives in the trenches, toiled in the factories, contributed to the Red Cross, or subscribed for war loans. But the masses neither planned the war, began the war, nor directed the war. They were merely the cannon fodder and the exploited factory and field hands who made the war possible.

The principal nations of the world are better armed and better equipped for war than they were in 1913. War machines are more efficient. The organization for war is more complete. Preparations for war are not secret. Scarcely a week passes in which the press or the movies do not carry pictures of the "largest" bombing plane, the "fastest" cruiser, the "finest" submarine, the "heaviest" coast defense gun, the "deadliest" gas. War preparations are extensive and they are being steadily extended.

The most spectacular form of military preparation is navy building. Because of the expense involved, only six or seven nations can afford the luxury of a modern navy. Even wealthy nations such as Britain, France and Japan are feeling the strain of the "cruiser-race." Yet, as the London Armament Conference of 1930 clearly showed, instead of a reduction in naval tonnage, the world may expect an increase. Certainly it can expect greater naval efficiency.

Since 1920, there has not been a single year in which a war did not take place somewhere in the world. A partial list of wars since 1920 shows:

1918–20	Imperialist campaigns against Soviet Russia.
1918–21	Civil Wars in Soviet Union.
1918–20	War of Poland against Russia.
1919–22	Wars between Greece and Turkey.
1919	Egyptian Revolt against Britain.
	Poles over-run Galicia.
	Afghan attack on India.
	Roumanian march into Hungary.
	Italian occupation of Fiume.
	Japanese suppression of Korean rebellion.
1920	French War on Arabs in Syria.
	Italian attack on Albania.
	Polish attack on Vilna.
1921	Montenegrin revolt against Jugoslavs.
1916–26	Spanish and French Wars in the Riff.
1922	Chinese Civil War.
1923	Lithuanians seize Mervel.
	Italy bombards Corfu.
	Military occupation of the Ruhr.

1924	China, Civil War.
	Mexico, Civil War.
1925	French Wars against Druses.
1926–30	China, general Civil War.
1928–29	Afghan, Civil War.
1929	Mexico, Civil War.
1929	Russo-Chinese War in Manchuria.
1926–28	Nicaraguan War.
1929	Arab revolt in Palestine.
1930	India, Civil War.
	Argentina, Civil War.
	Spain, Civil War.
	Brazil, Civil War.

To be sure, no one of these conflicts was a "world war," but several of them contained world war possibilities at least as great as the Balkan Wars of 1912. In any case, they showed that the formula: economic expansion and conflict; political expansion and conflict; military preparation, and finally, war, is as true of the years following 1920 as it was in the preceding epochs.

Even the most casual student of history would not argue that the great masses of people want war or make war. Periodically, they are forced into war—cajoled, misinformed, goaded, terrified, conscripted. But how many times, in the past hundred years, have the masses clamored for war? War is not a popular form of entertainment. Despite all of the glorification, the tinsel, the brass bands, the masses everywhere must be whipped into a frenzy of fear and hate before they will support war.

Wars are today unquestionably wars between groups of profit-makers. Modern war is part of the struggle for wealth and power. Never since the foundation of modern capitalism has the total volume of profit been so great. Never has the struggle to monopolize this profit been so intensive or so extensive.

The volume of profit has been increasing by the introduction of a steadily broadening variety of labor replacing machines. Each one of these machines involves an "investment" upon which the capitalist demands and receives a "reasonable rate of profit". As the complexity and variety of the machines mount, their "investment" value grows correspondingly. That is, from his ownership of the growing volume of machines the capitalist is able to secure a mounting volume of profit.

It would be utopian for a practical politician to talk about a warless world because he is a part of an economic and social system that was built by war and that relies upon war for its maintenance. But for those who see a new world now in the making, the idea of abolishing war is no more utopian than the idea of abolishing illiteracy, poverty, or contagious diseases.

War-making has been one phase of an aggressive struggle for wealth and power. The peace dream has been a negative reaction to the excesses of war.

The frequent recurrence of war has made men pessimistic. Humanity accepts war fatalistically as it accepts any other stroke of fate. "History repeats itself," they complain. "Since war always has been, war always will be." Thus, the commonly accepted argument runs, and in its support is ranged almost the entire history of civilization.

According to a second argument, "War is the result of human nature. Since human nature does not change, wars must continue." If the premises of this argument are accepted, the conclusion inevitably follows, and there is no hope for peace.

The primary lesson of history is not repetition but change. Wherever the historic record is examined, whether in the field of discovery and invention, in the character of implements and tools, in the forms of transport, food, and housing, in the means of communication, in the arts, or in any other avenue of human activity, change is the foreground of the picture. Where there is repetition the process is spiral rather than circular.

Economic, political, and social institutions have alike been modified, remade, discarded, and replaced. The ancient world gave way before classical society. Slavery passed into feudalism; feudalism into wagery. The city-state became the nation; the nation, the modern federation of sovereign states. There is no reason to believe that these changes have come to an end. On the contrary, they are more rapid and widespread today than at any other known period of social history.

This culture stream was flowing before the writing of history began. The modifications in its character and in its direction have taken place with increasing frequency. It is flowing today, broader, deeper, more swiftly.

The argument "war always has been and always will be" is true of any social institution and of any human activity up to a certain point. Beyond that point it ceases to be true.

The argument was true for cannibalism until the domestication of animals provided a permanent food supply. There are remains of cannibalism in various parts of the world today, but the race passed that stage in its development when it discovered and adopted a surer food supply.

The argument was true for slavery until the development of machine industry furnished a substitute in the form of wage labor. Slavery remains in certain out of the way parts of the world, but wherever the

machine process has gained a foothold it has eliminated the institution
of slavery because the two systems are essentially incompatible. With
more efficient methods, the less effective means of production is inevitably displaced.

The argument that war always has been and always will be remains
true until there is some basic economic and social change that will make
war as unnecessary as cannibalism and slavery. After that point has
been reached war will continue in certain out of the way parts of the
world and in certain minor instances. It may even recur spasmodically
as cannibalism does during a severe famine. But just as more efficient
forms of economic and social organization have successfully banished
cannibalism and slavery, a more efficient form of economic and social
organization will banish war.

The argument that a certain phase of social activity always has been
and always will be, holds true up to the point at which this phase of activity is permanently replaced by another phase. These "culture corners"
or points of drastic change in social organization have usually been the
result of some significant change in the method by which human beings
have made their living. At present, when economic changes are taking
place with such rapidity, there are unusually great possibilities of essential political and social modifications.

War-making is a human institution. In that sense, of course, it is a
product of human nature. So is every other phase of human activity. But
is it human nature that makes war?

Man is not any one unit urge or drive, but a complexity of urges and
drives. Russell distinguishes between the possessive urges, which lead
toward war and the creative urges, which lead toward peace. Even the
most ardent militarist cannot contend that all human urges lead toward
war.

The elimination of war is a problem of social reconstruction. Certainly war will not be abolished in a civilized society where war-makers
and war-making play a central role. While wealth and power are the
returns of economic and political expansion, war will remain the chief
agency for their attainment.

Peace can be hoped for only in a world whose major economic and
social institutions provide a foundation for peace in the same sense that
the major economic and social institutions of civilized society provide a
foundation for war. Until this essential foundation for a peace world has
replaced the war foundation of civilized society, war-making will continue to be one of the principal activities of the human race.

There is no more pressing social duty before mankind today than this
duty of building the foundations for a warless world. The task will tax
the human capacities to the uttermost. It is a gigantic social undertaking.

The building of a warless world is more than an engineering task. It is an enterprise requiring an organized, aggressive militant struggle by those who believe in the possibilities of peace against those individuals, institutions, customs, and traditions which represent centuries of war.

When the Yangtse or the Mississippi overflow their banks, men do not content themselves by tamely describing the terrors of the flood, by magnifying the potency of the river, and by detailing the impossibility of handling such huge volumes of water as are tearing away levees and dykes. Instead, they organize, plan, prepare, and attack the problem of flood control.

In the same way, a world inundated by war must organize, plan, prepare, and attack the problem of war control. Specifically: (1) The urge toward war must be reduced or eliminated by modifications in the economic organization of society that will reduce or eliminate economic and political expansion. Practically speaking, this means wiping out private profit in industry, trade, and finance through the socialization of the essential productive machinery and the setting up of a general economic plan as a substitute for economic competition. (2) Armaments, organizations for war-making, and training for war must be abolished, in order that no one, neither officer, soldier, nor war profiteer, may be in a position to derive an income directly or indirectly from war. (3) A war taboo must be set up. The machinery for the control of public opinion must be utilized to build a disapprobation of war, just as it is now used to establish pro-war sentiment. (4) The war-making man must be segregated. Persistent aggressors who insist upon cut-throat struggle in the economic, political, social, or military fields must be treated like any other persistent destroyers or meddlers. (5) Any such suggestions for the reorganization of society remain utopian unless those who are directing the social process are able to construct a social system that will survive without the making of war. This is the essential task in the building of a warless world: To create a body of economic and social institutions from which the drive toward war will have been successfully eliminated.

How should this change be directed if the desired goal is a form of economic life that will serve as the foundation for a warless world? The question may be answered in these words: economic changes should be directed toward a system of socialized, planned, world economy.

Socialization of productive machinery is the first economic step in the direction of a warless world. It involves a fundamental modification in the property conceptions of civilization and a complete reversal of capitalist practice under which private profiteers are entitled to the economic surplus.

Factories, mines, railways, telephone systems, power plants, banks—
all parts of the economic structure, the private ownership of which
makes it possible for one man to live, without labor, on the labor
performed by others—would, in a system of socialized economy, pass
under social control. The title to these properties would be a social title
just as the present title to streets, public school buildings, post offices,
and public hospitals is a social title.

Under the present system of private economy in production goods,
the owner of a factory secures a profit; that is, a portion of the product
turned out in a factory is regularly paid in the form of interest and
dividends and profits to those individuals who hold title, deeds, stocks,
bonds, mortgages, or other evidences of property ownership.

A street, on the contrary, pays no profit. The capital for its original
construction is supplied from the community funds and the upkeep costs
are paid out of current community income. The street is "for use" and
not "for profit".

The books kept by all enterprises which are operating under a system
of private economy include charges for rent, interest, and profit which
must ordinarily be paid before the privately owned enterprises are permitted to operate. Bread is not baked because people are hungry. When
profit ceases the bakery closes.

The economy of street construction is exactly the opposite of the
economy of baking for profit. Streets are constructed because they are
needed. Often, in sparsely settled sections, years pass before the tax
income is sufficient to pay the costs of a particular pavement. Still, the
pavement is laid and maintained.

A league of industries made up of socialized, planned, cooperating
economic groups already functioning as part of a world economic order
would have neither the pressure toward war-making nor the traditions of
war-making. Its needs would urge it in the direction of cooperation
rather than in the direction of war.

The functions of a league of industries—the distribution of resources,
the handling of transport, the direction of finance and credit, and the
administration of other world economic problems—would make of this
league of industries an active anti-war organization, since its success
would necessarily depend upon the maintenance of peace and the continuance of co-operation. The basic drive in each sovereign civil state is
a drive toward self-sufficiency, competition, and war. The basic drive
of a league of world industries would be a drive toward cooperation and
peace.

The administration machinery necessary for the successful functioning of a world league of industries would be provided by a world
parliament, the members of which would be selected from the occupational groups engaged in those industries of which the world league of

industries was composed. This world parliament, representing productive units, would establish subordinate administrative and judicial organs, charged with the detail of world administration.

Paralleling the economic basis for a warless world, a socialized, planned world economy would be the political or administrative structure consisting of citizenship in economic groups, the organization of public affairs along occupational lines, and a world league of industries. Such an economic and social structure would bring within the control of one administrative area the major world economic conflicts which are now the root causes of war. The existence of such a piece of social machinery would not in itself prevent war. On the negative side it would remove some of the most insistent causes of war, but on the positive side it would provide an administrative organization which might be used in adjusting the economic differences that now lead to war.

War-making civil states like those which have been in control of world affairs during historic times concentrate property control in the hands of a minority, establish social divisions between this property-controlling minority and the working majority, direct public policy in the interests of the profit-making minority, and exploit the majority. Under such an economic system, conflicts between rival ruling-class groups are the order of the day, and friction between the exploiting class and the exploited class recurs with insistent regularity.

Class divisions and class conflict are distinguishing characteristics of civil society. The clan and the tribe were, for the most part, classless. It was the introduction of private property in production goods that laid the basis, in the civil state, for class divisions.

A socialized, planned world economy would produce fundamental changes in the forms of social organization. The social structure necessary for the establishment of a warless world would be distinguished from the present social order by the absence of class divisions.

A class is a more or less permanent social group enjoying some economic special privilege. Usually this special privilege takes the form of the private ownership of productive tools, or some other means with which the masses of the people are forced to gain a livelihood. Socialize these productive tools, and the chief source of private profit is eliminated.

The chief sources of domestic and of international conflict, in a capitalist society, are the accumulation and the use of profit. Once the productive tools are socialized, the economic surplus, instead of going into the channels of private profit would be converted into various forms of social income. A classless society would of necessity be a cooperative society. If the economic system was planned on a world scale, cooperation likewise would be organized on a world scale. Hence the social base of a warless order of society would be a classless, cooperating world.

A classless world society, depending for its livelihood upon a socialized, planned world economy and operating its industries for use and not for profit, would guarantee the livelihood of its individual members. This guarantee of livelihood would be the ultimate material test of the success of a system of world economy, and as soon as the guarantee proved effective would remove one of the most fruitful causes of human unrest—want, and the fear of want.

The military machine has been built by the ruling classes in various parts of the world. During thousands of years it has been developed to its present level of efficiency.

The proletarian revolution has just stepped upon the stage of history. Compared with the organization of ruling class military might, it is new and untried. Nevertheless, in its first serious baptism of fire during the last twenty-five years it has scored a tremendous victory in the Soviet Union and has won notable successes elsewhere in Europe and Asia. No other movement, and no other group of organizations, can, or will, build the structure of a warless world.

At some stage in social history the world will again be warless, as it was at the time of the early food gatherers. Among them peace was local. They were scattered in isolated, tiny groups. Since the world has become unified through trade, transport, and communication, it has been a war world. Throughout the era of civilization men have fought, and written history is a record of organized destruction and mass murder. Exploitation, expansion, and military organization—the root forces of civilization—make war inevitable.

The great revolutions in agriculture, manufacturing, transport, exchange, and communications have remade economic and social life. A socialized, planned, world economy is now an immediate possibility. Such an economy can be established only through the agency of a militant labor movement, whose leaders and members will take advantage of each revolutionary situation in their efforts to replace exploitation and war by a socialized, planned world economy—the basis for a warless world.

20   FASCISM (1933)

THIS 56-PAGE MONOGRAPH was finished in Jamaica, Vermont, a year after Scott and Helen bought their homestead there. The Great Depression had tightened the economic life of the country and that of the Nearings as well. The opportunities for lecturing, teaching, and publication had diminished their livelihood greatly; in Lower East Side New York they burned Scott's old pamphlets to keep warm in winter. They decided it was easier to be poor in the country, and moved to New England.

This year fascism (which Nearing considered an aspect of unleashed capitalism) was in the world news. Hitler became chancellor of Germany; reports of violent Brown Shirts in Germany and Black Shirts in Italy were widespread. In Germany labor unions and political parties other than the Nazi were suppressed.

Nearing wrote this analysis to inform readers about how fascism arose, how its leaders maintained power, and what the social and economic theories behind the movement meant. He considered the study the first to be published.

In 1933 in this country, radical changes occurred. President Franklin D. Roosevelt established a battery of federal agencies to deal with the depressed economy; the Tennessee Valley Authority, the first publicly owned American corporation, was instituted; and the United States went off the gold standard. Human misery was rampant and Congress gave the federal government powers to relieve it. This was the era in which 67,000 homeless children were reported in New York City, according to one study.

The competitive economy of capitalism in its early stages was a happy hunting ground for the small business man. But capitalist economy did not stay competitive. Instead, it passed quickly into the monopoly era.

Cut-throat competition might be the life of trade, but it was the death of profits. Keen business men soon realized that they could keep a surer grip on their affairs and make a larger volume of profit if they consolidated the many small competing enterprises into a few big combines or trusts. Accumulating surpluses drove business-for-profit to establish larger and larger productive units.

The harassed middle class elements in one country after another have adopted programs of action directed in part against the more aggressive phases of trust economy, imperialism and rationalization, but especially against the forces of the proletarian revolution. They were also driven to seek allies, first among the members of the ruling class, and later among the working masses. The fascist movement was organized, financed and supported as the instrument for executing this program.

The major task of those who drew up the fascist program was to find a middle ground between trustification, imperial expansion and rationalization on the right, and a working class revolution on the left. The program may be summed up in four sentences: Unite the propertied and privileged. Smash the proletarian revolution. Organize self-sufficient nations. Establish a strong state.

As the fascists moved toward power, their attacks on the big capitalists grew less severe. The fascist seizure of power was greatly facilitated by the fact that, with minor exceptions, such as Soviet Bavaria and Bolshevik Hungary, much of the economic and political machinery was already in the hands of fascist supporters, who owned property, held important jobs, dominated and in many respects controlled the technical and professional fields. If, as is almost always the case, these key positions include important posts in the army and navy, the war and naval ministries, the post, telegraph and other agencies which are likely to be determining factors in a revolutionary situation, the fascists merely proclaim the possession of that which they already occupy.

Fascism aims to perpetuate such basic institutions as private property; individual enterprise; small scale farming and trading; the church; and the political state. Since most property and privilege are based on one or more of these institutions, the fascists in bidding for power, can promise security to the well-to-do and also to those workers who hold a position above the level of bare subsistence.

Such a situation eases the struggle for power. The fascist movement, through its control of so many strategic positions, expropriates fewer individuals and makes fewer enemies than would the proletarian movement under similar circumstances. Even where it employs direct action, fascism respects and defends most of the existing institutions.

The fascist movement did not begin among the masses, or even among the rank and file of the middle class. Rather it has had its origin in the conspiratorial activities of a few adventurers and soldiers of fortune. Fascists scoff at the voice-of-the-people slogan of the democrats.

Fascism became a political factor in central and western Europe during the years when the wave of proletarian revolution was sweeping through Russia, Germany, Austria-Hungary, and Italy. It grew most rapidly in precisely those countries where the proletarian revolution showed the greatest vigor. There were two reasons for this: first, the menace of revolution drove the propertied and privileged into a united front; and second, the sharper the revolutionary situation, the greater was the need for fascism to take form organizationally and to take action politically.

Fascism is the reaction of the propertied and privileged to the general crisis in capitalist imperialism. War, economic collapse, colonial revolt and the proletarian revolution are all aspects of the general crisis, and in that sense only they are all responsible for fascism. Even were there no working class movement, the propertied and privileged would be compelled to retreat to fascism as the superstructure of capitalist imperialism comes tumbling down about their ears. The suppression of the communist movement does not prevent the rise of fascism. It merely destroys the militant and aggressive leadership of the proletarian revolution.

Fascism and the proletarian revolutionary movement are strongly antagonistic. Fascism builds on private property and profit economy. The proletarian class-conscious wage-workers aim to replace both institutions, by a socialized use economy. The success of one of these movements involves the destruction of the other. The fascist road to power lies through the consolidation of the middle class; cooperation between the unified middle class and the ruling class; the winning over a vacillating working-class elements, and a united attack against the organizations of the proletarian revolution.

Fascist society is built upon profit economy. It contains an owning class and a working class. It accepts exploitation. Despite revolutionary promises, fascist society does not differ essentially from any other phase of profit economy.

Private property, in its more familiar aspects, dominates the economic life of every nation that has moved along the path toward fascism. Italy, having gone farthest in the organization of a fascist society, provides the best illustration of the relation between fascism and private property.

Fascism has drawn its chief support from middle class elements that almost without exception own land, houses, productive tools or other private property forms that represent exploitive power. Since the fascist leaders desire to broaden the social basis for their movement, they have aimed at increasing the number of small property holders and of small business men.

Fascist policy seeks to return to the stage of small-scale, competitive, private economy that preceded the trust movement. Such an economy increases the number of property owners and thus provides a constituency that will fight for the perpetuation of private property forms. Furthermore, small-scale farming, manufacturing and trade are more nearly self-sustaining than are large scale business activities, and they involve a smaller proportion of wage-workers. Hence they fit more satisfactorily into the picture of a self-sufficient economy.

The word *fascism* has been employed to describe the policies of Mussolini in Italy, of Horthy in Hungary, of Rivera in Spain, of Pilsudsky in Poland, and of Hitler in Germany. In its more generalized form the word has been used to designate a movement that is sweeping over central and western Europe and over certain non-European countries. It is now necessary to summarize certain aspects of the fascist movement into five terse generalizations concerning the nature of fascism:

1. Fascism is a movement of the propertied and privileged, who are seeking a way of escape from the destruction that threatens them during the general crisis of capitalism.
2. The movement begins in the middle class, gains allies in the ruling class and working class, and as it grows in power becomes the chief weapon of the propertied and privileged in their survival struggle.
3. Fascism flourishes best in regions where the breakdown of capitalist imperialism is most complete and where property and privilege must fight a life and death battle with the proletarian revolution.
4. The root principle of fascism is local or regional economic self-sufficiency, in a private profit economy. Its chief institutional weapon is a unitary, authoritarian state backed by an equally authoritarian church.
5. Fascism in action rejects the principles of democracy, emphasises the role of social inequality, relies for its efficacy on the autocratic rule of the elite, and establishes institutions and practices that differ fundamentally from those of capitalist imperialism.

Fascism gropes, planlessly. It was not until five years after the seizure of power that the Italian Fascists formulated their Charter of Labor and their Law of Corporations. In the interval, they had organized a nation-wide movement and had consolidated the state power. The present-day fascist movements of Germany and other countries are almost equally without philosophy or definite plans. The propertied and privileged, using the fascist movement to escape from decimation or annihilation, have no clear understanding of the path they should follow. They are merely determined at all hazards and by every necessary means to retain control of their property and privileges.

The necessity for preserving an established institution such as private property, makes the Fascist movement essentially opportunistic. It can have no great ideal. Its driving force is the desire to keep. It is necessarily a narrow, restrictive movement.

Whatever differences may arise over the philosophy of fascism, there can be little question regarding its medium of action. Fascism is working through the self-sufficient corporative state, using national boundary lines as the bulwarks of its power and the limitations on its field of activity. The directors of fascist policy are the elite, who discipline the masses in the interests of the nation. An adequate description would run something like this:

1. Fascism is a movement of the propertied and privileged, initiated by the middle class, and led first by members of the middle class and later by members of the ruling class,
2. who are retreating from the system of capitalist imperialism, rendered untenable by war, economic crisis and colonial revolt,
3. and who at the same time are defending themselves from the threat of proletarian revolution.
4. These elements are trying to barricade themselves behind strong national boundary lines; to exterminate the working-class revolutionary movement, and to provide themselves with the means of existence through a system of self-sufficient economy.

The fascists are leading the western world back from those unworkable forms of imperialism and internationalism which were built beyond the boundary lines of individual states, while wealth and ruling class authority remained centered within national boundaries. The fascists are pursuing this policy as the spokemen for propertied, privileged elements that cannot make use of the advances scored by modern science, and that are willing to wreck the entire social structure rather than surrender their out-worn system of profit economy.

Fascism to the masses means a continued life under a decaying social order, with the insecurity that accompanies chronic unemployment;

with wages cut so low that living standards fall below the level of physical starvation; with war; with the growing corruption of a putrescent social organism. For the masses, especially the proletarian masses, fascism is the way of death.

21   UNITED WORLD (1944)

IN 1926 NEARING FINISHED an outline for this book. During the next ten years he wrote many other books and pamphlets and traveled for research and eyewitness studies of China, Russia, Germany, France, Austria, Spain, Switzerland, Italy, and Great Britain. He saw World War II as inevitable and set out to offer *United World* in reaction.

Originally, the manuscript numbered 800 pages. He could not get it published and, on recommendation, reduced it to half the size. Still, he could not find a publisher. He cut the manuscript further and still the 20 or so publishers who saw it in the next three years rejected it. Finally, in May 1943 after he had arranged to have it privately printed, the Open Road Press, Inc., of Mays Landing, New Jersey, accepted it.

Nearing thought that the only way to break the cycle of world war was to establish a united, federated world. He held that structured cooperation led to peace; competition led to war. The design for this united world reflected the federal structure of the United States in preserving appropriate local autonomy. He called for a radical change of attitude while pointing out that the seeds of this wholesale change had been planted already through the increase of world opinion, world buying and selling, world athletics, world culture, communications, and travel.

The peoples in different countries and on different continents must sink their differences and find a common meeting ground on which they can work together for peace, bread and freedom. No single people or country or continent can hope to win peace for itself. Peace, to be enduring, must be world-wide.

Isolationists propagate the doctrine of peace for one country. They urge defensive armament and the avoidance of entangling relationships or alliances with other nations.

They forget that no modern government considers itself an aggressor. All are defending their vital interests against the actual or threatened aggression of their neighbors.

Much has been said and written about the virtues of competition. Nor can it be denied that competition has been an important stimulant at various times during the evolution of mankind.

But since competition involves war, those who desire peace must find a substitute for competitive struggle. Cooperation is the answer. Competition arouses and stimulates the individual. It is a driving, aggressive force. Cooperation links up the individual with the social group. It provides a pattern for his activities and coordinates his energies with those of his fellows.

The more complex forms of competition undermine and destroy. Business men discovered this after generations of experimentation. Their answer was a form of coordination (monopoly or trust economy) under which competition was banished from one field after another.

While competition has been largely eliminated from the business world, it persists in international relations. The results are so costly and disastrous that some form of coordination must be discovered under which the suicidal losses of modern wars can be avoided.

Cooperation is more difficult than competition. Its ways are less known, its possibilities less explored. Modern man has learned how to compete. His whole training has been directed into competitive channels. Now he must learn to cooperate.

A day may dawn when it will again be necessary to use competition as a stimulus to human endeavor. At the moment, however, peace can be won only through world-wide cooperation in the conquest of nature and the organization of human society.

Those who see and feel the possibilities of world organization are world men. Their ultimate loyalty is world loyalty. Their ultimate form of organization is world organization. They accept and assume the responsibilities of world citizenship under the slogan: "The world is our country."

A world community will not come of itself, any more than the wheat in the fields will make bread of itself. The forces of nature provide the fertility, moisture and sunlight. Human beings must fertilize and cultivate the earth, select the seed, plant it, watch over the crop, harvest it and carry through the many stages that intervene between wheat on the stalk and bread on the table. Historic forces provide the opportunities for a world culture pattern. Human beings must plan and organize the world society and must also see to it that living conditions in that society are more tolerable and inviting than they are in the old social order.

A world commonwealth will not come of itself, but world disorder and disintegration will come of themselves. Indeed, they are here. The world crisis is not the result of a human desire for chaos, but of the failure of human ingenuity and human will to resolve the contradictions and conflicts that have arisen within the old social order. It requires an affirmative act to upset nature's balance and begin the construction of a social environment. After the natural balance has been disturbed, however, it tends constantly to return to its former state of equilibrium, as a stone in a wall tends constantly to fall back to the earth. The breakdown of society today is like the decay of an old wall. It will continue until it is checked by the world builders.

The experience of the British Empire, of the United States of North America, of the Soviet Union, and of other extended groupings of land masses and peoples into effectively functioning units, suggests that the limit of collective action has not yet been reached; that on the contrary, the human beings inhabiting territories covering millions of square miles seem quite as capable of successful and continued collective action as those living within the narrow confines of tribe, village or city. All of these far-flung communities are of course built upon the modern technique of mass commodity production, trade, transport, communication, finance and accounting.

Between the discovery and invention of the technical facilities that make possible planet-wide collective action and the organization of a world community stretches a no-man's-land of social experimentation. After two centuries of technical development and of conflict between the contending forces of localism and worldism, important beginnings have been made in the establishment of a world-wide social pattern.

The technical basis for world economic activity lies in the worldizing of the means of production. Paralleling this worldizing process, economic activity assumes such forms as buying and selling; carrying; banking and investing; insuring; organizing branch planets and agencies; communication, including the dissemination of news; migration; conquest, and exploitation. While no one of these activities has reached world proportions in the sense of being completely diffused over the planet, all are inter-national, in that they include more than one country, and most of them are participated in by individuals and organizations from all of the leading nations and empires.

Buying and selling between the nations is perhaps the most widespread of all forms of planet-wide economic activity. The sum-total of these transactions make up world trade, or, as it is usually called, inter-national trade. Inter-national trade arises directly from specialization and division of labor. It is based on two assumptions: first, that certain goods can be produced at lower costs in one locality than in others; and second, that goods should be produced in low-cost areas and transported to areas less favorably situated.

Improved transport has made it possible for millions to move about the world from one place to another. Improved communication has made it possible for certain culture traits connected with the sciences and the arts to move with even greater facility. Printing and lithography, the postal service, trade journals, news distributing agencies, conferences and conventions have combined to broadcast achievements, discoveries and creations in science, arts, music and literature. The work of Pasteur, Lister, Edison, Weissman, Darwin, Haeckel, Marx, Wagner, Beethoven, Tschaikowsky, Goethe, Whistler and Picasso is world work. Their discoveries, inventions and creations are studied, utilized and appreciated by workers in the same fields in all parts of the planet. The sciences and the arts are built up by human endeavor. Achievements in these fields are human achievements. The tools of science and art—mathematics, physics, chemistry, logic, color and rhythm, are not restricted by frontiers or by language. Discoveries, inventions, productions and creations pass from country to country on their merits. The sciences and the arts are of world import, with only incidental elements of localism clinging about their more detailed and concrete applications. Despite repeated attempts by fanatical nationalists to put national labels on the sciences and arts, the achievements of scientists and artists are primarily human and only incidentally national.

Sport, likewise, leaps easily over national frontiers. Football, tennis, skiing, golf, boxing, wrestling, swimming, skating and the rest have their devotees everywhere. Inter-national sport meets, and particularly the revival of the Olympic games, have made sport an outstanding world activity. World records are made and preserved and world champions are recognized and acclaimed with little reference to nationality, language and the other barriers that help to make political frontiers formidable.

Non-institutionalized activities and institutions are separated by no sharp line. The two are parts of a unified process and merge imperceptibly into each other. Codes of inter-national practice (law) existed for centuries before the organization of the Hague Tribunal or the World Court. Haphazard inter-national postal relations were maintained for many years before the formation of the Universal Postal Union. Numerous attempts have been made to regulate armaments and the arms trade. The world-wide demand for arms limitation raised by the War of 1914, was embodied in a clause of the League Covenant, in the Washington

Treaties of 1921–2 and in the series of arms conferences that culminated in the General Disarmament Conference of 1932. This conference, failing of its purpose, was followed by a new armament race and another general war. The demand for disarmament will be formulated in one conference after another until it institutionalizes itself in a world authority with power to regulate the production and sales of arms. The continuance of world-wide activities leads sooner or later to the establishment of world-wide institutions.

World public opinion can come into its own as a factor in world life only insofar as a world community has been developed. Perhaps the maturity and influence of world opinion is a good yardstick with which to measure the development of world unity and solidarity. The recent growth of world activities and institutions and the world-wide diffusion of information and of ideas have brought into existence a world opinion that is a force with which men must reckon.

World opinion is always present, but it may take a notable event or a crisis to crystallize it. Every general war focuses world opinion. This was noticeable during the wars from 1793 to 1815. It was much more in evidence during the 1914–18 war. The Russian Revolution of 1917 led to a sharp division of world opinion, pro and con. Hundreds of millions watched with deep concern the struggle for Manchuria, the conquest of Abyssinia and the Spanish Civil War. The Czechoslovakian crisis of 1938, the invasion of Poland, the battles of France, Britain and Russia, all aroused and focussed world opinion.

Political news is not alone in providing the stimulus to world opinion. An important sporting event such as a tennis championship, an international yacht race or an Olympic meet is widely reported. A spectacular ocean flight; a sea disaster; flood, fire, storm, earthquake and other catastrophes are announced over the radio, pictured and described.

Extreme nationalists denounce inter-nationalism and plead for the concentration of thought and attention upon national affairs. Their efforts are vain so long as the agencies of communication keep mankind informed as to what is happening across the frontiers. Human beings are curious. They are also sympathetic. They wish to know what their fellows are doing, and in many cases they are anxious to share joys and sorrows, regardless of political frontiers. Easy and quick communication has called into existence a world opinion that those in high places can ignore only at grave costs to themselves and the interests they represent.

The transition from civism to worldism is part of a social process that extends both in time and in space. The entire human race cannot shift from civism to worldism in a moment. The transition, even for the race vanguard, will require a considerable period of time. For the bulk of the race, the process will cover centuries. Indeed, it has already covered centuries if in it are included the all-important technical improvements which provide the framework for a world society.

Nor is it necessary that a particular attempt to establish a world community succeed. History records many efforts to found world empires. While none attained the objective, at the apex of each imperial cycle the idea of an ordered world was generally accepted by those who thought in social terms. The failures of ambitious world-uniters, who tried to do their work before the era of machine technology, should in no wise discourage those moderns who believe in and work for a world community. Every discovery, every invention, every advance in social organization began at some point in history. Before that point was reached, repeated unsuccessful efforts were made to achieve the desired result. Only with a workable confluence of historic circumstance, talent and human will was success possible.

The most complete knowledge concerning the possibility of world organization and the most elaborate and attractive plans for its establishment are of little avail unless and until they are backed by the mass will to change and improve. So long as the masses of mankind are satisfied with the established order and are ready and willing to fight for its preservation, there will be no world society. It is only when the masses have grown dissatisfied and restive that the actual shift of power from the nationists to the worldists will take place. Even then, as the experience of 1917–1933 so abundantly proves, unless the masses are conscious of their purpose to improve the social order and are willing to assume and exercise power, advance may be swallowed up in a wave of reaction.

Worldism is not yet a reality any more than nationism was a reality during the early stages of the founding of the first nation, or than empireism was a reality during the early stages of the founding of the first empire. But the initial steps in the organization of a world community have already been taken and the technical facilities are available for still further advances. Whether the final steps are to be taken during this present period depends upon the success attending the efforts of those who are leading the movement from civism to worldism.

Worldism, as a cultural stage, will be reached when the dominant activities of mankind take place on a world scale. The success of the movement toward a world community is therefore measured by the effectiveness with which the activities, the institutional life, and the thinking and planning of the world can be formulated and maintained at a world level.

World activities, world consciousness and world thinking exist today in the lives of tens of millions of human beings who have families, friends and acquaintances, and who live in cities, states, nations, empires. To all of these social groups they have a sense of loyalty. But they have become aware of a broader loyalty that extends beyond and includes family, city and nation,—loyalty to the human race.

A stable economy of abundance for the world's population can be attained only under the direction of an authority competent to handle world issues. Matters of local concern such as the water supply or the bus service in a city can be dealt with by the community in question. Other matters, such as the distribution of world resources and the handling of world-wide transport are matters of world concern and can be successfully dealt with only through a world administrative apparatus. Matters that are of general world concern cannot be adequately dealt with by localities. The organization of a world authority provides a means of handling those problems that are broader than the jurisdiction of any single locality, people or nation.

A competent world administrative authority or world government will be composed of representatives from such population units as nations, peoples and economic areas. Membership in the world parliament will be open to all groups without distinction of race, color, creed or political outlook. Some may be radical; others conservative. It is not the function of the world administration to insist upon a pre-determined social philosophy, but to transact the world's business in exactly the same way that the Congress of the United States transacts this country's business. Lines of policy will be worked out in the world parliament as in any other body that is responsible for public policy.

Democratic mass control of public policy may be an ultimate goal toward which various regions are moving. But in the immediate future democratic institutions will exist only in their most rudimentary forms. If a functioning world authority is to be constituted, its membership must include the existing units of world life,—whether they be proletarian democracies or plutocratic dictatorships. Peoples are entitled to representation in the world parliament irrespective of the views that they may hold.

The essential economic basis for a world society is access to the resources of nature. Instead of the monopoly of world resources by a few individuals or nations, the oil, iron, coal and water power would be shared in accordance with a ratio determined by the relative requirements of nations and groups. There is no more pressing issue in the world today than resource conservation and distribution.

A world organization will be a complex of lesser organizations, in the same sense that the United States of North America is a complex of states, counties, townships and municipalities. Each of these units has its own organization. Each represents a specialized aspect of American society, and each is, in its internal structure, highly specialized.

The individual who lives in a complex modern society is bound by a variety of social duties and responsibilities to a number of social institutions. He is loyal to his family, his union, his church, his city, state and country. As world organization progresses, the individual must add to his other social relationships, membership in the human race, responsibility for its well-being, and loyalty to a world community.

A world federal administration, with authority to handle matters of general import, would act as a counter-weight to this extreme localism, just as the Federal Government of the United States checked the destructive localism that followed the War of 1776. A central world administrative apparatus would be organized along the following lines:

1. A parliament or legislative body composed of representatives from all states or local units of the federation. The parliament would be elective and would say the final word in all matters of world concern. It would meet from time to time to discuss and formulate policies.
2. An executive committee in constant session, elected by the parliament and small enough to be a working body. This executive group would be divided into committees or commissions,—each responsible for one of the major problems of world administration,—transportation, finance, the allocation of raw materials, migration, boundaries, and controversies between constituent groups. Each committee would employ its experts and technicians and provide itself with a competent staff.
3. A responsible ministry, consisting of representatives from each of the committees or departments into which the executive committee was divided. The ministry would be a steering committee of the executive committee, and would be responsible to it and to the parliament for the day to day conduct of world affairs.
4. A judiciary responsible to the parliament, and authorized to pass on all matters brought to its attention that involved disputes between local groups or between departments of the central world authority. The parliament, like the House of Lords in the British system, would be the court of last resort.

The central administrative authority would deal with those matters that lay outside the jurisdiction of any single member of the federation. Its constituents would be not individual citizens, except in unusual cases, but members of the world federation. Its authority would be exercised over the following general fields:

1. A world plan and world budget, covering economic and administrative needs and relationships.
2. Resources and raw materials; their survey, development and allocation.
3. World utilities including transport, communication and exchange.
4. Migration and travel.
5. Conflicts that might arise in any field between local units of the world federation.

A world federation, securely established and in control of world affairs should be able to stabilize world relations at least as effectively as the Federal Government of the United States has stabilized relations between the states and localities. A world government would not resolve the world's contradictions and antagonisms. On the contrary, differences of interests, misunderstandings, disputes, aggressions, and conflicts would fill the legislative halls of the world capital with clamor, besiege commission hearings and clog the dockets of the world courts in much the same way that they now appear in the government of the United States. Under a world government as under the government of the United States, such differences would be handled by an appeal to law instead of an appeal to arms.

The states, districts and municipalities composing the world organization would maintain administrations corresponding to the functions that each must perform. The imprint of tradition and custom would necessarily appear in these local administrations, particularly if states like Bavaria or Holland were taken whole into the world organization.

Variation in local organization would be no disadvantage. Indeed, it would possess definite advantages in its avoidance of a mechanical uniformity. Experimentation and innovation would be as necessary here as in any other new field of human endeavor, and local groups might well make important contributions by initiating new forms of organization and administration. On the other hand, sufficient uniformity to stabilize central control and direction would of course be necessary. The local administrative apparatus of state, department and municipality would include:

1. A legislative body or parliament, elective and responsible for major policies to the electorate.
2. An executive head or board, responsible to the parliament.
3. A judiciary, also responsible to the parliament.
4. Administrative duties, carried out under the direction of technical boards or commissions.

Local administrative apparatus would not differ, in essentials, from the governments now functioning in many of the municipalities, states, and nations of the western world. Since the days of the Greek city states, human beings have been struggling to effectivize the apparatus of local government. They still have a long way to go, but the best local government machinery is undoubtedly effective enough to give satisfactory results when coordinated into the total structure of a world society.

World crisis and world chaos cannot be successfully handled in the absence of world authority. If the economic, political and social conflicts that are vexing mankind at the moment could be submitted to a competent legislative body for decision and to a competent judiciary for interpretation, more than nine-tenths of the issues could be disposed of without any resort to force, either by the police or the military. As it is, they have led to war. The rational, scientific answer to world crises and world chaos is the organized world community.

22 THE TRAGEDY OF EMPIRE (1945)

NEARING VIEWED HUMANKIND's long history of empire building as the building blocks of war. Nations have lusted after the resources and land of other nations for millennia, and this in turn has led to invasion, destruction, and suppression. He sought to break this cycle by suggesting that nations organize into a world government that would harmonize and share its differences rather than compete for them.

This book explores the history of empires and leads to an outline for a world federation. Nearing analyzes the patterns of empires, from Roman to American, as well as their decay. He warns that the Soviet Union could develop into a similar empire if its primary goal of a cooperative rather than a competitive society should give way to the seduction of power politics.

His emphasis on a beneficient world government springs from the World War II years; the book was published when an estimated 35 million people had been killed in the war, the atomic bomb had been exploded over Hiroshima and Nagasaki, the League of Nations had held its final meeting, and the United Nations had been planned as a confederation, not as a true system of federal government.

The 1789 Constitution provided for a legislature, a judiciary and an executive, each with specified powers. All persons born or naturalized in the United States were declared citizens thereof and of the states in which they resided. The federal government had jurisdiction over matters involving inter-state relations and over matters of general concern to all the states. Matters of concern to each state remained in the hands of the state governments. The Constitution also included a bill of civil rights.

The Constitution of 1789 embodied a series of compromises between the advocates of popular sovereignty and of minority rule; between the advocates of one-man government and of government by parliament; between the advocates of States Rights and of a strong federal authority; between the free labor interests and the slave owning interests; between manufacturing, trading, financial and agricultural interests.

The Confederate North American States in 1789 constituted a mixed community. Their interests were sharply divergent. But it was a question of order or chaos; of hanging together or hanging separately, and they decided to hang together.

Modern world conditions resemble those existing among the North American colonies in many important respects. The world is a mixed community that includes many divergent interests. For centuries the world community has been disputed by political conflict. For three decades it has been devastated by destructive wars. Shall the disruption and devastation continue or shall the world get together under an effective world government?

An effective world government is one having sufficient authority to make and enforce decisions on international issues and on issues involving the general welfare of mankind. A confederation establishes no such central authority. Its members retain their sovereignty as they did under the League of Nations and as they do under the proposed United Nations organization. If the world government is to be effective it must take a federal form: a central government exercising specifically delegated legislative, executive and judicial powers over member nation states whose sovereignty has been sufficiently restricted to permit the central authority to function.

Concretely, a world government, to be effective, must meet certain minimum requirements:

1. A basic agreement embodied in a constitution that is adopted by a world constitutional convention, ratified by the various member states of the world federation, and subject to amendment.
2. Provision for including within its constituent membership all groups of human beings on terms of substantial equality.
3. Authority to make and enforce decisions on matters of international or world-wide concern.
4. Sufficient power to restrain the strongest and to protect the weakest of its member states.

5. Jurisdiction over economic as well as political and administrative fields.
6. The world government must be so representative in character that the groups over which it exercises authority have a voice and vote in the determination of its policy.
7. All individuals living under the jurisdiction of the world government must be citizens of that government, with equal rights under its laws. Those rights must be specified in the world constitution.

Each person who gives serious consideration to the problem will have different ideas as to the minimum requirements for an effective world government. The seven items listed above do not exhaust the subject. They will be modified and perhaps substantially altered before a world constitution is adopted.

Ours is a world community in which international relations have become a commonplace. This is true of trade, travel, migration, diplomacy, war, the exchange of news and scientific information, sport, art, letters.

At the same time it is a mixed community, divided and separated by a network of procedural and institutional barriers that range from language, manners and customs, across the economic fields of capital investment, raw material monopoly, wage differentials and the control of strategic trade centres, to the modern armed state with its cult of patriotism and its political apparatus, designed to protect the vested interests of its nationals against all comers. Some of the world's peoples still live by picking nuts and berries, some by farming, some by digging coal, some by teaching school, some by dealing in stocks and bonds. Most of the world's people cannot read or write in any language; many are literate; a few have excellent technical trainings.

All of the 2,100 million human beings now on the earth have this in common: they want to go on living. Many desire to improve their lives. Multitudes are willing to share the good things with others. This is the common denominator of the human nature about which we hear so much.

Social contacts will continue to unite the world for an indefinite period. Divisive social procedures and institutions will continue to work against world unity. The hundreds of millions who make up the human race will continue their struggle for survival and their efforts to improve and to share.

The same sociological problems that puzzle and frustrate in every complex social situation will continue to puzzle and frustrate the architects and builders of a planet-wide social order:

1. How to keep likenesses and common interests paramount and to subordinate differences and sectional interests.

2. How to keep the forces of cooperation paramount and to subordinate the forces of competition.
3. How to keep the spirit of service paramount and to subordinate predacity and parasitism.

The world is a functioning whole. Planet-wide function must be so directed that it results in the greatest net human advantage. The world order and peace necessary to the fulfilment of that task can be established and maintained by a world government based, at this juncture, upon a world federation.

World federation seems to be the only available alternative to the empire pattern in the world as it is now constituted. Those who argue that it is improbable or impossible are merely asserting that the human race will probably or certainly continue to live in accordance with the empire pattern, based upon the preservation of differences, competition and predacity. Since the present imperial cycle is moving along a declining arc, those who reject the possibility of world federation must accept the inevitability of continued conflict and deepening chaos.

There is no likelihood that either collectivism or decentralism will establish itself as a world-wide pattern at any time in the immediate future. In the century-long interval that must elapse before the world's culture pattern reaches a substantially equal level of development, world federation seems to be the only likely alternative to the conflict and chaos that are the present outstanding characteristics of the empire way of life.

23   THE SOVIET UNION AS
A WORLD POWER (1945)

T HIS BOOK IS a collection of lectures delivered during
1944–45. Nearing was asked frequently to publish
these and other lectures and finally did through The Island
Press, a nonprofit cooperative, and the World Events Committee, an independent socialist organization.

During this time, he and Helen were living a country life
on their Vermont homestead but were far from inactive with
their traveling, lecturing, and writing. In these years the
Nearings evolved a pattern of working their maple sugar
orchard, land, and buildings in the spring and summer before traveling and lecturing during the winter when they
could. (In this excerpt Nearing mentions six visits to the
Soviet Union, some of which occurred before he and Helen
moved to Vermont.)

The book contains much history of the Soviet Union and
its struggle for world recognition and power. What is of
particular interest is Nearing's view of the Russian Revolution as an alternative to the economic and moral turmoil he
saw in the Western society in which he lived. He writes of
this in the preface, which is included here in its entirety.

There is peculiar timeliness in a discussion of the role of the Soviet
Union in world affairs—(1) because the part played, and to be played,
by the Soviet Union is so substantial, (2) because it is so little understood and (3) because it is so frequently misrepresented. I have studied
closely the Russian Revolution and the Soviet Union, have made six
trips to Soviet Russia and have had opportunities to discuss Soviet

policy with many well informed persons. While I have no idea that I can set the reading public right on the much discussed issue of Soviet foreign policy, I hope that I can make some contribution toward brushing away the cobwebs of traditionalism and providing a reasonable viewpoint from which to consider the position of the Soviet Union in the world of today and tomorrow.

Anyone attempting to write or speak on a general subject such as the relations between the Soviet Union and other nations is confronted by three serious difficulties: (1) the bigness and complexity of the matter, (2) its unfamiliarity to an outsider (foreigner) and (3) the great body of prejudices, preconceptions and half-truths that all of us carry about. These difficulties are present in the consideration of many controversial questions, but in the case of the Soviet Union, with its land mass flung across two continents, its conglomeration of cultures, races, peoples and nationalities and its bold attempt to replace an old social system by a new one, the difficulties are magnified and multiplied.

Writers and speakers on the Soviet Union fall into two main classes, those who deal with some technical subject, such as the construction of hydro-electric plants or the handling of tuberculosis, and those who discuss the economic and social structure and policies. The first group has an easy time of it, since it is necessary merely to survey and report; the second group is hampered by personal bias and harassed by special interests.

If there is a wholly unprejudiced report on the Soviet Union, I have never seen it. Some writers, like the Webbs, make an effort at neutrality. I make no such pretense, I am not neutral on the Soviet Union. I have been a partisan of the Russian Revolution since its inception and I am still a partisan of it. Anything I say or write on the subject will necessarily be colored by that partisanship.

Why am I partisan? I am not Russian, nor were any of my ancestors, so far as I know. I am not and never have been in the pay of the Soviet government and, with the exception of two years, 1927–29, I have not been and am not a member of the Communist Party. But I am a student of sociology and I am profoundly convinced that a time has come in the development of social theory and practice when mankind can undertake what Lester F. Ward called "the conscious improvement of society by society".

I have lived my life in an outmoded social order that is tearing itself to pieces in a manner which has proved highly expensive in terms of material wealth, health, life, hopes, aspirations and ideals. As a teacher of social science, I came in contact with the youthful victims of this social death agony and was casting about for some proposal or proposals that would provide a way out for the lost generation.

This search led me through the literature of social reform and social revolution. At the outset I was inclined to believe that the established order could be reformed—that is, preserved in principle and changed only in detail. The economic breakdowns that preceded World War I and then the war itself convinced me that the present social order is unsound in principle and must therefore be radically altered—that is to say, uprooted and replaced.

I was not and am not committed to any particular technique of social revolution. I disagree with Bolshevik theory and practice in a number of important particulars. But, while we in the west swallowed the bitter pill of economic paralysis and war, the Bolsheviks worked out an alternative theory and, at the risk of their lives, tried to put it into practice. Here was a group of people with a passionate belief in an ideal, a willingness to make immense sacrifices in its behalf and wide backing among a sturdy, uncorrupted people.

Had the Zapata brothers in Mexico or Sun Yat-sen and his Chinese followers or Gandhi and his Indian multitudes stepped out with equal boldness, I would have been equally partisan in their behalf. I felt and feel confident that capitalist imperialism has outlived its usefulness. I am convinced that any effort to keep the old carcass alive by the injection of artificial stimulants will result in disillusionment and much unnecessary suffering. I welcome any and every attempt to find a workable substitute.

Soviet Russia to date embodies the most ambitious attempt to find a way out of the world-wide social crisis precipitated by the decay of capitalist imperialism and accentuated by the rush of technological changes and the rapid spread of social science. In the same sense that the years from 1780 to 1840 are known as the era of the French Revolution, the years from 1900 to 1950 will be known in history as the era of the Russian Revolution.

Bolshevism has already profoundly altered the social pattern of this half-century. Its influence will extend far into the future. Anyone who pretends to be well informed on the major social movements of our time must devote serious study to the rise and development of the Soviet Union. Anyone who is concerned for the future of mankind must do his thinking, plan his social strategy and formulate his program of social action only after a careful survey of Soviet experience.

In the field of world politics Soviet influence has been felt ever since the revolution of 1917. During the past five years the Soviet Union has played a leading political role in both Europe and Asia. There is every reason to believe that this role will be enlarged and will extend to the Americas and perhaps to Africa. Under these circumstances the subject of the role of the Soviet Union in world affairs becomes a matter of prime importance for every thinking person.

24 DEMOCRACY IS NOT
ENOUGH (1945)

FOR AN EPIGRAM, Nearing quotes Henry David Thoreau
from *Civil Disobedience* in which he asks whether democracy is the last improvement possible in government.
Thoreau suggests that it is possible to take democracy a step
further toward recognizing and organizing the rights of
man.

In the first chapter, Nearing lists seven presupposed freedoms for a democracy—freedom of body, movement, livelihood, thought, expression, investigation, and association.
Then he builds his case toward the disciplines necessary for
a democracy, the next step in detail that Thoreau proposes
in theory. These disciplines, Nearing asserts, include those
of the body, movement, livelihood, mind, creative expression, truth seeking, and organization. These he maintains
are what citizens of a democracy must give in return for the
freedoms given them.

Government by the many pre-supposes certain freedoms. If the common man is to decide matters of public policy and to take part in
determining the life pattern under which he is to live, he must have:

1. *Body freedom.* Chattel slavery cannot exist in a democracy. Each
   member of a democratic community must own himself.
2. *Freedom of movement.* Serfs and peons are bound both to the land
   and the land owner. In a democracy men may move from place to
   place, subject only to traffic rules which are the same for all.

3. *Livelihood freedom,* either in choices between various means of making a living (free enterprise) or a voice in determining economic policy (industrial democracy).
4. *Freedom of thought,* including an equal opportunity to learn and to seek truth, and a choice in the matter of belief and faith.
5. *Freedom of expression* in speech, writing, drama, the pictorial arts, music.
6. *Freedom of investigation,* inquiry, invention and discovery.
7. *Freedom of association* in private or public meetings and in private or public organizations.

These freedoms measure the extent to which democratic practices are present in any community. If all seven freedoms are enjoyed and exercised without restraint by the adult members of a social group, the term democracy may be justly applied to such a community. If some of the necessary freedoms are absent, the social processes fail in that degree to be democratic.

Woodrow Wilson, campaigning for the presidency in 1912, stated the issue admirably. "The government of the United States in recent years has not been administered by the common people of the United States", he said. "Our government has been for the past few years under the control of great allied corporations with special interests". "The government, which was designed for the people, has got into the hands of bosses and their employers, the special interests". "An invisible empire has been set up above the forms of democracy". (*New Freedom,* pp. 59, 25 and 35.)

Big business was in control of the industrialized democracies. Those who owned the wealth made the vital political and economic decisions. The government was still called democratic, but the job-owning plutocracy was better organized and more vocal than were the common people.

Until the 19th century, the new middle and working class forces hardly existed in their modern form. Up to that time, class rivalries were largely confined to the struggle between the landed aristocracy and the rising business class. In the 19th century, however, the new class elements began to act in their own right. The Paris Commune (1871) marks the historical turning point in the shifting class conflict. From that time onward, the working masses, rather than the business class, took the initiative in European struggles against privilege.

Landed aristocrats drew their power from the ownership of the soil. Business class power resided in the ownership of the job. Both land and job ownership involved the ancient formula: I own—you work—I eat. There was nothing democratic about the formula. It had been the foundation-stone of privilege and arbitrary authority through the ages.

Jack London, Ida Tarbell, Lincoln Steffens, Charles Edward Russell, Ray Stannard Baker, Upton Sinclair and others pointed to the growing menace of plutocratic power and the need for mass action to forestall and check it. Populists, green-backers, free silverists, progressives and socialists campaigned for an entire generation against the menace of predatory wealth.

Democratic masses are slow to move. In the United States and in Western Europe they were enjoying their new-won freedoms to agitate, to organize and to vote. They were being lulled into a sense of false security by the rapidly increasing stream of goods and services with which the new economy was flooding the market. The security was on the surface. People were in for a rude awakening.

Democratic freedoms were not yet deeply rooted. They scarcely penetrated the economic sphere. The profound social changes that had destroyed feudal privileges had at the same time altered the traditional life patterns of the masses. The machine and the city had replaced landlordism and the village, and opened up long vistas before the working masses and the growing middle classes. At the same time they had destroyed village neighborliness, undermined the functions of the family and regimented leisure time as well as work time. Inquiry and invention were releasing new forces that the people did not understand and were quite unprepared to control. Several aspects of this shifting social scene merit special mention.

Applied science released gigantic forces that tore, masterless, through the traditional patterns of society. These forces included a great increase in production, wealth and income; a multiplication of the available supply of commodities; a considerable extension of transportation, communication and information; immense growth in the volume of profit and in the concentration of wealth; a considerable extension of economic relationships beyond the boundaries of localities such as villages, of regions such as river valleys and of national frontiers.

Mass production, plus accumulating profits in the hands of the capitalists, speedily glutted both domestic and foreign markets. Millions of workers and billions of capital stood idle during each business depression.

Ultimately, of course, the social ownership of the means of production will provide the economic basis for freedom. Agriculture will follow merchandizing into the mass production field and collective activity in both production and in the distribution of goods will be the obvious means of preserving individual liberty and popular government.

State ownership of public utilities or other economic agencies provides no guarantee of freedom to the workers who carry on the enterprises. A government department such as the United States Post Office may be as authoritarian in its organization and operation as the Standard

Oil Company or General Motors. Letter carriers and mail clerks—the rank and file of post office workers—do not select their superior officers and do not have a voice in deciding Post Office policy. Like the rank and file in any great enterprise, they do as they are told or take the consequences. Policy is decided and orders come from the top. The Post Office, like General Motors, is run by an oligarchy,—plutocratic in the case of General Motors, statist in the Post Office.

Social ownership of the means of production is a step in the direction of popular control of public affairs only in so far as the principles of popular sovereignty are incorporated in the socially owned enterprise. Recent experience in Germany and elsewhere makes it quite clear that a ruling oligarchy in control of economic, political and propaganda institutions can reduce an entire population to servitude in a phenomenally short period.

The huge, intricate apparatus needed to plan, organize and administer a mass production economy on a continental or a world scale will centre a formidable amount of power in a small ruling clique. Jobs, police, armed forces and propaganda agencies will all be in the same hands. Future experience will decide the issue; but it seems clear that in the long run, efficiency will be secured through central planning, and liberty through decentralization and local autonomy. The issue is not immediate. But those who are striving for the establishment of a democratic community cannot afford to ignore it, since it is in all probability the ultimate economic base for democracy.

People usually think of democracy in connection with politics. In the realm of politics they relate the idea to the expression of public opinion on public questions. Spokesmen for democracy are generally agreed that in the field of politics the citizen must be free to discuss public issues, decide upon policy, and record his choice on election day.

In the light of modern experience this interpretation of democracy is clearly not inclusive enough to meet the most pressing issues that confront the western world. On one hand, the definition of public questions must be broadened to cover essential economic areas such as natural resources and basic industries and such means of social education and control as the cinema and the radio. On the other hand, the people must develop new techniques for selecting and training their public servants. The 19th century ideas of democracy must be extended to embrace economic as well as political freedoms.

There are still other directions in which the generally accepted techniques of democracy are not adequate to meet modern conditions. These pertain to the relationship between rights and duties on one hand and freedoms and disciplines on the other.

Nineteenth century democracy matured in an atmosphere of laissez-faire. "That government governs best which governs least" expressed the viewpoint of the period. Jefferson and other spokesmen for minimal government associated government with tyranny and coercion. They were opposed to both and tried to avoid them by limiting governmental powers to the barest minimum compatible with the performance of elementary governmental functions.

Subsequent experience with the development of large complex social units has forced democratic communities to modify their views of government. Public utilities which provide transportation and communication and the agencies which supply municipal water, light and power are handled, on the whole, more cheaply and efficiently by the public than by private interests. Furthermore, the private vested interests controlling public utilities have been among the chief agencies that have engaged in the corruption of public servants. Needed regulations of health, the safeguarding of food supplies and the control of other economic activities have re-written the formula: "that government governs best which governs least," so that today it reads: "enough government to safeguard and promote public well-being." Governments that represent the interests of owning exploiting classes will continue to fall under the Jeffersonian formula, but communities under popular control will carry on the functions of government in order to provide necessary social services.

Bills of rights, drawn up in 18th and 19th century Europe and America, emphasized rights and freedoms as means of protecting the citizen against the state. Twentieth century constitutions must parallel rights and freedoms with duties and disciplines as one means of linking the citizen with the tasks of government. Freedoms detail the rights of the individual as against the authority of the social group. Disciplines assert the duties of the individual to the social group. If popular government is to survive and enlarge the sphere of its influence it must lay at least as great an emphasis on disciplines as it lays on freedoms.

If democracy is to survive the present social crisis the freedoms listed in the opening chapter of this study must be balanced by an equally weighty group of disciplines. The freedoms are taken for granted by all advocates of democracy. There is no such agreement, however, either upon the place of disciplines in a democratic community or, if the disciplines are to be imposed, upon their character.

The material presented in this chapter is based on the assumption that mass betterment through democratic procedures requires the imposition by the community of certain disciplines upon its citizens. If the common man is to decide matters of public policy he must require of himself and of his fellow citizens:

1. *Body discipline.* Each human being owes it to the community to build his body with the best available materials, to maintain it in health,

to train it to perform necessary tasks and safeguard it against accident. The body is a tool through which each citizen performs his share of socially useful labor, contacts his fellows and cooperates with them in carrying out community projects.

The body is constantly being worn out. Muscles, nerves, bones and other body tissues are rebuilt with the sunshine that reaches the body, with the fresh air that supplies oxygen to the blood stream and with the food that passes through the digestive tract. What householder would use poor materials in rebuilding his home? Body users should be even more careful of the materials used in rebuilding the body.

Health is in part the result of the sunshine, air and food intake, in part the result of exercise, and in part of adaptation to the environment. It is a well-known fact that some peoples enjoy excellent health while other peoples, suffering under no greater handicaps, are beset with diseases. The difference between health and disease is probably determined in great measure by diet. Studies of nutrition are adding to the knowledge of the subject and furnishing at least one answer to the question: What is the path to health?

Householders enjoy a wider margin of safety than body users. If a house is damaged, it may be repaired. If it is destroyed, it may be rebuilt.

No such margin offers itself to the body dweller. While some body damage can be repaired, eyes, hands and feet cannot be replaced. And if the body is severely damaged it is useless as far as its occupant is concerned and may become a charge on the community.

Safeguarding the body is therefore a public duty of first importance. The strength of the community is in direct proportion to the strength of its constituent members. Every citizen owes it to the community to rebuild his body with the best available materials and to safeguard it as effectively as possible.

A body, no matter how sturdy, is next to useless unless it is trained. The mind and the senses are trainable. So are many of the organs. So too are the hands and feet. So are other members of the body.

The citizen who would be useful to his community must, in the first instance, have a sound, disciplined body. This is the least he can offer to his fellows as his contribution toward community well-being.

2. *Disciplined movement.* Movement may be aimless or purposeful. The citizen who moves aimlessly gets nowhere and may very well interfere with others whose movements are of some social consequence. Having won his freedom from the limitations on movement imposed by slavery and serfdom, the citizen of a democracy must first take root somewhere; second, move from his neighborhood only when necessary; third, when he moves, he must obey the traffic rules which he helps to make; and fourth, when he moves, he must be constantly and keenly aware of the rights of his fellows.

Among the bad turns that industrialization has done to modern society, none is worse than the multitudes of unattached individuals and families that it has sent wandering about the planet. Some among these wanderers drift about within the frontiers of their homeland. Others migrate across frontiers. Similar migrations take place from countryside to city.

Wanderers sometimes move with their families. In newly settled centres such as Detroit or in great trade-commerce aggregates like London, numbers of men and women live by themselves. They are attached neither to a family nor to a neighborhood. They are socially footloose.

The first duty of every community is to establish and safeguard social institutions to which all individuals may belong. The most universal of these institutions is the family. Legally a person born in the United States is a citizen of the country. Under ordinary circumstances citizenship in a nation composed of millions of persons is too general a relationship to be of intimate use to the individual. Day to day experiences must be shared with small groups: a family, a club, a trade union. Firmly rooted in an intimate institution, the individual plays his part in society as a member of that group.

A community of unattached individuals would be as lacking in cohesion as pebbles in a bucket. The fabric of community life is made up of the inter-relationship between individuals and social groups and between social groups.

Since individuals serve their communities better by remaining in them than by leaving them, their movements should be confined to the neighborhood except when movement to other communities is desirable or necessary. Social discipline demands rootedness. Would-be migrants assume the burden of proof when they decide to wander.

During the horse and buggy age and before, the slowness of movement confined people, perforce, to the neighborhood. A journey of even fifty miles was a serious undertaking.

Motor vehicles have transformed the situation. A fifty-mile journey in a car is merely an after-supper jaunt. Five hundred miles over the weekend is a commonplace. The wider use of airplanes will multiply this figure by at least three.

Bicycles, autos and planes have made it possible to move, easily and pleasantly, merely for the sake of movement. The entire community being on wheels, relations with a coordinated neighborhood are replaced by relations with an unintegrated traffic jam.

Speedy transportation, legitimately used, is a boon to the whole of humanity. It makes possible a degree of mobility never before achieved and thus enhances the flexibility and multiplies the possible number of human contacts and relationships. It loses its point, however, when it enables teen-aged boys and girls to "go sixty," or when otherwise useful citizens clutter up the crossroads at 3 o'clock Sunday afternoons.

The duty to abide by traffic rules is axiomatic. Social order is not possible on any other basis.

Fourth among the duties related to movement is the necessary awareness of other people's rights. The bicycle "scorcher," riding at twenty miles an hour, raised the issue. The speed maniac in an automobile has made it a matter of life and death. An annual auto death toll in the United States alone of 35,000 makes further comment superfluous.

Drivers of autos and pilots of planes hold in their hands the safety of great numbers of their fellows. They can scarcely do less than limit their movements to necessary journeys and always proceed with reasonable care.

Mechanical transport is not only disruptive of neighborly relations and dangerous to life and limb; it is expensive. The construction and operation of motor vehicles has put a heavy drain on metals, fuels and other essential resources. The maintenance of such vehicles has disorganized many a balanced family budget. Furthermore, a disproportionate amount of each twenty-four hours has gone into aimless and costly movement. Neither the individual nor the community can afford these extravagances.

Freedom of movement is a boon to mankind. Like every other freedom, it must be balanced by the disciplines of rootedness, of restriction to necessary movement, of obedience to traffic regulations and of a keen awareness of the rights of others to move or to remain at home.

3. *Livelihood discipline* requires each able-bodied individual to carry a fair share of the livelihood load. Most natural resources are limited in amount. Goods and services are the result of human labor and are likewise limited in amount. The citizen must not only do his part in producing them, but must make every effort to conserve them.

Private property in both producer and consumer goods is one of the basic institutions of western civilization. Its presence has confused the livelihood problem by introducing the antithesis between the owning (unearned income) class and the working (earned income) class. The presence of these two classes with the resulting class conflict has obscured the basic livelihood issues.

Any community in which the means of production are owned by one group and used by another will in the long run be controlled by the owning group. No matter how often such a community labels itself "democratic," if it tolerates the private ownership of productive tools until their control is thoroughly concentrated, it will inevitably become a plutocratic oligarchy—a community in which essential decisions on public policy are made by the wealth-owning minority.

The essential livelihood duty in a democracy is for every able-bodied adult to do his share in providing the goods and services upon which the well-being of the community depends. If "every man an end, no man a means" is a fundamental principle of democracy, private ownership of the means of production must be terminated; all forms of vested, un-earned income must cease, and each citizen must be expected to per-form a part of the necessary social labor.

The first livelihood discipline is therefore an adequate training in some useful occupation. The community must make the final decision as to what is and what is not useful and will establish the educational facilities requisite to provide training in useful fields.

The second livelihood discipline involves the conservation and care-ful use of natural resources, of producer goods and of consumer goods and services. The moment land and tools cease to be the property of a vested owning class and become "ours," the property of the communi-ty, they must be treated like our schools or parks or commons. They are ours to use, not to abuse.

The third livelihood discipline demands the constructive use of re-sources, tools and consumer goods and services. Periodically, in all class-divided communities, the livelihood apparatus has been diverted from civilian to military use. Instead of aiming at production, it has been aimed at destruction. So long as the profit motive dominated economic relations, this result was inevitable. With the social owner-ship of the means of production the livelihood apparatus can be used only for production.

4. *Mind discipline.* Freedom of thought and of belief carries with it the duty to train the mind to observe, examine, to draw conclusions and verify them, and to subject all beliefs to rigorous analysis. The mind, like the body, may be untrained and flabby or trained to vigorous, flexible usefulness.

Everything that was written in a previous section on the duty to maintain the body in the best of health applies with equal effectiveness to the mind. A healthy mind in a healthy body is a well-worn adage.

Men, like other animals, have bodies; but so far as we know no other animal has achieved a level of mental development comparable with that of human beings. The mind is an invaluable and irreplaceable tool. It should be fed, disciplined and safeguarded with the utmost care.

Mind conservation like body conservation is in part a duty of the individual, in part a community responsibility. Mental energy can be wasted or employed anti-socially. It can also be conserved, and directed into creative and social channels. Community well-being and advance-ment depends upon creative, social thinking.

5. *Creative expression.* Man, more than any other creature, is a creator. The results of his creative endeavor through thousands of years

are embodied in his arts and sciences, in his stabilized food supply, in his protection against the elements, in short, in the social environment that mankind has built out of the natural environment.

Invention, discovery, planning, organization, administration and a huge expenditure of will and energy have established the social environment. Its maintenance and its improvement demand a continuance of the same creative activity.

Human faculties and energies must be stimulated, developed, given opportunity for expression, conserved, safeguarded and dedicated to the highest purposes within the capacity of the individual and the community.

Freedom of expression must be balanced by trained creativeness. The man or woman who feels the urge to discover, invent, organize, administer or labor must take advantage of training and freedom of choice in these directions and through creative expression must add his mite to the sum total of human achievement.

6. *Truth seeking* is the necessary basis for investigation, inquiry, invention and discovery. Human achievement has been built upon the uncovering of new truths.

What is truth? It is in the essence of the manifested world; it is revealed in form, color, function, relationship. The understanding of truth depends upon observation; the accumulation of knowledge; upon critical comparisons; upon flights of imagination or intuition that reveal meanings not heretofore perceived. The pursuit of truth requires the exercise of the highest human faculties.

The search for new truths is arduous and frequently dangerous. Convention, habit, comfort and the vested interests cry out against any unsettlement of the established life pattern. The more militant conservatives are ready to penalize and punish the innovator. Truth seeking is nonetheless the duty of every human being who feels a call to press forward along the frontiers of discovery or to step aside from the beaten paths.

7. *Organization* is an indispensable element in social achievement. Many things can be accompanied by individuals working singly. This is particularly true of creative effort in the arts and sciences. But the translation of newly discovered truth into the function and structure of society requires specialization and cooperative effort.

Banded together under competent leadership, and practicing division of labor, social groups can achieve results wholly beyond the reach of individuals. They can master nature, build cities, transport and communicate, dramatize and orchestrate. But only insofar as the individual remains a disciplined member of the group.

Organization presupposes and imposes discipline. In a free society, the needed discipline may be largely self-imposed. A community built in terms of coercion will impose the disciplines from above. In either case the discipline is indispensable to effective organization.

Irrespective of names, the maintenance of a complex social system is impossible in terms of rights and freedoms alone. Community survival depends, in the first instance, not upon rights-freedoms, but upon duties-disciplines. In the absence of duties and disciplines, there will be no rights and freedoms because there will be no community.

25   THE MAPLE SUGAR BOOK (1950)

T HIS IS THE FIRST of the jointly written works that Helen
  calls "the sweet books." It is a thorough study of the
subject with chapters on the history of sugaring, the right
weather, tools, equipment, and how to make syrup and
sugar. The final chapter, which they titled "A Life as Well
as a Living," delves into some of the thinking about their
homesteading, and is included here.

Originally, we had no intention of going into maple production. On
the contrary, we were unaware that maple offered us an opportunity to
try out the life pattern we had in mind. Broadly, the purposes we had in
mind when we turned our backs on the city and our faces toward the
country might be summed up in this manner:

First, we wanted to control our own source of livelihood. The community had left us no choice in the matter by denying the chief wage
earner of our family group the opportunity to practice his profession—
which is teaching. While we were not anxious to own land, we were
compelled to face the fact that under existing conditions in North America, the renter, share-tenant, or worker was at the mercy of the landlord
or job owner. The weakness of the teacher's position, for example, lay
in the fact that the businessmen who made up the boards of education
and the boards of college trustees could deprive a teacher of his job and
blacklist him in his profession, not on the basis of academic efficiency,
but because of differences in political and social viewpoints. What was
true of teaching was more or less true of any field in which one man
owned or controlled the job on which another depended for his liveli-

234

hood. Under these circumstances we were looking for a source of livelihood that was beyond the reach of the privateers who were operating big
business.

Second, we wanted to get away from the cities, which seemed to us
more and more hectic, disorganized, and disorderly. We had lived in
cities all over the world, and with minor exceptions, the story was the
same everywhere. The city was artificial from top to bottom, imposing
upon its victims a life pattern based upon superficialities and upon an
endless grind of routine that had as its chief purpose the fleecing of the
poor and weak for the profit of the rich and powerful. Furthermore, we
found cities in general squalid and corrupt; ruthless, policemanized
concentration camps in which men and women were persuaded or compelled to spend their lives and in which children were forced to grow up
unaware of any alternative to the wealth-power pattern.

Third, we wanted to get our feet on the earth and to get our hands into
it—to make and keep that incomparably important contact with nature
which balances life at the same time that it cleanses it; rejuvenates it,
and keeps it sane. We also wanted to find a place near a large body of
water—preferably the ocean. This wish we did not realize, in part
because the capital outlay involved in such choice spots was so heavy
that the place could hardly be self-supporting, and in part because
waterside areas were being rapidly converted into stately and select
summer colonies or into miniature Coney Islands.

Fourth, we wanted to live simply, doing as much good as possible to
our fellow humans and fellow beings, and at the same time doing them
as little harm as possible. The negative part of this aim could be fulfilled
anywhere on earth.The positive part made it impossible for us to withdraw to the inaccessible mountains of Guatemala or India or to the
remote Pacific Islands, to which, indeed, we were inclined to go. The
place had to be so located as to enable us to reach other people and to
enable people who so desired to reach us.

Fifth, we wanted to live solvently. That is, we did not want to beg or
borrow or steal, and we did want to produce our living with our hands
and in the closest possible contact with the earth. That meant an annual
budget that would cover a simple but adequate livelihood and show a
surplus rather than a deficit.

Sixth, we wanted, in one sense most important of all, to make a living in about half of our working time—say four or five hours a day—so
that we would be freed from the livelihood problem and enabled to
devote the other half of our time to study, teaching, writing, music,
travel. We had frequently read and heard theoretical advocacies of such
a daily time schedule: four hours for bread labor, four hours for one's
vocation, and four hours for social intercourse, but we had seldom seen
it practiced in our acquisitive society. We have succeeded, better than

we dared to hope, in putting such a formula into practice, but subject to minor modifications. There are times during the year, such as the syrup-making weeks, when we work eight or ten or twelve hours a day. These we balance with at least an equal number of weeks when we do no bread labor whatever. During the balance of the year, we succeed moderately well in carrying out the daily 4-4-4 formula.

Last, we wanted to demonstrate a pattern that might be followed by those who felt with us that self-respect could properly be maintained only at arms' length from the centers of exploitation and only under conditions where the able-bodied individual was doing his share of the necessary social labor at the same time that he was satisfying his own creative urges in his chosen fields of the sciences, the arts, and social intercourse.

That sounds like a big order. It was and is. We spent years in the search for a locale, finally picking on an area in southern Vermont that seemed to come as near as any we had seen to meeting the varied requirements for a place to try out our ideas. The district we selected is in a high valley in the chain of Green Mountains that stretches from the Canadian border southward. "But why not the summerlands of Florida or southern California?" might be asked. We have a theory, which we are not able to defend to our complete satisfaction, that soft climates probably produce soft people and certainly produce parasitic people. Life, like a magnetic field, cannot operate without its positive and its negative poles. A year of all summer is as deadening as a year of all winter would be. A sequence of varied seasons maintains interest by providing the basic ingredient of climatic change. We look forward to winter with as much or perhaps more anticipation than to any other season. But more than that, we enjoy the procession of the seasons across the hills and through the varied activities of our daily lives.

We are located on a side hill of a valley directly facing Stratton Mountain, the highest peak in southern Vermont. The first place we bought required an outlay of $300 cash, and the assumption of an $800 mortgage. It had a farmhouse in poor repair, a good barn, and sixty-five acres of land well stripped of timber, but with plenty of firewood in the wood-lot. That was in 1932. We soon added a much larger piece of land, lumbered over between 1916 and 1919, which we were able to buy for $3 an acre. As things then stood, we decided that by foresting this area, beginning with the cutting of cordwood and going on with logging as the timber matured, we could make our cash income and set up a solvent economy. We began our venture with some minor house repairs, built a stone cabin off in the woods, dug a swimming pool beside it in a brook, established a garden, and got out our firewood.

We had no sooner stabilized our thinking in terms of forestry as a source of cash income than we discovered that we were in the heart of the Vermont maple country. The valley where we had settled contained thousands of sugar maples at all stages of growth from tiny seedlings to mighty trees twelve feet in girth. There were maples on our place. We accepted our destiny, tapped half a dozen trees near the house and made a few gallons of maple syrup on the kitchen stove. We hired out, free of charge, to neighboring farmers, watched their system (or lack of system, as the case might be), and learned while we helped them.

Within a year we were so fortunate as to be able to buy the place next door. It had a fairly good stand of timber and included an old but excellent sugar bush, several buildings in bad repair, and a decrepit sugarhouse. When we bought the place, it was being sugared on shares by a neighboring family. We continued the share arrangement and worked under the guidance of these competent sugar makers for five years.

At the outset we accepted the local pattern in sugar making and followed it implicitly, as though we had been hired hands. We were told what to do—in the typical indirect manner of mountain folk—and to the best of our ability we did it. Our neighbors were patient and we learned as quickly as we were able.

While we took orders, we kept looking for ways to improve the plant and the techniques. As recounted in the pages of this book, we invested a little money and a deal of labor in good tools and housing, improved the bush, and "learned maple" until it now affords a comfortable living, country style, with a minimum of gadgets and a maximum of leisure time to do other work, to study, and to travel.

We have said perhaps enough to show how, in a few years, novices in maple production can turn their energy and ingenuity into a craft that offers scope for imagination and new ideas, and pays sufficient financial returns to provide a simple but adequate living.

We were now turning about half of our annual syrup crop into sugar. Roughly, a gallon of syrup, which sells for three or four dollars, converted into cake sugar will sell for about double, and made into fancy shapes and packs will sell for nearly triple. Our gross sugar sales therefore greatly exceeded our syrup sales and gave us a considerable margin, a part of which was used for capital improvements.

Much of the equipment used by our sugar-making neighbors was primitive and inadequate. We made various improvements and innovations and, by doing much of the work in our spare time, we cut money costs and paid the expenses out of our syrup income.

For instance, our first sugarhouse was completed for $242 cash outlay. At the then retail price of syrup ($1.50 a gallon) this made the building cost about 160 gallons of syrup, or something more than a third of our share of the year's syrup crop. With a little attention the building should last anywhere up to thirty or forty years, and was as completely fireproof as such a building could be. The concrete stack that we later attached to the building cost us $66, making the total cost of the sugar-house not much more than $300.

The woodshed was erected in 1944 at high-price levels for both labor and materials, and cost $167 in cash, or the equivalent of 50 gallons of syrup at the price of syrup that year.

Our second sugarhouse, including its concrete stack and the attached woodshed, cost $457. Compared with the cost of the sugarhouse built in 1935, it seemed excessive. But at 1935 price levels the first sugarhouse, with its stack, cost us 205 gallons of syrup, whereas on the 1946–1947 price levels the new sugarhouse, with stack and woodshed, cost us only 65 gallons of syrup.

Our first evaporator, bought in 1935, cost about $450, which at that time represented the value of 300 gallons of fancy syrup. Our second evaporator, bought in the autumn of 1946, cost around $650, which in terms of 1947 syrup prices (the first season in which the evaporator was used) cost less than 100 gallons of syrup. If we had had a good run of sap in 1947 the new evaporator would have made 100 gallons of syrup in two days. Actually the season was disappointing. However, like all farmers, we look ahead with the slogan, "Things will be better next year."

Furthermore, with the two sugarhouse units and added boiling capacity, we were in a position to take two more people into our enter-prise and virtually assure them a minimum cash income in exchange for about three months work per year.

We have gone into this detail concerning our capital improvements because we want to urge the desirability of: (1) improving a capital plant, instead of letting it deteriorate; (2) using modern methods of accounting, setting aside depreciation and similar funds; and (3) using these funds to replace and, where possible, to improve capital equip-ment as it wears out.

We like to be connected with a solvent enterprise. Still more do we like to have it a bit better equipped at the end of each year than it was at the beginning. We like to look ahead, make plans, try them out, modify them where they prove inadequate, better them, and finally see them embodied in workmanlike, useful, and pleasing forms that are fulfilling their share of a general program. Such developments are particularly satisfying to one who has helped carry the stone, gravel, and sand, mix the concrete, cut the trees, peel and hew the timbers, prepare them, put them in place, lay the roof, put in windows and doors, and install the tools and implements. Those who have not felt the joy of seeing an enterprise pay its way, and improve itself as it goes along, would do well to test out the experience and find out how profoundly satisfying it is to man's urge for growth and betterment. We are convinced that a city family, spending ten thousand dollars on amusement, diversion, and entertainment during a social season, will not get a tithe of the solid satisfaction that we get from an experience that pays us while we have the joy of participating in a productive, creative, going enterprise.

Improvements in capital equipment provide the economic foundations for broadening social equipment. We enjoy seeing our capital plant improving from year to year. We would not be satisfied unless parallel improvements were being made in our social equipment. This is not the place for a detailed description of the changes we have made in our social setup, but we might mention some of them in order to show that our project yields a fuller life as well as a living.

For seven years we stayed on in the rather unsatisfactory wooden farmhouse that we bought when we first went to Vermont. We then selected a site about a quarter of a mile distant for a combination dwelling and work unit, built a stone lumbershed as the first structure in the project, filled it with green lumber straight from the mill, and let it season for a year. Next, we laid out and constructed a road to the new house site. The dwelling, in three units, we constructed over several years. We needed a place to make, pack, and store sugar and house the necessary supplies of boxes and other packing materials essential to such a business. We incorporated such a unit into our plans and made the work place a part of our living place. Four years after we began work on the new house we left the old farmhouse and moved in.

The whole project we built of stone and concrete, using a modified Flagg system of double movable forms. We believe we have demonstrated what Flagg claimed: that people of moderate intelligence, with no particular training, can build satisfactory stone houses easily and cheaply if they take their time, dispense with architects and contractors, and do much of their own work. Suffice it to say that we have a combined stone and concrete dwelling and workshop, equipped with stone floors, hewed timbers, fireplaces, and wood-paneled walls, cool in summer and warm in winter, good to look upon and pleasant to live in. We paid for it as we went, by making and selling syrup and sugar, and going only as fast as we had cash to buy materials. Throughout the entire operation we paid no interest on loans and no fees to architects or contractors.

This is literally a home that sugar built. With the exception of logs, cordwood, maple syrup, and maple sugar, upon which we relied for our cash income, we did not sell anything. Whenever there was a surplus in the garden or on the place we shared it with neighbors or visitors. When the guesthouse was empty, the next comer was welcome to use it. Whoever set foot on the place at mealtime was invited to share what there was on the table. We were trying to combine the techniques of efficient, simple living with the essential social principle: each for all and all for each.

We have our social theories and we expound them whenever we get a chance. We also have our pattern of living. In this book we have by-passed the theories almost entirely and have concentrated our attention on practical economic and social detail dealing with syrup and sugar production. We have done this deliberately because we believe that a solvent, sane life pattern can be set up even under conditions of comparative difficulty and adversity. Furthermore, we believe that this can be done by foresight, determination, and hard work, quite irrespective of the social theories held by the pioneer in these directions.

We have been trying to demonstrate four livelihood propositions in the fifteen years of experimentation and construction that we have put into the Vermont enterprise.

1. A modest subsistence may be secured and all but guaranteed in exchange for approximately half time, devoted to planned, well-organized, co-ordinated labor.
2. The other half of the time (taken off in daily hours or in larger units) is leisure, which may be spent in active outside, or sedentary inside, pursuits.
3. The capital tools of a household economic unit are neither complicated nor unduly expensive, provided they are acquired gradually in exchange for labor and are not based on borrowing, mortgaging, and interest payments.
4. Facilities for the effective use of leisure time and for building up and maintaining satisfactory, co-operative, creative relations with neighbors, friends, and acquaintances may be enlarged at the same time that the productive enterprise is set going.

In short, what we have been developing is a source of livelihood from the earth—from maple, as it happens, for any one of many household crafts would have served the same purpose. It is hardly possible to overemphasize the importance of this relationship with the earth, its rhythms, seasons, and cycles.

It is semi-independent in that a family or small group is able to make its plans, lay out its programs, put them into action, and see them come to fruition, day by day, season by season, year by year, with little or no necessary help or contact with the outside world.

It is social because we have the time and means to share our livelihood and our lives with people outside of our immediate circle. Thus we play our part in setting up a good town, state, nation, and world. We are not isolated in any but a very limited sense of that word.

Life is interesting, full, rewarding. The day is never long enough to finish all of the things that seem worth doing. Each dawn renews the promise of a multitude of opportunities for planning, building, planting, harvesting, improving, sharing, learning. There are difficulties, obstacles, mistakes, setbacks, but never a dull moment.

We think we are rediscovering the secrets that some of our forebears in the Green Mountains knew so well: the secrets of simplicity, adequacy, decency, neighborliness, self-respect, and a never ending attachment to the marvels of the life of nature and of society that we contact on every side and of which we are integral parts.

We have earned from maple and found a means of livelihood. We have also learned from maple. The occupation of sugaring has been a thorough-going education and broadened our contacts with life in its many aspects. The young Thoreau in his Journal wrote, "Had a dispute with father about the *use* of my making this sugar. . . . He said it took me from my studies. I said I made it my study and felt as if I had been to a university." A complete syrup and sugar maker comprises in himself a woodcutter, a forester, a botanist, an ecologist, a meteorologist, an agronomist, a chemist, a cook, an economist, and a merchant. Sugaring is an art, an education, and a maintenance. "May it long be the mission of the maple thus to sweeten the cup of life."

26 ECONOMICS FOR THE POWER AGE (1952)

IN THE FOREWORD, Nearing says that academic economists will be dissatisfied with this book because it contains no sections on utility, value, money, rent, interest, or profits. "Marxians will be displeased," he continues, "because it lays no emphasis on the labor theory of value. That is as it should be. In this country academic economists and Marxians talk and write as though the steam engine were still the chief source of mechanical power and as though we lived in an economy of scarcity."

He lists 10 "First Principles of Economics" at the opening of the book and then discusses each one at length. The seventh principle, "The economy should be owned by those who use it," a recurring theme of Nearing, is included partially here.

The year of publication dated the beginning of the H-bomb era (the United States first tested one in the Pacific) and Great Britain announced it had developed its own atomic bomb. The Korean War continued, the federal government seized steel mills to avert a strike (the action was later declared illegal by the Supreme Court), President Eisenhower was elected president, Charlie Chaplin was forced into exile for his political opinions. In Harborside, Maine, Helen and Scott incorporated the Social Science Institute to help obviate any future "frame-up" by the government to intimidate them.

First Principles of Economics

Principle 1. Individual and social life are conditioned by subsistence.
Principle 2. All subsistence originates with nature.
Principle 3. Western man utilizes nature by means of science and technology.
Principle 4. Subsistence is the result of productive effort and, increasingly, of group effort.
Principle 5. Subsistence should be apportioned according to need.
Principle 6. The less overhead, the better.
Principle 7. The economy should be owned by those who use it.
Principle 8. The economy should furnish a stable, secure subsistence.
Principle 9. The economy must assure justice and provide incentive that will lead the individual and the social group to assume and carry a full share of responsibility for the production and apportionment of livelihood.
Principle 10. The economy should afford opportunity for the growth and development of successive human generations.

For our purposes, the objects of ownership may be divided into four general groups: (1) fellow creatures; (2) nature; (3) the social environment; and (4) the product of human ingenuity and creativity. Fellow creatures are living beings whose endowments of mass, energy, creativity, will, and purpose make them useful to the potential owner. They may be fellow humans, domesticated animals, or wild animals, captured and held in a state of involuntary servitude by their owners. Nature is a broad term which includes all factors and forces not shaped or determined by man—resources of energy, fertility, topography, water, air, and sunlight. Among natural resources the land has been considered an object of ownership; the high seas theoretically may be used by all comers. Air and sunshine are classed as free goods, available to all in proportion to need. The social environment includes the modifications which man has made in nature; the uses to which man has put nature; the capital equipment embodied in buildings, implements, transport facilities; and the results of collective thinking represented by the arts and sciences. The fourth group contains the results of one man's activity—the music of a composer, the canvasses of a painter, the books of a philosopher, the inventions of an engineer, the discoveries of a scientist, the output of a craftsman or of a working team of craftsmen.

Property titles to fellow creatures may be absolute or limited. Absolute titles carry with them the right of the owner to end the life of the owned. Among certain peoples, the head of a household may put to death wives, children, and servants. The ownership of chattel slaves usually carries the power of life and death. Owners of horses, cattle, sheep, dogs, and other domestic animals may terminate their lives.

Fellow creatures afford various advantages to their owners. (1) Their bodies and bodily functions may provide food. (2) Their energy may supplant the energy of the owner and serve his purposes. (3) They may reproduce themselves and thus provide a continuous supply of food and energy for their masters. (4) Fellow creatures may be turned into cannon fodder. (5) Fellow creatures may provide diversion and amusement. Fellow creatures are used by modern man in all of these ways. The carcasses of animals form one of the chief food sources of the Western world. Bodily secretions, such as milk from mammals and honey from bees, are even more extensively used. Horses and other quadrupeds are bred and trained as burden bearers and draft animals. Labor power is sold and bought in the open market, as a part of the regular procedure of a wage-labor economy. Owners breed domestic animals to suit their purposes. Genetics is a recognized science, whose aim is to enable the owner to turn out types of fellow creatures better adapted to serve the ends that he has in view.

Modern states have developed a novel variant of fellow-creature ownership in the form of conscription for military service and for compulsory labor. The war-making epoch which began in 1910 extended the area of compulsory military service and transferred industrial conscription from the colonies to the centers of Western civilization.

Military and industrial conscription are based on the assumption that the state may dispose of the individual citizen as it sees fit. It owns, not the body of the citizen, but his loyalty. Those who make state policy and who play the game of power politics have at their disposal the property of the nation and the services of its people. Both may be expended, at the behest of the policy makers, until the property is destroyed and the lives of the citizens are snuffed out.

Custom, law, and the agencies for shaping public opinion not only sanction these procedures and justify them in terms of ethics and morals, but the leaders who implement such policies have their statues set up in the public squares and the perpetrators of the policies are loaded with decorations and honors. Since the development of mechanized warfare, the living creatures who perish in war are chiefly human beings.

In our final category, the use of fellow creatures for diversion and amusement, the victims are usually animals, birds, and fish. A few of these creatures are penned and caged, to be stared at and poked by the idle and curious. The great majority are hunted, tortured, and murdered for sport. Each year, throughout the civilized world, tens of millions of men and women, equipped with rod and gun and served by dogs, horses, and elephants, spend their leisure hooking and spearing fish and blowing the lives out of animals and birds. Next to war, "the sport of kings and king of sports," fishing and hunting are relied upon by civilized men to offset the tedium and strain of daily routine. Daily routine is monotonous and exacting; of that there can be no question. But by what right do the victims of routine recoup themselves at the expense of innocent and for the most part defenseless and helpless fellow creatures? The answer is simple—by the right of the strong to coerce, exploit and, when they wish, to destroy the weak. This is the right behind every phase of the ownership and use of fellow creatures to serve the purposes of those who occupy positions of authority and mastery.

Ownership, coercion, exploitation, and extermination of fellow creatures pervades the entire structure of contemporary society. While forms and practices vary, the essential feature of the procedure is the sacrifice of the interests and purposes of the victim to the interests and purposes of the owner and master.

We turn, now, from the ownership of fellow creatures to the ownership of the earth. Men may, and frequently do, breed the fellow humans and fellow creatures which they later utilize for food, for services, for power, and for sport. The earth is in a different category. No man and no group of men made the earth, with its fertility, its water supply, its atmosphere, and its quota of sunlight and starshine. The natural environment existed before man arrived on the scene. The earth is a common heritage of various forms of life, including human beings. Each creature is born upon its bosom. Earth is the common mother of man and of his fellows.

Anyone fortunate enough to own fertile, useful acres therefore occupies a privileged position. He can either cultivate the land, use what he requires and exchange the surplus for the surpluses of other producers, or he can permit others to use his land in return for rent payments. In this second case the landowner is able to say to the land user: "You may farm my land, provided you give me a share of the product." By this device of renting out land, the landowner may live without work on the proceeds of the tenant's labor.

A community which aims at the provision of equal opportunity for its members must treat the earth as common property. Several accepted practices conform to this requirement. The right of eminent domain is all but universally recognized. Under it, community need may lead to the requisitioning of a segment of the earth, with or without the consent of the owner and with or without compensation. The law has embodied this practice in the theory of dual ownership. Each piece of land has two titles, that held by the state and that held by the citizen. At any time, on the plea of public safety and well-being, the state may assert its title, take the property, and let the private owner shift for himself as best he can.

The principle of dual sovereignty and eminent domain places the interests of the community above those of the individual owner. Under this principle the earth and its resources may be declared the common heritage of mankind to be owned, utilized, and administered in the interest of the community rather than of the private property owner.

We come now to the third subject of ownership, the social environment. We have written of the ownership of fellow creatures and of the earth. The social environment presents peculiar ownership problems.

The social environment is man made, the product of past and present human ingenuity and effort. Productive techniques; methods of communication; institutions of government and social administration; the arts, sciences, and philosophies proceed from human imagination, ingenuity, energy, and will. Beset by the rigors of nature and in response to his concepts of need and want, man has built up the complicated fabric of practices, techniques, formulas, and ideas to which we apply the name "social environment."

Both in space and in time the social environment is being added to and subtracted from ceaselessly by discovery and invention, by diffusion, by supercession, and by abolition. To this process of culture modification, individual humans contribute minutely, while humanity in the aggregate is the chief artificer.

Large sections of the social environment are communally owned and communally shared. This is true of public buildings, highways, and public educational facilities. The extent of communal ownership and direction is greater in commercial cities than in the countryside, but it develops wherever technology advances.

Like the earth, therefore, the social environment is collective in its origin and its function. It has been built up by successive generations over periods of time which are more extensive than the life span of single human beings. Numbers of individuals in each generation have helped to construct and to modify the social environment. The advantages and disadvantages of the culture pattern have been shared by the members of the culture group. The social environment is produced by the social group and used by the group. While individuals make contributions to it and derive benefits from it, the social environment is an expression of the group rather than of the individual.

Following the principle that an economy should be owned by those who use it, those aspects of the social environment which are related to the livelihood process should be the common property of groups which have produced them and which depend upon them for survival and improvement.

Thus far, in our analysis of the subjects of ownership, we have dealt with three areas—fellow creatures, the earth, and the social environment. In each case we have concluded that in terms of both origin and use, the ownership should be vested in the social group rather than the individual. There remains, among the subjects of ownership, the extensive category of personalia, or items of personal use.

In terms of ownership and use, personalia may be divided into those items which are common to the family or household and those which are more strictly personal. House and lot, household furniture, tools, implements, and supplies are usually the legal property of the head of the family. In usage, however, they are the common property of the group, and become personal only when they are in actual use. "My towel," for example, is taken from the common store, used by me for a time, and then returned to the common store. Clothing is largely personal. Food does not become personal until it leaves the common source of supply and is placed on a piece of household crockery before the individual who is to consume it.

Consumer goods, after they leave the workshop, garden, warehouse, or store, are in the main the property of a small social group. They become strictly personal in use terms, only at the point of consumption.

While there are a few consumer goods, chiefly items of clothing and personal adornment, which are essentially individual and personal, durable consumer goods like durable producer goods are essentially social in character. They are used by a group and for the advantage of the group. They are "ours for us" rather than "mine for me."

We have now reached the fourth item mentioned in the second section of this chapter—ownership of the products of human ingenuity and creativity. These products cover a wide range, from the output of a self-sufficient household, through the various fields of mechanized agriculture, industry, transportation, and commerce to the arts, sciences, and philosophies. They extend from unleavened bread, baked on a warm hearth, to the abstract ideas of a mathematical philosopher.

There can be no question as to the great variety and vast quantity of artifacts, formulas, and ideas turned out in the past and present by human effort. This output involved conceptions, plans, techniques of execution, organization, direction, will, determination, and persistence. Why have human beings put time and energy into productive effort and built up the elaborate social environment in which they live? The answer most commonly given and accepted in the West is that men have suffered the pangs of creation and endured the labor of production because of the incentive provided by ownership. Men agonized, suffered, and struggled in order to possess necessaries, comforts, conveniences, superfluities.

There can be no question that in an acquisitive society, like that now prevailing in the United States, the urge to have and to hold is one of the major incentives to effort. If incentive to sustained effort is of primary importance in an economy, certainly the possibility of getting and keeping large quantities of a variety of commodities has been a potent incentive in the Western world.

Acquisition, as an urge to human action, is doubtless based upon certain characteristics born into members of the human race. But the absence of this urge in certain primitive communities, side by side with its omnipresence in the industrialized areas of the planet lend strong support to the contention that the present-day drive to get and keep, which is so outstanding in the West, is the result, not of forces inherent in human nature, but of social pressures, skillfully and ceaselessly applied by seekers after profit and power.

These speculations concerning the origin of the acquisitive urge among moderns is of historical interest. Its answer will furnish guidance for the future. The immediate question, however, is of a different nature, namely, what has the social emphasis on acquisition as a way of life done to human beings and to the communities in which they live? Let us attempt a brief answer to this question, first for individuals and then for the community, approaching the matter from the standpoint of livelihood.

Individuals, in an acquisitive, mass production culture (a) devote a large portion of their adult years to uncongenial, sterile, and often to destructive occupational activities in order that they may get the income necessary to satisfy artificially created wants. (b) They clutter up their lives with a quantity and variety of commodities which, on the whole, are cheaply made, unnecessary, unbeautiful, and in the case of processed food unhealthful. (c) They compensate for the uncongeniality of their work by leaving it as soon as possible each day, staying away from it over long week ends, increasing the number and length of holidays, and consuming habit-forming drugs to lower tensions and forget their troubles. (d) They are lured into cities, and once there are held like flies on sticky paper, by habit, poverty, and inertia. (d) They live in cities under high tension, overstimulated by proximity to other individuals, by sights and sounds, by constant movement, shift, and change. (f) They learn and practice the principle "every one for himself and the devil take those who fall behind." Thus they live their adult lives, caught on the horns of a frightful dilemma. Their ideals and ethical standards demand fraternity and neighborliness while in practice each is engaged in a perpetual struggle to get the better of his neighbor. This conflict between theory and practice confuses, dismays, frustrates, and finally paralyzes the individual by turning him into an embittered opportunist, cynic, and pessimist.

Acquisitive, mass production communities (a) concentrate wealth, and therefore power, in the hands of the greedy; (b) follow policies which are formulated by acquisitors; (c) exhaust their natural resources by converting them into nonessentials; (d) build a culture pattern around the principle that human happiness and well-being depend upon the abundance and variety of possessions; (e) sanction and encourage a competitive struggle for wealth and power, waged between individuals, between private social groups, and between governments and nations. This competitive struggle leads, on one hand, through accumulations of wealth and income, to economic unbalance, depression, deficit spending, inflation, and bankruptcy, and on the other hand, through artificially stimulated loyalties and rivalries to economic conflict, wars, destruction, and eventual extermination. While the acquisitive community pattern is being wrecked by competitive struggle, it is undermined by internal disintegration due to excessive mobility in the population and the overemphasis on acquisition. Mobility by breaking up families and neighborhoods weakens the basic building units of the social structure. Greed leads to corruption in the public service and to an emphasis upon individual enrichment at the expense of community well-being.

Perhaps the whole position may be summed up in a sentence. An acquisitive competitive social pattern produces unhappy individuals and unstable, self-liquidating communities. Such a conclusion does not mean that Proudhon was right when he wrote: Ownership is theft. Ownership has its uses, for individuals as well as for communities. At the same time antisocial uses of ownership restrict livelihood, develop inequality and undermine the entire social structure.

Ownership in a rationally organized economy will be partly individual and partly social. This formula holds for all economies, which differ only as to the relative proportions of the economy which are owned individually and socially.

Those aspects of the economy which are technically integrated and therefore inseparable into autonomous units should be socially owned and administered. A highway or a telephone network is integral and cannot be divided into separate useful parts. A local strip of highway is all but useless. A single telephone instrument is a museum piece. If they are to give maximum service, highways and telephone systems must be group enterprises, jointly owned and managed for communal use and advantage.

Social ownership varies in character from a voluntary group of consumers holding equal shares in a co-operative store; a nonprofit corporation like a university, owning its buildings; a business corporation, owned by stockholders; a municipality owning its schools, parks, and hospitals; and a state government owning and operating highways, power plants, railways, mines, and factories. In each of these instances the enterprise is essentially social rather than individual in nature. In each case the enterprise reaches its maximum usefulness through group participation in ownership and use.

Individual ownership continues, even in the most collective economies. Its basic formula: "It is mine because I need it." The need is personal. With personal need goes personal ownership. This formula applies to food, shelter, clothing, and other necessities. The wheat in the bread, the lumber in the house, and the cotton in the clothing may have come from a collective or state farm, and have been supplied through a co-operative store. At a certain point, however, these forms of group property lose their collective character and minister directly to the needs of an individual. At that point they become individual property. They cease to be "ours" and become "mine" because they supply my personal need.

Goods and services which the consumer needs vary in character with the individual. First, there are the simple necessities of physical survival. Second, there are the goods and services which custom, social pressures, and habit make desirable or essential. Third, there are the goods and services which add to personal efficiency, convenience, and comfort. Fourth, there are the goods and services which meet the demands of personal whim or vanity or which add to prestige. Among these goods and services some, such as food, are consumed at one sitting. Others such as houses, clothing, and labor-saving devices are used on more than one occasion. To all of these the same rule applies. If they meet the need of an individual and are consumed by an individual, they are the property of the individual who consumes them. Thinking in these terms, it is clear that the principle of individual property will become dominant at some point in the process of converting nature's stores into the goods and services which individual human beings consume.

There is a second formula which justifies individual ownership: "It is mine because I produced it." Especially in a use economy there are goods and services which are made available to the individual as a result of his own efforts. Food gatherers pick berries and fruits; woodsmen cut wood for fuel; cultivators prepare the soil, sow the seed, and harvest crops; craftsmen convert wood, stone, clay, and fibers into implements, and use the products of their own labor. In most instances the members of a tribe or household work together on such projects, but there are cases, in preurban communities, in which the individual produces commodities and consumes them.

A third justification for individual property ownership: "It is mine because I have the power to command the labor of others," lies at the basis of the exploitation of man by man. One man holds property titles, whether to land or capital. Another uses the land, paying rent (or interest) for the privilege. The job owner may therefore live, without labor, upon the unearned income derived from his job ownership. Property owners are not asked how they acquired their titles. The fact of their possession is a sufficient justification to allow them to live without labor on the labor of others.

The position of the job owner is secured by custom and law. He holds title to land, capital goods, patents, franchises, monopolies. Whether he gained possession of the titles by hard labor, double-dealing, fraud, exploitation, or inheritance is not made a subject of inquiry. Ownership provides him with a source of unearned income.

Wherever such a claim is recognized, the foundation is laid for special privilege. Resulting inequalities in wealth and income, coupled with the principle of inheritance lead to class distinctions and the ultimate division of the community into rival groups. Since no rationally organized community can accept such a possibility, it must reject all those forms of private ownership which threaten to establish division, conflict, and disruption.

Individual enterprise and individual ownership have a place in an integrated, complex economy, dependent upon an advanced technology. But it is a minor place. If such a community is to survive, group ownership and group enterprise must dominate and direct the economy.

An integrated, urban, technically based economy is, of necessity, a group economy. Capital is secured not from an individual, but from a group. Labor is performed by a group. A group of consumers utilizes the product. In no sense, except a legalistic one, is such an economy personal or individual. Its structure and its function are unquestionably collective.

Therefore, the economy must be regarded as a public enterprise rather than a private one. The trend in this direction is unmistakable. Corporate (group) ownership and management by a group of business executives have already replaced the individual capitalist and the individual entrepreneur.

If the economy is collective in fact the group which depends upon it for a livelihood faces a simple alternative. Either private ownership and direction will dominate the economy and therefore leave the community at the mercy of greedy profit seekers, or the economy will be regarded as one aspect of communal life, owned collectively and managed, like every other form of public business, by representatives of the collectivity and in the collective interest.

Ownership is a factor of prime importance in any economy. The guiding principle in determining ownership is axiomatic. The economy must be owned by those who need its products and by those who are associated with it, either as producers or consumers.

Pretechnical economy based on hunting and fishing, animal husbandry and agriculture provided livelihood for such self-contained population units as enlarged households, tribes, and villages. It functioned, therefore, locally and on a use basis of self-sufficiency.

Since each local unit was self-sufficient, need, production, consumption, and ownership were limited by the area of the household, the tribe, and the village. In all of these social groups there were large and often predominant segments of collective or group ownership.

Economics relying upon mass production concentrated around towns and cities. They draw their raw materials and food supplies from widely scattered parts of the planet and market their output over equally wide areas. They are not local in scope, but international or planet-wide in their relationships. Hence the area of ownership must be enlarged to meet the enlarged area of economic function.

We are all familiar with ownership by persons, tribes, villages, cities, and nations. The conception "property of mankind" or "owned by the human family" is less usual. It is made inevitable by the development of planet-wide economic function.

When we say that in the era which is dawning, various aspects of the economy such as natural resources, means of transport, and communication, the facilities for exchange and the like will be communally owned (or collectively owned), it is necessary to add that the community or collectivity in question, in certain instances, will be the human family or the world community. Under such circumstances the word ownership will be associated with groups from households to humanity. Such an outcome is made inevitable by the structure and function of present-day technology.

Voluntary groups such as co-operatives and clubs organized to carry on certain social activities will own small segments of the economy. Likewise there will be individual ownership of the commodities and capital goods which provide for personal needs. The bulk of ownership will, however, be collective in the sense that it is vested in official bodies, delegated or directed to conduct the public business of the community.

27 LIVING THE GOOD LIFE (1954)

T HIS IS THE BOOK that drew thousands of visitors to
Helen and Scott's Forest Farm in Vermont and Maine.
The original few curious guests grew into multitudes when
descriptions of the Nearing way of living and working,
based on the book, were printed in magazine and newspaper
articles. The Nearing's efficient, methodical life, their respect for land and organic gardening, their vegetarian diet,
their concern for the welfare of the world appealed as a
better lifestyle.

Originally, the book was to be a larger work. They showed
the manuscript to their friend and writer Pearl Buck, who
saw two books in it. She suggested that one focus on the
practicality of living the good life and the other on the more
abstract side of it. The Nearings took the advice and Scott
then published his side of it under the title *Man's Search for
the Good Life*.

Reception of the book was modest at first publication, but
the Nearings' reputation for homesteading spread along with
the disaffection young people had with the general American society of the late 1960s and early 1970s. The reissue of
the book in 1970 met this disaffection head-on, turning the
book into a counterculture bestseller and source of inspiration for millions of people. The Nearings became the grand-
parents of the back-to-the-land and environmental move-

ments. Excerpts from the preface here tells some of their
rationale for homesteading.

We might have followed the example of many of our compatriots,
moved to Paris, Mexico or Paraguay, and allowed the United States to
go its chosen way to destruction. We could not accept this alternative
because our sense of responsibility as teachers, and as members of the
human race, compelled us to do what we could (1) to help our fellow
citizens understand the complex and rapidly maturing situation; (2) to
assist in building up a psychological and political resistance to the
plutocratic military oligarchy that was sweeping into power in North
America; (3) to share in salvaging what was still usable from the
wreckage of the decaying social order in North America and western
Europe; (4) to have a part in formulating the principles and practices of
an alternative social system, while meanwhile (5) demonstrating one
possibility of living sanely in a troubled world. The ideal answer to this
problem seemed to be an independent economy which would require
only a small capital outlay, could operate with low overhead costs,
would yield a modest living in exchange for half-time work, and therefore would leave half of the year for research, reading, writing and
speaking. We decided these tasks could better be performed from a
Vermont valley than from a large city or from some point outside the
United States. As it turned out, we saved enough time and energy from
the bread labor and the association required by our Vermont experiment
to take an active though minor part in United States adult education and
in the shaping of public opinion, at the same time that we were living
what we regarded as a self-respecting, decent, simple life.

We had tried living in several cities, at home and abroad. In varying
degrees we met the same obstacles to a simple, quiet life,—complexity,
tension, strain, artificiality, and heavy overhead costs. These costs were
payable only in cash, which had to be earned under conditions imposed
upon one by the city,—for its benefit and advantage. Even if cash
income had been of no concern to us, we were convinced that it was
virtually impossible to counter city pressures and preserve physical
health, mental balance and social sanity through long periods of city
dwelling. After careful consideration we decided that we could live a
saner, quieter, more worthwhile life in the country than in any urban or
suburban center.

We left the city with three objectives in mind. *The first was economic.* We sought to make a depression-free living, as independent as
possible of the commodity and labor markets, which could not be interfered with by employers, whether businessmen, politicians or educational administrators. *Our second aim was hygienic.* We wanted to

maintain and improve our health. We knew that the pressures of city life were exacting, and we sought a simple basis of well-being where contact with the earth, and home-grown organic food, would play a large part. *Our third objective was social and ethical.* We desired to liberate and dissociate ourselves, as much as possible, from the cruder forms of exploitation: the plunder of the planet; the slavery of man and beast; the slaughter of men in war, and of animals for food.

We were against the accumulation of profit and unearned income by non-producers, and we wanted to make our living with our own hands, yet with time and leisure for avocational pursuits. We wanted to replace regimentation and coercion with respect for life. Instead of exploitation, we wanted a use economy. Simplicity should take the place of multiplicity, complexity and confusion. Instead of the hectic mad rush of busyness we intended a quiet pace, with time to wonder, ponder and observe. We hoped to replace worry, fear and hate with serenity, purpose and at-one-ness.

After twenty years of experience, some of it satisfactory and some of it quite the reverse, we are able to report that:

1. A piece of eroded, depleted mountain land was restored to fertility, and produced fine crops of high quality vegetables, fruits and flowers.
2. A farm economy was conducted successfully without the use of animals or animal products or chemicalized fertilizers.
3. A subsistence homestead was established, paying its own way and yielding a modest but adequate surplus. About three-quarters of the goods and services we consumed were the direct result of our own efforts. Thus we made ourselves independent of the labor market and largely independent of the commodity markets. In short, we had an economic unit which depression could affect but little and which could survive the gradual dissolution of United States economy.
4. A successful small-scale business enterprise was organized and operated, from which wagery was virtually eliminated.
5. Health was maintained at a level upon which we neither saw nor needed a doctor for the two decades.
6. The complexities of city existence were replaced by a fairly simple life pattern.
7. We were able to organize our work time so that six months of bread labor each year gave us six months of leisure, for research, travelling, writing, speaking and teaching.
8. In addition, we kept open house, fed, lodged, and visited with hundreds of people, who stayed with us for days or weeks, or much longer.

We have not solved the problem of living. Far from it. But our experience convinces us that no family group possessing a normal share of vigor, energy, purpose, imagination and determination need continue to wear the yoke of a competitive, acquisitive, predatory culture. Unless vigilante mobs or the police interfere, the family can live with nature, make themselves a living that will preserve and enhance their efficiency, and give them leisure in which they can do their bit to make the world a better place.

28 TO PROMOTE THE
GENERAL WELFARE (1956)

T HIS PAMPHLET TAKES the "General Welfare" clause of
   the "Preamble" of the U.S. Constitution for its central
theme, a phrase that Nearing argues has preeminent priority.

Halfway through the pamphlet, he cites what he calls the
"cold civil war" of the House Un-American Activities
Committee and Senator Joseph R. McCarthy's pursuit of
Communists. McCarthy told President Truman publicly in
1950 that the State Department was filled with Communists
and Communist sympathizers. The campaign developed
momentum in the next few years. By 1954 nationally tele-
vised hearings were conducted like dictatorial trials to prove
that Communists had infiltrated the U.S. Army and important industries, such as the General Electric plant in Lynn,
Massachusetts, that Nearing refers to here. McCarthy was
censored by his Congressional colleagues; he died in 1957.

"We the people of the United States, in order to . . . promote the
general welfare, . . . do ordain and establish this Constitution for the
United States of North America." This statement is embedded in the
Preamble to the United States Constitution. It is known as The General
Welfare Clause.

Six purposes are set forth in the Preamble as the underlying objectives which led to the writing of the Constitution. "To promote the
general welfare" is one of the six. The authors of the Constitution laid
down a proposition which was widely accepted among the political
scientists and popular leaders of the day: Human beings must work
together to promote the general welfare.

During the years since the Constitution was written, the General Welfare Clause has been given less attention than those parts of the constitution concerned with special interests, such as the provision that private property may not be taken for public uses without just compensation. There has been a tendency, particularly since the rise of the big corporations, to pass up the general welfare with a cursory glance, while treating the special interests of property owners with a consideration bordering on tenderness. As the country has grown in size, wealth and complexity, there have been more special groups demanding priorities, protection and assistance. Consequently, the general welfare has been pushed further and further into the background of public attention. The result of this emphasis on the particular, and neglect of the general welfare, has been a growing babel and confusion as particular claimants have advanced their interests at the expense of the general public, of which the individual contenders are integral parts.

General welfare presupposes the particular welfare. You cannot hope for health in a body where tissues and organs are diseased and whose functions are deranged. The welfare of the whole is dependent upon the welfare of the parts composing the whole. Interdependence works both ways. General welfare is essential to particular welfare, and particular welfare enhances general welfare up to the point at which particular welfare upsets the balance of the whole.

We have now thought our way through to the problem of checks and balances in society and in government. Society and government are wholes or aggregates composed of interdependent parts, held in balance by the forces which they contain and express. If the forces are properly adjusted to one another, the community and the government enjoy order and peace. If the adjustment is faulty, the result will be disorder and conflict.

Demagogues in many parts of the world have risen to power because of instability and insecurity engendered by a major change in the culture pattern. American demagogues are taking advantage of the confusion, disorder and uncertainty that the social hurricane has left in its wake—particularly during the anxious cold war years and the wracking epoch of the Korean War.

Locally, United States demagogues are harrying dissidents, denouncing heretics, closing public forums, banning meetings, boycotting magazines, burning books, terrorizing the wives and children of the unorthodox, hounding teachers, preachers and editors who have the temerity to speak or write in opposition to the official line on matters of public policy. At the state level, the demagogues are prescribing loyalty oaths, purging the schools, enforcing state sedition laws, and in a few instances, sending their most stubborn opponents to serve long terms in the penitentiary. At the federal level, the demagogues are working out from the office of the Attorney General, the secret police (F.B.I.), the White House, the House of Representatives and the Senate—encouraging denunciations of private citizens, cataloging neighborhood gossip, listing and attacking organizations which express minority opinion, putting millions of office holders through humiliating loyalty tests, indicting and convicting men and women for the crime of "conspiracy to teach." The most spectacular performances have been the inquisitions directed by Congressional committees into the beliefs, ideas, associations, political leanings and activities of trade unionists, movie producers, writers and actors, educators, scientists, publicists, and the determined efforts, backed by threats of public smearing, fines and jail sentences, to extort from witnesses the names of others, who in their turn may be put on the grill for the delectation of the committee members and to satisfy the cravings of a sensation-sated press, radio and television audience.

Legislative committees are raiding parallel government agencies, private associations, the prerogatives of professionals and the privacy of individuals, asking questions, making demands and uttering threats which contravene both constitutional guarantees and the fundamental principles underlying the pluralistic make-up of the United States community. Interrogations center around the question: "Are you or have you ever been a member of the Communist Party?" Demands center around the citing of names and the furnishing of lists of individuals—a demand that compels the witness to become an informer against his neighbors, associates, fellow workers and fellow citizens. The witnesses are under oath. If they make an inaccurate or incorrect statement, they are indicted for perjury; if they refuse to answer, they are charged with contempt of Congress and, if convicted, are fined and/or imprisoned. If witnesses invoke the Fifth Amendment, written to prevent self-incrimination as the result of torture, they are *ipso facto* considered to be guilty, dismissed from their jobs and denounced as subversives. When one of the inquisitorial committees goes to a community like Los Angeles or Detroit, staff members summon educators, doctors, lawyers, trade union leaders, ministers, workers, editors. Anyone, man or woman, who is known as an upstanding, energetic advocate of minority causes and a supporter of unpopular ideas is called before the inquisitors, grilled, badgered, insulted, bullied and threatened. The unhappy victims of this procedure are not charged with any overt or illegal act. They are accused of holding ideas and of associating with groups which are out of favor with the American Oligarchy.

Conducted in any form, public grillings such as those of the House Committee on Un-American Activities and the Senate Permanent Committee on Investigation would be annoying and aggravating, even to the most experienced public figure. To the uninitiated, they are as terrifying as a child's first appearance on a public platform.

As an example of such procedure, take the hearings which the Senate Subcommittee on Permanent Investigation staged in Boston, Massachusetts, on November 19, 1953. Private hearings, held previously, had convinced the Committee that it had savory morsels for the avid press, radio and television audiences. The press and camera men were alerted, the public was informed of the approaching spectacle and at 9 o'clock on Wednesday morning the Committee turned on the Kleig lights and produced a hero and several villains. The hero, William Teto, was a former worker at the General Electric Plant in Lynn, Mass., who, in 1941 had decided that it was his patriotic duty to join the Communist Party and report his findings to the secret police (F.B.I.). Before a packed hearing room and a breathless radio and television audience he went through the act which had been rehearsed the previous day in the private committee session.

The secret police spy told his local, his radio and television and his newspaper audience that he was a Communist. Senator McCarthy: "Mr. Teto, as of this moment are you a member of the Communist Party?" Answer: "Yes sir."

Teto then told how in 1941, he had decided to provide the secret police with what information he could gather by joining the Party, and of the thirteen terrible years from 1941 to 1953 during which his reputation as a Communist had alienated his father, wrung the heart of his mother, separated him from his brother and kept him from going to church. The under-cover man had been elected secretary of his Communist Party branch and was thus in possession of the membership list and of branch records. He knew who worked in the factory, the reports they made at meetings and the private conversations which he was able to over-hear. Thus he could inform the Committee: (1) that Communist Party members were employed in the General Electric plant; (2) that some of them worked on government contracts; (3) and were in a position to sabotage defense production, and (4) that they could bring secret information concerning government contracts to the Communist Party branch. He did not report a single example of sabotage nor an instance in which secret information had been brought to the branch.

The spy was then asked to identify his fellow Communist Party members. Since they were waiting, conveniently, with their attorney, in the hearing room, and stood up when requested, the Committee was able to confront the police-spy hero with the Communist villains. Whereupon the following interrogation took place: Question (to Teto): "Did you know a man named Robert Goodwin?" Answer: "Yes, sir."

Q. Does he work for the General Electric? A. Yes, sir. Q. Did you know him as a member of the Communist Party? A. Yes, sir. Q. I think Mr. Goodwin is here. Would he stand up? [The marshall called Goodwin.] Q. Will you take a look at this man. Is this Mr. Goodwin a member of the Communist Party as far as you know? [Goodwin started to talk before Teto could answer but McCarthy interrupted:] No Communist will cross-examine our witness. **Goodwin:** You are making a political speech here. **McCarthy:** Marshall, will you remove the witness. [The witness was removed.] **Q.** [To Teto:] As far as you know is he a member of the Communist Party at this moment? **A.** Yes, sir. **Q.** In his work at the General Electric plant in Lynn would he be in the position to sabotage facilities there in case of war with Communist Russia? **A.** Yes, sir. **Q.** Do you consider it an extremely dangerous situation to have men who are Communists at this moment working in the GE plant? **A.** Yes, sir. [Another witness was then called to the stand and the act was repeated.]

At 10 A.M. the hearing adjourned in order that the Committee Chairman might fly out to his home state to make a speech. Whereupon the spy-hero, under police escort to heighten the dramatic effect, went home and was received into the bosom of his family amid the flashing of bulbs and the clicking of cameras. The General Electric Company played its part in the drama by sending telegrams suspending from work two villains who had refused to say whether they were or were not Communists. Verbatim reports of this affair were carried in the Boston papers on Nov. 20, and detailed stories were telephoned, telegraphed and radioed across the United States.

There was an anti-climax next day when newspapers reported that the spy-hero had a record as an army deserter, that he had pleaded guilty to passing bad checks, that in his garage were two expensive autos and that he had been living a life of comfort not as a GE worker but as an upholsterer. A spokesman for the Communist Party threw more cold water by announcing that the spy-hero had been expelled from the Party in 1949 on charges of being a government agent. He was therefore guilty of perjury when he had said, under oath, that he was a Party member in 1953. This information, however, appeared in an inconspicuous place and in small type, while the name and fame of the Committee Chairman had been headlined and broadcast across the nation. Millions had heard and seen evidence that the General Electric plant at Lynn, Massachusetts had been the scene of a horrendous Communist plot.

Now comes the most devastating aspect of this squalid episode. In the course of a controversy over espionage in government, Senator McCarthy had secured time on a nation-wide radio and television hook-up (on Nov. 24th) to answer charges made against him by Ex-President Harry Truman. In the course of his radio address, the Senator attacked the Eisenhower Administration, of which, in theory at least, he is a part. At his next press conference, on December 2, President Eisenhower, without mentioning McCarthy by name, read this statement: "In all that we do to combat subversion, it is imperative that we protect the basic rights of loyal American citizens. I am determined to protect those rights to the limit of the powers of the office with which I have been entrusted by the American people."

The President read the words slowly, emphatically, dramatically, to a hushed press audience. Presumably he was silencing Senator McCarthy. In fact, he was endorsing the entire McCarthy program of insult, slander, purge and terror by referring to "the basic rights of loyal American citizens."

What is a "loyal" citizen? Has the President the authority to define it? The word does not appear in the Constitution. The Bill of Rights refers to "the right of every citizen." This would include those critical of the government as well as McCarthy men. Senator McCarthy would agree with the President's statement one hundred percent—if McCarthy were permitted to decide who are loyal and who disloyal.

American citizens have a right to disapprove and oppose everything for which the Senator or the President stands. The term "loyal" as used by the President contravenes the Constitution and violates the fundamental concepts of the part played by the citizenry in a society of checks and balances.

The Romans threw subversives to the lions. In the United States they are subpoenaed before legislative committees. The Committee members emerge from the hearings as high priests of patriotism and defenders of freedom and justice. The victims of the public circus lose their jobs and are smeared as disloyal.

At the time the Senate Committee staged its rehearsed television show in Boston, there was no United States law which made Communist Party membership a crime. If there were such a law, it would contravene the constitutionally guaranteed rights of private association and personal privacy. If these constitutional guarantees are swept aside, the social balance will be upset and the life, liberty and happiness of the population will be endangered by the demagogues and the tyrannical actions of despots. The Constitution also provides that a citizen must be presumed innocent until guilt is proven. The Senate Committee began the hearing with the presumption that a Communist is guilty of anything and everything until proved innocent.

General welfare depends upon the establishment and maintenance of an orderly, peaceful community—made up of an effective coordination of healthy parts. We mention the whole first because unless the whole is functioning normally, the parts are bound to suffer.

Until the people of the United States put their own house in order, the entire human family faces the unceasing threat of untimely and violent death. The cold civil war now raging in the United States is a matter of grave concern to men and women everywhere. The ending of that civil war and the redirection of United States competence and experience towards the solution of world stability and security problems may be approached from many angles and at several levels. It is not enough for government to act wisely and courageously in the interest of the general welfare, desirable and necessary as such a course would be. The people must also act, individually and through their non-governmental associations, first because as sovereign people, they are the final authority in determining the direction of public affairs, and second, because the existing government is so frankly the spokesman of private, special interests and so patently unconcerned with the general welfare. Therefore, the sovereign people must act individually and collectively, through existing associations and organizations or through such organizations and associations as may be developed to meet the present threat to the general welfare.

Our first task is to resist the invaders and usurpers who are waging cold civil war in the United States. Our second task is to liberate North America from the plutocratic Oligarchy which is violating the Constitution and threatening the life, liberty and happiness of the American people. Our third task is to set up institutions and practices which will use science and technology to provide peace and plenty for the entire human family.

Here is our program. To our posts. No defections or desertions. When the Oligarchs threaten, preserve discipline and move ahead. If some are jailed or shot, close ranks and keep contact. Let us play our parts well today—the best we know how. And on each tomorrow, carry on as before—to promote the general welfare.

29 OUR RIGHT TO TRAVEL (1959)

HELEN AND SCOTT had traveled widely over the years, but they found political roadblocks during the Cold War fifties. After their trips to Europe and China, they were denied passports by the State Department. The Nearings drove to Washington for a hearing to present their side of the case before the final decision.

They wrote this pamphlet as a result of the affair, explaining how no passports were required before 1914 and World War I, and how travel restrictions increased the power of governments to control movement of their citizens. Reasons for denial of passports in this country often rested on political beliefs, and the Nearings were among those who viewed such restrictions as unreasonable and unconstitutional according to both U.S. and UN provisions.

What the Nearings found astonishing was that no curiosity whatsoever was aroused in State Department personnel. The officials saw no opportunity to question these two seasoned, observant travelers to a China that loomed such a threatening mystery to the United States. Prophetically, Helen stated at the hearing how our future national relations with China might change.

United States citizens, before 1914, traveled abroad when and where they pleased. They bought steamer tickets and made reservations for Europe or Asia as easily as they bought stamps in a post office or a railroad ticket for New Orleans or San Francisco. Passports, or travel papers, were necessary only for a few "backward" countries. International travel was no more hampered by national regulations than travel in the homeland.

After 1914 the United States, along with most of the European governments, issued passports to those of its citizens who wished to travel abroad. Eventually Congress made it a crime for an American citizen to travel abroad without a passport, except in Canada and certain neighboring Latin American countries. Passport policy in the United States was completely reversed from "no passports needed" in 1910 to "no travel without passports" in the 1950s.

Travel restrictions came with general war in 1914; the second general war saw even tougher limitations and prohibitions on travel. After 1946, Washington, having become a major power, developed a policy toward travel which was more restrictive than that of other powers such as Britain and France, and differed from pre-1914 State Department policy as night differs from day.

United States citizens who traveled abroad were not only required to have passports, but elaborate passport applications forms were drawn up and used until 1958, in which applicants were asked to state their political affiliations as well as the countries to which they were proposing to go and their reasons for going there. Further, files were built up in the Passport Office consisting of information used in determining whether an American citizen was or was not entitled to a passport. These files were secret. The sources from which the information came were not revealed to passport applicants. The State Department was penalizing those who differed from the Administration and preventing American citizens who expressed radical ideas from exercising their right to move about the world. The victims of these restrictions were given no evidence against them nor a chance to confront their accusers. Only after suits were brought by private citizens and private organizations against the Secretary of State, and the issue had been fought out in court, did the State Department make provision for the appeal of rejected passport applications to a board set up within the Passport Office and staffed by State Department personnel.

Applications for passports which we had made in former years had passed through the usual routine. Applicants answered a page of questions on date and place of birth, names of parents and their birthplaces, and gave the names of two local citizens who would vouch for them. This material was sent to Washington with photographs and the necessary fee. Passports were returned by registered mail in a week or ten days.

The passport for which we applied in 1952 reached us at the end of 15 months, after long haggling by mail and a trip to Washington for an interview with Mrs. Ruth Shipley, then head of the Passport Office.

In the fall of 1952, after months of silence from the Passport Office, we asked for and obtained our interview with Mrs. Shipley. She was barely polite, not even asking us to sit down when we were ushered into her office. Standing by her desk, she questioned us rather sharply on some of our expressions of opinion and activities. Then she said in a hard, accusatory voice, "I have evidence here that you advocate the overthrow of the United States Government by force and violence."

We demurred, quietly and explicitly, saying we were pacifists and not in favor of killing or violence. "We would like to see the evidence," we added.

Mrs. Shipley searched nervously thoroughly the large dossier of papers on her desk. "The security officer who was to have been here for this interview has not shown up," she said finally and rather helplessly. "Can you come back at this same hour tomorrow?" We agreed.

The next day we went back to a very different reception. On the previous day Mrs. Shipley had made a public accusation against us. Obviously neither she nor her security officer had been able to discover any evidence that would support the accusation. After some conversation, in the course of which Mrs. Shipley explained the months of delay since we filed our passport application by saying that our papers had been "placed in the wrong file". She promised to help expedite the matter, and we went on about our business.

After more months of silence with no passports from Washington, we finally wrote a peremptory letter saying we thought it was now high time for the Passport Office to cut the red tape and issue us our passports,—that we had waited long enough. A registered letter arrived fairly promptly, with a joint passport enclosed, and a note from Mrs. Shipley (clearing her skirts) saying she was sorry we did not approve of the American form of government. This passport was good for only six months instead of the usual two years. It was not renewable, and gave us permission to visit only four countries,—respectable Sweden, Britain, France and Holland. Other West European countries we had desired to visit were struck off the list as "too unsettled" for our proposed visit.

Once in Europe we learned that a United States passport, specifically validated for travel only in Sweden, France, Britain and Holland, was perfectly good for other countries through which we transited. Local officials took our passport, looked at the date, glanced at our photographs, thanked us politely and turned to the next passenger. Visas were not necessary; they were interested in identification, and were not particularly concerned with State Department regulations or restrictions.

We filled out new passport applications in October 1954, asking for separate passports this time, and with no special restrictions. Our passports reached us in January, 1956.

One day early in October, 1958, each of us received an identical letter from the State Department.

October 2, 1958

Dear Mr. Nearing:

Your continued entitlement to a passport is being considered under the provisions of Section 51.136 (b) and (c) of the Passport Regulations.

Pending consideration of our entitlement to passport facilities, passport No. 816975, issued on January 3, 1956, is hereby tentatively withdrawn and you are requested to surrender it. . . .

This action is predicated upon information indicating that you traveled to and in that area of China under Communist control in violation of the restrictions contained in your passport and in contravention of United States foreign policy.

Under Section 51.137 of the Passport Regulations, you are entitled to present informally to this office any relevant information before the tentative withdrawal becomes final. You also have the right to appear personally at an informal hearing in this office at which you may be represented by counsel.

If, after presentation of your case and compliance with the applicable provisions of the Regulations, the Department's decision should be adverse, you may appeal to the Board of Passport Appeals. . . .

On November 29, 1958, we sent our reply to the State Department.

Harborside, Maine

Edward J. Hickey,   Nov. 29, 1958
Acting director,
Passport Office.

Dear Mr. Hickey,

We have your letters of October 3, 1958 (PT/LS-130-Nearing, Scott), advising us that the Passport Office is considering the withdrawal of our passport Numbers 816,975 and 816,976 because we traveled "to and in that area of China under Communist control in violation of the restrictions contained in your passport and in contravention of United States foreign policy". You request the surrender of our passports and give us sixty days to file this answer.

1. There is no question as to the facts. We did travel in People's China in December, 1957. We have reported upon our observations in numerous public addresses, in newspaper and magazine articles, and in a book, *The Brave New World,* published November 15, 1958.
2. We consider the restriction which forbids us to travel in People's China as unreasonable and unconstitutional.
   a. The right to go and come across frontiers is a fundamental or "natural" right of citizens, under the United Nations Declaration of Human Rights.
   b. The right to go and come is guaranteed, by implication, in the first ten Amendments to the United States Constitution.

    c. If the State Department has the authority to issue passports, it may prescribe reasonable regulations upon travel, but the right to go and come cannot be generally denied.

    d. Therefore we believe that the general prohibition of travel to and in People's China is unreasonable and unconstitutional.

3. We hold that our desire to visit People's China is reasonable.

    a. We are students of social science and writers on public affairs.

    b. The developments in People's China since October 1, 1949, when the present regime was established, are of great significance, not only to the citizens of China but to peoples the world over.

    c. If the experiments now being made in People's China provide a workable alternative to the Western way of life, and our visit has convinced us that they may do so, it is vitally important for people everywhere to know the facts.

    d. Hence it is not only our right as students of public affairs but it is our duty as responsible citizens to inquire into the facts and publicize them to the extent of our abilities.

    e. Under circumstances as stated above, instead of obstructing, the State Department should make every effort to encourage and facilitate our travel in China in order that our report on developments there should be as informative and complete as possible.

4. Under the Constitution of the United States, we, the people, are the residual holders of power and authority. We believe that the policies adopted by the present administration in Washington in its dealings with People's China are not only short-sighted and self-defeating but that they threaten the peace and happiness of millions of people in Asia and Europe as well as in the United States. We consider it our duty and responsibility to oppose such policies by every reasonable means.

5. We have decided not to surrender our passports.

    a. They are our property. We paid the required fee for the passports when they were issued on January 3, 1956 and again when they were renewed by the United States Embassy in Moscow on January 2, 1958.

    b. Our passports are the record of a contract entered into by the Government of the United States with one or more of its citizens. A contract may not be repudiated at will by one of the parties to the agreement.

As students of public affairs it is our right and our duty to study and report significant social developments. We believe that the economic and social changes now being made in People's China are significant. Within a year we should like to revisit People's China to observe the communes now being established there, to study the spectacular advances in agricultural and industrial production and the alterations in the general standards of living. If you withdraw our present passports, we shall apply for new ones and will continue to press for our rights as citizens and as students and reporters of public affairs, to go and come across our national frontiers.

We went to Washington, and on April 14th at 10 A.M. reported at the Passport Office where we were faced by three officials.

Mr. Brooks: Mr. Nearing, prior to your entry into Communist China in December of 1957 were you generally aware of the foreign policy of the United States with respect to travel by American citizens to and in Communist China?

Mr. Nearing: Yes, and I thoroughly disagree with it as an American citizen. I thoroughly disagree with the policy of Washington in this respect.

Mr. Brooks: What was your concept of the policy with respect to travel by American citizens?

Mr. Nearing: I believe that the right to go and come, as stated in the United Nations Declaration of Human Rights, is a natural right, or a basic right which may not be denied. Am I answering your question?

Mr. Brooks: What I meant is what was your concept of what the United States Government policy was?

Mr. Nearing: It is quite clear on the passport. The passport said "Not good for traveling in Communist China." So we did not use the passport in Communist China.

Mr. Brooks: But your general concept was that an American citizen was not permitted to travel in Communist China?

Mr. Nearing: No, my concept was that the Passport Office had issued a statement to the effect that this passport is not good for travel in Communist China. I know of no law which forbids us to travel in China. I knew of the passport restriction. It was stated clearly on the passport.

Mr. Brooks thereupon introduced Exhibits 7 and 8 which were a press release of October 31, 1955, and a statement of William Sebald, Deputy Associate Secretary of State for Far Eastern Affairs before the House of Representatives on March 28, 1959, regarding the policy of the United States Government with respect to travel by American citizens to and in China.

Exhibit 9 was a statement we had signed in the American Consulate at Hong Kong on January 7, 1959: "I, Scott Nearing, an American citizen, declare that my wife, Helen, and I wish to travel to Communist China but do not intend to travel there on this October, 1956 to May, 1957, trip in contravention of the regulations of the Department of State, Washington, D.C."

We identified this singular document and said: "It states very clearly that we did not intend to go into Communist China then."

Said Mr. Brooks: "I would like to introduce this into the record to show that Mr. and Mrs. Nearing were aware of the policy of the United States Government with respect to travel in Communist China."

Then from Mr. Brooks: "Do you have Passport #816,975 and Passport #816,976 with you this morning?"

Mr. Nearing: No, sir.

Mr. Seeley: Would you be willing to submit them to the Department if we requested them?

Mr. Nearing: You have requested them. Will the Department return them?

Mr. Seeley: Well, we will have to come to a decision on that.

Mr. Nearing: Good. We will come to a decision on our side. This is our property. We paid for it just as we pay for a postage stamp, and we regard it as our property and we propose to hold on to it.

Then we were asked as to our travel itinerary from the United States to China. We gave it: from New York to Paris, to Prague, to Moscow, and by jet plane to Peking.

Mr. Brooks: When did you first formulate your plans to enter Communist China or to travel to Communist China?

Mr. Nearing: I have been in China before and I regard the developments in China today as probably the most significant developments, politically, economically and socially, that are taking place anywhere in the world.

Mr. Brooks: Did you contemplate this journey before you left the United States.?

Mr. Nearing: Let me state one additional thing, and that is that after 1952 we considered the position of the United States as increasingly critical, both domestic and foreign, and we spent three years travelling in the United States. We traveled about 60,000 miles by car and spent about 17 months doing it to get a thorough grounding as to what was happening inside the United States. Then for the next two years we went abroad and covered large parts of both Asia and Europe in order to fill out this picture as to what was going on. So, generally speaking, the developments in China we consider more important than the developments in Russia, and we think that the developments in Russia are among the major developments of this period.

Mr. Brooks: At any rate, you did contemplate, prior to your departure from the United States on this trip, touring Communist China?

Mr. Nearing: Oh yes, we were very definitely committed to cover those parts of the world in which socialist construction is being attempted or carried forward. We spent a long period in India; we spent a period in Japan; we spent considerable time in other Asian countries, and then we spent a considerable period in USSR and Communist China.

Much of the time in the hearing room was then devoted to haggling over whether or not we used our passports in China. We said the visas granted us by the Chinese Embassy in Moscow were on separate pieces of paper and our passports as such were not used. Exhibits 10 and 11 were then inserted in the record. They were copies of a China News Agency story giving rules for exit, entry and residence of foreign nationals in China, and statements by an official of the All China Federation of Democratic Youth and by the Rev. Warren H. McKenna in late 1957 with respect to the requirement of passports in entering Communist China.

At this point an article by Scott Nearing, "China Then and Now," from the May 1958 issue of *China Reconstructs,* was marked as Exhibit 12.

Mr. Brooks: The next is an article which appeared in the September 1958 issue of the *New World Review,* entitled "China's Good Earth," which is written by both Mr. and Mrs. Nearing. I would like to have this admitted into the record [Exhibit 13].

Mr. Brooks: The third and final exhibit is a book entitled *The Brave New World,* which is written by Mr. and Mrs. Nearing and published in 1958, concerning their travels in Communist China.

Mr. Nearing: You observe from this book that we have made no secret of our procedures.

Mr. Brooks: I would like to have this book entered into the record, Mr. Chairman.

The Chairman: It will be admitted [Exhibit 14].

We were then questioned as to our itinerary and dates in China, what if any American monies we had spent there. (We had spent none, as our expenses had been paid in large part by the Chinese People's Association for Cultural Relations with Foreign Countries, whose guests we had been, and partly from our own locally obtained royalties on books and articles published there.)

Mr. Seeley: While you were in China, did you contact any other Americans?

Mr. Nearing: Oh yes.

Mr. Seeley: Could you give us the names?

Mr. Nearing: No.

Mr. Seeley: Don't you recall them?

Mr. Nearing: Oh no. I am not an informer, not an agent, and I don't mention names or addresses or anything of that kind. I don't want to involve anyone else.

Mr. Seeley: What was the general reaction of the people toward you? Did they know you were Americans?

Mr. Nearing: The last time I was in China, in 1927, . . . there was real enmity, hatred. This time we were received with utmost friendliness from everybody, from kindergartener up to public officials. They don't like the government policy of the United States, but as far as we were concerned, we were greeted in the most friendly and hospitable fashion wherever we went. In fact, we were over-fed and over-entertained.

There were further questions as to our itinerary returning home from Peking, when we had stopped off for a few weeks in Moscow and a week in Hungary.

Mr. Brooks: Now, Mr. Nearing, if you are furnished with further passport facilities, that is, if your passport is returned to you or invalidated, will you again travel in violation of the geographical limitations of general applicability which are contained in the passport at the present time?

Mr. Nearing: You see, the same answer which I presented in my letter to the Passport Office, the same answer still holds true. My loyalties to my science and to my constituency (I both write and talk, write and teach) come before my loyalties to the Government of the United States. I happen to have been born on the 6th of August, and President Truman saw fit on the 6th of August to drop a bomb on the women and children of Hiroshima. Since that time I have been pretty much alien to the Government of the United States, pretty much in opposition. I realize we are living under conditions where opposition is not encouraged in the United States, but I not only differ with the policies of the State Department, I also differ with the policies of the Untied States Government. I therefore don't feel committed, I don't feel loyal, to the Washington Government or its agencies or bureaus. I do feel loyal to my science and I do feel loyal to the people who read my writings and attend my classes.

Mr. Brooks: Would you then say, Mr. Nearing, that you would have no hesitancy in traveling contrary to the foreign policy of the United States?

Mr. Nearing: I don't accept the foreign policy of the United States. This is not my policy. I am in opposition. I am in outspoken and vigorous opposition to the foreign policy of the United States Government as now enunciated and practiced by the State Department and by the Washington Government.

Mr. Brooks: Then, if the opportunity arose for you to re-enter a restricted area, you would have no hesitancy about doing so?

Mr. Nearing: I have the opportunity to do that at any time. . . . You see, you have to realize that where you call "beyond the iron curtain" people are happy to do anything for Americans who are not in harmony with the policy of the United States Government. So that, in a sense, when you are in China you are more among friends than you are when you are in the United States. We are more in agreement with the Chinese Taiwan policy than with the State Department Taiwan policy. You see, the limitation of nationalism which has become so universal in the last hundred and fifty years or so does not restrict us, because we do not accept the limitation of nationalism any more than we accept the limitation of national statism. We happen to live in the State of Maine; but Augusta, the capital of Maine, doesn't limit our actions. We pay our taxes and do what we are supposed to do. We feel exactly the same way about the United States. The world today is in a very perilous situation and one of the steps we have to take is to get beyond national loyalties and national frontiers to a higher loyalty, which is the loyalty to the human race, humanly speaking and to an international authority, politically speaking.

Mr. Brooks: I have no further questions, Mr. Chairman.

The Chairman: Now, as we have informed you in the letters, the Department of State indicates that your passports were tentatively withdrawn. As far as the Department is concerned, we do not consider these passports are valid for travel at this time, so that the purpose of this hearing, of course, is to afford you an opportunity to present your side of the case, and also to furnish us with whatever information is necessary to arrive at a decision. Now, do you have anything at this time you would like to state in addition to what you have already said?

Mr. Nearing: I think that in our letter of November 29th we stated our case. Of course, the feeling that I have is that this hearing is of a sort of legalistic nature and I am not concerned with legalisms. I am concerned with things that are very much more important than legalisms. So all of these exhibits and this record and so on have already been covered. We are not denying that we went to China. The facts of the case are accepted. The question of law is whether we have a right to passports as American citizens. And the question of fact is whether the State Department, under the circumstances, will either revalidate or issue new passports to us. We regard the passport as a sort of an impertinence. We think that people ought to be free to go and come, and we would like to live in a world where people are free to go and come. Now, if passports are required, it is like vaccination. We don't believe in vaccination, but we put up with it because we have to. That is also an impertinence. We do what we have to in order to carry on our activities. We would like to have a passport because there are certain things that we like to do outside the United States. If the State Department refuses a passport, then we will stay home and carry on our work here.

The Chairman: Sir, from what you have already stated, I gather you would not abide by the geographical restrictions that would be placed in your passport, the restrictions that apply to all Americans generally. As you will notice, all the passports we issue at the present time restrict geographical areas of the world.

Mrs. Nearing: But they shift and change. I think our passports still have the prohibition on going to Israel. That was on account of the Suez crisis. That is now over and probably Americans can go to Israel. There are other prohibited countries stamped on our passports. There will be other shifts and changes. We think that it may shift and change on China.

The Chairman: But if it did not shift or change, as far as China was concerned, you would still go there, irrespective of the restriction that might be in your passport? Is that correct?

Mr. Nearing: If necessity arose. We drive a great deal, and when we drive on highways we obey the traffic restrictions punctiliously unless something happens that leads us to depart from traffic regulations. We feel the same way about any regulations. If they are reasonable, we abide by them. If necessity arises, they are only traffic regulations. They are routine restrictions. We think of a passport as an impertinence, and we think of the limitations written into the passport as routine regulations.

This, except for the placing of our letter of November 29th on record as Exhibit 15, concluded the hearing.

After the April 14th hearing in the Passport Office it was only a question of time before the State Department got around to finalize the tentative cancellation of our passports.

One fact stands out with unequivocal clarity. Unless people of the United States stand together and struggle persistently and valiantly they will be reduced to vassalage by the all-powerful oligarchy which owns the crucial segments of the economy, manipulates the government and manufactures public opinion.

Aware that conditions and situations differ in various parts of the globe, we feel that Americans should understand the dangers which confront them. They should organize and determine their course of action. Meanwhile, there is nothing for a self-respecting United States citizen to do but to follow his conscience, use his best judgment, unite with his fellows, and challenge the oligarchy by every means which he can conscientiously use until the usurpers are driven from public life and a commonwealth of the people is reestablished. The ultimate measure of judgment for self-respecting United States citizen is his sense of right and wrong and his feeling of responsibility for preserving and enhancing the general welfare.

30 The Conscience of a Radical
(1965)

A T 82 YEARS OF AGE, Nearing continued to work the land
at Forest Farm and write books. He reached an age of
assessing and explaining his life, prompting him to write
this work to balance Chester Bowles's *Conscience of a
Liberal* and Barry Goldwater's *Conscience of a Conservative.* The book juxtaposes many differences among liberals,
conservatives, and radicals. Part of the foreword excerpted
here describes some of the events and observations in Nearing's early years that led to his commitment as a radical.

My conscience is aroused, outraged and anguished by the dangerous
drift of mankind toward self-destruction, and by the satanic role which
the United States is playing in the fateful drama. My conscience assails
me so unbearably that I have no choice in the matter—I must speak out.

More than sixty years ago, while still in high school, I began to look
around and wonder why in a pleasant, beautiful, fruitful world so many
people were living such hard, dismal, limited, unrewarding lives. At
this early age I felt that there was more to life than my own personal
interests, needs and satisfactions, that all about me and at many levels
there were social problems. Heartless disregard for the general welfare
seemed all too prevalent. My own family was well enough off, so there
was no need to worry about their welfare. But round about me people
lived in slums; children tended machines in factories, picked slate in
coal breakers; working hours for adults and children were long; wages
were low; prices and profits were high; big businesses forced little businessmen to the wall, gobbled them up and organized huge combines and
trusts. Why were not individuals and families concerned about other
individuals and families? Why the "me and my wife, my son John and

his wife, we four, no more?" attitude? Why were not people consumingly concerned with the welfare of the whole race and every last one of its members?

As a result of what I saw, heard, read and felt in those early days I decided to devote my life to a study of the problems of living and livelihood and to search for solutions that would increase security and enhance happiness. My studies and my personal experiences led me to avoid superficial living, led me to dig to the roots of personal life and social problems; led me, in other words, to become a radical. And I have remained a radical to this day.

In my early years I went into the slums and helped out in settlement houses. I took jobs in mines and mills for long hours at low pay. I saw at close range how hard people worked for the little they got, while grinding poverty twisted, warped and stunted them. I saw rich idlers wasting their inherited money and their purposeless lives. Many of them did nothing useful—only chased after happiness like children after butterflies. In some ways they were worse off than the poor; in the end their lives were even more barren than the lives of poverty-stricken workers.

The inequalities and injustices and immoralities I saw profoundly concerned and plagued me. I asked myself: "Is this the best we humans can make of life's opportunities on this green planet? Is it for this rat race that discoveries and inventions have brought us such marvelous powers over nature and society?" The waste in daily living particularly horrified me—waste on frivolities, waste of food, waste of productive energies, waste of talent. Human life, which might be so wonderful, rich, rewarding, was so small, so mean, so selfish, thoughtless, so close to the barnyard and the jungle.

More glaring and inexcusable were the wastes of war: small-scale war in Cuba, South Africa and the Philippines; world wars that swept over Europe and Asia. Petty waste in homes and neighborhoods was bad enough; war waste was cruel, degrading, horrible. Was there no escape from such a senseless, shameful, sterile life pattern? Were sympathy and kindness, human imagination and aspiration, human talent and genius able to turn away from such folly and wickedness without increased determination to organize and act? Could we not make an end to these stupidities, immoralities and injustices and move forward to higher levels of action and broader fields of endeavor?

Over the years, I have been forced to the conclusion that we human beings are doing something less than our best in our personal and our social lives. If that is the case, surely our social conscience as well as our individual consciences must stab and must continue to prod until we have elevated our feelings, thoughts and actions to something more unselfish, inspiring and ennobling.

That "something" must be big, broad and deep enough to command our loyalties and lead us to make the best possible use of our abilities and talents in order to deal with the social and individual issues which face us. If things are not right, we have no business turning aside until we have done our share and more than our share in our efforts to set them right. A radical who merely plays with theory should continue to feel the pricks of conscience until he has pulled off his jacket and lent a hand.

I was brought up in a family of engineers where we were taught to get the foundations broad and deep and to see that the structure was plumb, square and according to plan. If we failed in any essential respect, we tore the whole thing out and started over again.

Liberal patching here and there will not fill the bill. If we are losing water from a pond, it is useless to cut the grass or plant shrubs along the bank. We must find the leaks and plug them, even if we have to build a new retaining wall to make the pond tight. We must go far enough to get to the root of our troubles, to reach the source of our difficulties. We must stay on the job until the leaks are stopped and the water back where we want it.

What conscientious civil engineers do on construction jobs, conscientious social engineers must do on jobs involving the livelihood and well-being of their fellow workers and fellow citizens. If they fail to reach their highest possible standards of excellence, their consciences should and will continue to gnaw until they have done the best job possible with the available materials and know-how.

Like responsible civil engineers on a construction job, we social engineers must scan history for its lessons, pool our knowledge and experiences, survey the field, make our plans and estimates, check and recheck our figures, and utilize our individual and collective energies to help build a life that will bring the greatest degree of wealth and well-being to the greatest possible number of our fellows. If we fail in any essential particular, our consciences should continue to bother us until we have set matters to rights.

31 THE MAKING OF A RADICAL (1972)

A T 88 YEARS OF AGE, Nearing finally got to the task his
friends and colleagues had requested of him for many
years but that he had refused until he was 80—an autobiography. Characteristically, he refused a personal life story
and instead wrote a political autobiography, the story of what
influenced his ideas and how he put the ideas into action.
This excerpt at the end of the book tells of his lifelong
commitment to teaching and to assigning his energies and
talents to something worthy and larger than himself.

I had the good fortune to be born in 1883 and to live consciously
through more than half a century of transformation of a class culture
into a mass culture. I have watched the doors of opportunity swing open
for larger and larger segments of my fellowmen. I never thought the
world would move so quickly, that socialism would spread so far so
fast. Not only have I watched the process, but I have played a part in
the big drama. Indeed, I consider that I came with an assignment to
do my level best to help convert our time of troubles into an era of
opportunities.

Act by act, day by day, year by year, age by age, the Inspector has
come around asking: "How are you getting on today, this year, this life,
in this period? Let's have a look at your records." This autobiography is
part of my report to the Inspector. One of these days the Head Office

Pages 298–301 from *The Making of a Radical: A Political Autobiography* by
Scott Nearing. Copyright © 1972 by Scott Nearing. Reprinted by permission of
Harper & Row, Publishers, Inc.

will acknowledge the receipt of my report and will, I hope, give me another assignment. Meanwhile, the books are open. The auditors are at work. Balances are being struck.

The assignment was definite: to learn, understand, report, interpret, to help in applying and spreading knowledge and in realizing the greatly enlarged potential of human creativity, to help in making the broadest possible use of the new knowledge and the vastly improved techniques. To this end I was born and educated in a technically advanced community, in a mineral-rich and fertile land.

After the turn of the century the United States became a happy hunting ground for the ambitious, greedy, power-hungry few. But in the process, the North American mass culture made notable contributions to the sum total of economic productivity and scientific and technical advance. For half a century I have been an educator and teacher with no academic position and a random, shifting, negligible "student" body. I have been living in a technically advanced, fabulously rich country, run by a power-drunk oligarchy, rushing themselves, their dupes and victims into a cul de sac from which there is no escape and in which, if they remain, they, their associates, and possibly the planet earth may be denuded and rendered lifeless for ages to come.

Teaching is my job. Teaching, in its largest sense means searching out the truth, telling it to all who are willing to learn, and building it into the life of the community. Truth is often unpleasant, annoying, and unpalatable to those who hold a disproportionate amount of worldly goods, who are power hungry, and who are pushing a cause to the detriment of the many. So they try to avoid truth, to cover it up, to forget it. It is the job of the teaching profession, of which I have been a lifetime member, to keep on uncovering the truth, reminding the rich and powerful of its character and its significance, bringing it to public attention, and arguing that it be made the cornerstone of local, regional, national and planet-wide public life.

I came with an assignment: to seek out the truth, to teach the truth, to help weave truth, justice, and mercy into the fabric of human society. Through more than half a century of active participation in public affairs I have seen the opportunity for such activity in the United States decline from a broad stream to a tiny rivulet which periodically disappears into the desert sands of mob violence, martial law, declarations of emergency and war.

Opportunities to teach have dwindled. Restrictions, limitations, and prohibitions have multiplied. As a member of the teaching fraternity I continue to practice my chosen profession whenever I have a chance. Times have changed, drastically, radically; my assignment to search

out, teach and apply the truth in my field of social science remains
unaltered. I am as enthusiastic a teacher at eighty-eight as I was at
twenty. I am more concerned to teach and more dedicated to social
science now than I was then.

The teaching too is more needed. The social science field has broadened enormously. With the revolutionary advances in natural science
and technology, social science has opened wide the doors of opportunity for the entire human race. Under its auspices, mankind may learn
to leave the narrow confines of ignorance, superstition, exploitation,
class tyranny, insecurity, fear, and hatred and to step into the broader
fields of knowledge, reason, cooperation, mass culture, planned security, confidence, and brotherhood, establishing a planet-wide, federated human community. Coupled with this possibility is the urgency
created by tens of thousands of nuclear warheads, produced, stored, and
ready for use at the touch of a button.

Mishandled, this crisis will surely lead to the decimation of mankind
and perhaps to an end of human life on the earth. Understood, grasped,
and managed, the crisis gives humanity a chance to lift itself above
over-indulgence in personalia, racialism, nationalism, and factionalism
to the level of a planet-wide culture that will make the earth a fit
dwelling place and testing ground for many life forms, while linking up
with the cosmos in the space age.

Such a confrontation—involving the lives and destinies of more than
3000 million humans, as well as myriad nonhuman lives—challenges
every right-minded, socially conscious, cosmically aware man, woman,
child. It also pushes individual anxieties and worries into the background and forces collective thought and action to the center of the
planetary stage.

The perilous fight goes on. While there is life, energy, purpose, skill,
and experience, advances may be made. As human beings, we are part
of the environment in which we live. So long as we live we cannot
escape from this identification. The individual human is thus part of the
human race and of the social natural environment of the period in which
he lives.

In order to live fully, therefore, the individual human must reach
beyond self: to another human and/or to a cause or project and/or to an
idea or purpose. By identifying oneself with the interests of another
person, of a group (the family or the community), or with some purpose, cause, or idea, life is broadened and may be greatly deepened.
One does not have to choose "either/or." One can reach out in all these
and other directions. The important thing is to identify with some thing
or things beyond the self. Actually, each is part of the whole. The

immediate task is first to grasp this universal truth and second to act upon it.

Part of this essential process of growing up or maturing is the maintenance at one and the same time of the self-respect and dignity of the individual and the responsibility which one has for other individuals, for the community and for the mastery and improvement of the environment.

My assignment requires me to state and restate these truths, urging that they be recognized and utilized in a vast crusade aimed at the wise use of nature's priceless stores and the planned improvement of society by society.

32 THE GOOD LIFE
   UNIVERSAL (1974)

PERHAPS THE MOST FITTING WORDS to end, even summarize, this reader are these that Nearing wrote and
delivered as a commencement address to the graduating
class of Gould Academy in Bethel, Maine. In this typical
rounded approach, he speaks of the ragged edges of American society, proposes the alternative of a constitution and
citizenship in a Federated World, spells out specific steps
necessary to establish social decency, and exhorts young
people not to settle for second best but to work for their
future as "builders of the good life universal."

At 91 years of age, Nearing had nine more years of life.
He spent them helping to build a large stone house, lecturing,
growing exquisite gardens, and writing—separately and with
Helen—three more books.

———————————

Sixty-four members of the 1974 Gould Academy graduating class
have asked me to say a few words of greeting, of encouragement, and of
warning, as they leave academia and enter the teetering, treacherous
adult world called western civilization.

I am glad to comply with this request because it will enable me,
through this class, to address some of the twenty million high school
and college students in the United States and perhaps a few of the young
people in the capitalist segment of present-day human society.

You graduates are entering adult life in a nation and a world caught in
the crunch of a deep and widening economic, political, social and moral
crisis. The society built up by western man during the past ten centuries
is at the same time breaking down and breaking up. The full impact of
this general social crisis will be felt during your entire adult lives.

Americans born as you were, between 1950 and 1960, should have a life span of around 70 years. That life span should carry graduates of your class and of your generation to 2020–2030 A.D. That period will probably witness the dissolution of capitalist society to a point at which it will no longer be a viable social system anywhere on our planet. Speaking sociologically (if you stay in the United States) you will probably live most or all of your adult lives in a dying society.

The United States of America, richest and most powerful among western nations, is passing through the early stages of a general social crisis marked by five million unemployed among its 80 million gainfully employables. The percentage of unemployment among American youth is nearly twice as great as it is among all American employables. Widespread unemployment means for you graduates a growing difficulty in finding congenial, meaningful life careers.

Our general social crisis involves social and economic insecurity, a break-up of normal family life, a rising crime rate, a sharp increase of suicides, particularly among young people. It includes government by rival gangs of law-breaking lawyers, led by our elected representatives and financed by big business money.

The general social crisis is not confined to the United States. It exists throughout western civilization. It is expressed in the instability of governments, in inflation, in two general wars in one generation (1914 and 1945) and extensive preparation for a third general war, which may be fought with nuclear weapons.

This assumption is based on a careful study which I have been making of western society during the 73 years since I graduated from high school—in 1901.

Immediately after the second general war, nearly half the human race threw off the yoke of the chief empires and in the name of self-determination, organized sovereign states and took the thorny path to self-government. Currently they are known as the Third World.

During the same period, socialist-communist governments emerged,— the first in Soviet Russia, after 1917. After 1943 socialist governments multiplied, especially in Asia and East Europe. Today about one-third of the human family lives in countries dedicated to the construction, first, of socialism and ultimately, of communism.

The general social crisis through which the western world is passing is the logical and probable result of the competitive struggle for pelf and power among individuals and among nations which has occupied western man during the past five centuries—from 1450 to 1974. It is the tangled, twisted, inter-dependent social chaos which we incompetent, irresponsible adults are passing on to your generation. It is to our eternal shame that we have not found a way to avoid economic instability and social insecurity, and to build a society patterned on justice, mercy, love and right living.

With this confession of our failure, we pass the current crisis of the western world on to you. It is your challenge; your opportunity.

We Americans, old and young, face a common problem: we must learn to govern ourselves,—locally and planet-wide. We must govern ourselves as a nation. We must govern ourselves as a human family.

Our forebears approached the national problem two centuries ago in the preamble to the Constitution of 1789: "We, the people of the United States, in order to form a more perfect union, establish justice, insure domestic tranquility, provide for the common defense, promote the general welfare and secure the blessings of liberty to ourselves and our posterity, do ordain and establish this Constitution for the United States of America."

What do these words mean in June 1974? They mean that we as a nation of 205 million people should take the steps necessary to establish justice, order and social decency in this country. Specifically:

- We must own, preserve and conserve our natural heritage—the land of the United States, and its resources.

- We must own, plan and manage our national economy to ensure our general welfare.

- We must provide all necessary public services at local, state and national levels.

- We must take our place and play our part as a member of the family of nations.

- Planet-wide, as a human family, we must conserve and improve the earth, its resources and its inhabitants.

- We must own, plan and manage our planetary economy.

- We must provide and develop all necessary public services at the planetary level, and for the general good.

- We must formulate and enact world law and preserve world order.

As a member of the family of nations we should help in writing a preamble to the Constitution of a Federated World. The preamble of this Constitution should read: "We, the people of the Federated Nations, in order to establish and maintain fraternity, cooperation, order, decency, self-respect and peace among the nations and peoples of the earth, do ordain and establish this Constitution for the Federated Nations."

At the outset, this Constitution should declare: "All persons born or naturalized in any of the Federated Nations are citizens of the Federated Nations and of the nation in which they reside." As citizens of each nation, and as citizens of the Earth, they must learn to govern themselves.

These things we must do as soon as possible. The situation is critical. The time is short. We must act for our own well-being and for that of our children's children.

Some of your elders may wag their heads and repeat the time-worn admonition: "Let well enough alone. We never had it so good. A bird in the hand is worth two in the bush."

You graduates should not be deceived. This is only a side-step. It is their confession of their failure to lay the foundation for a good life for the people of the United States and for the human family on this earth.

A great economic, political and social revolution surfaced about two hundred years ago. It has turned human society upside down during the past two centuries and has put in your hands the implements, agencies and institutions necessary to make the Earth a useful and beautiful homeland for the human family. As you graduates reach adulthood, the possibility of effective self-government passes into your hands.

If you will, you can learn to govern yourselves. You, as citizens of North America and citizens of the world, can join hands to make the Planet Earth a fit and fine home for mankind and for the many other forms of life which inhabit it.

This graduating class is a part and a potentially meaningful part of the total picture. Do not be satisfied with any "lesser evil" or any "second best." Demand only the best, and struggle valiantly until you have won it.

Observe, analyze, think, decide, resolve, organize, act. In your generation, you can build a world which will exalt and ennoble man and prepare humanity to play its part as planners and builders of the good life universal.

BIBLIOGRAPHY OF SCOTT NEARING'S MAJOR WRITINGS

1908   *Economics* (with Frank D. Watson). New York: Macmillan Company. 499 pp.

1911   *Social Adjustment.* New York: Macmillan Company. 377 pp.

   The Solution of the Child Labor Problem. New York: Moffat, Yard, & Company. 145 pp.

   Wages in the United States, 1908–1910: A Study of State and Federal Wage Statistics. New York: Macmillan Company. 220 pp.

1912   *Elements of Economics: With Special Reference to American Conditions* (with Henry Reed Burch). New York: Macmillan Company. 363 pp.

   The Super Race: An American Problem. New York: B. W. Huebsch. 89 pp.

   Woman and Social Progress: A Discussion of the Biologic, Domestic, Industrial, and Social Possibilities of American Women (with Nellie M. S. Nearing). New York: Macmillan Company. 285 pp.

1913   *Financing the Wage-Earner's Family: A Survey of the Facts Bearing on Income and Expenditures in the Families of American Wage-Earners.* New York: B. W. Huebsch. 171 pp.

   Social Religion: An Interpretation of Christianity in Terms of Modern Life. New York: Macmillan Company. 227 pp.

   Social Sanity: A Preface to the Book of Social Progress. New York: Moffat, Yard, & Company. 260 pp.

1914   *Reducing the Cost of Living.* Philadelphia: George W. Jacobs & Company. 343 pp.

1915   *Anthracite: An Instance of Natural Resource Monopoly.* Philadelphia: John C. Winston Company. 251 pp.

         The New Education: A Review of Progressive Educational Movements of the Day. Chicago: Row, Peterson, & Company. 264 pp.

         Income: An Examination of the Returns for Services Rendered and from Property Owned in the United States. New York: Macmillan Company. 238 pp.

1916   Debate. "Should Socialism Prevail?" Affirmative: Scott Nearing and Morris Hillquit. Negative: Rev. Dr. John L. Bedford and Professor Frederick M. Davenport. Held in Brooklyn, N.Y., October 21. New York: Rand School of Social Science. 47 pp.

         Poverty and Riches: A Study of the Industrial Regime. Philadelphia: John C. Winston Company. 261 pp.

1917   Debate. "Will Democracy Cure the Social Ills of the World?" Affirmative: Scott Nearing. Negative: Clarence S. Darrow. Held at Garrick Theatre, Chicago. Chicago: The Workers' University Society. 31 pp.

         The Great Madness. New York: Rand School of Social Science. 44 pp.

1918   "Who Should Pay for the War?" New York: People's Council of America. 4 pp.

1919   *The Trial of Scott Nearing and the American Socialist Society.* New York: Rand School of Social Science. 249 pp.

1921   *The American Empire.* New York: Rand School of Social Science. 265 pp.

         Debate. "Resolved: That Capitalism Has More to Offer to the Workers of the United States Than Has Socialism." Affirmative: E. R. A. Seligman. Negative: Scott Nearing. Held at the Lexington Theatre on January 23. New York: Fine Arts Guild. 46 pp.

1922   Debate. "Can the Church Be Radical?" Affirmative: John Haynes Holmes. Negative: Scott Nearing. Held at the Lexington Theatre, New York, on February 12. New York: Hanford Press. 39 pp.

         The Next Step: A Plan for Economic World Federation. Ridgewood, N.J.: Nellie Seeds Nearing. 175 pp.

1923   *Oil and the Germs of War*. Ridgewood, N.J.: Nellie Seeds Nearing. 32 pp.

1924   Debate. "Resolved: That the Soviet Form of Government Is Applicable to Western Civilization." Affirmative: Scott Nearing. Negative: Bertrand Russell. New York: League for Public Discussion. 69 pp.

1925   *Dollar Diplomacy: A Study in American Imperialism* (with Joseph Freeman). New York: B. W. Huebsch and Viking Press. 353 pp.

        Educational Frontiers: A Book about Simon Nelson Patten and Other Teachers. New York: Thomas Seltzer. 250 pp.

1926   *The British General Strike: An Economic Interpretation of Its Background and Its Significance*. New York: Vanguard Press. 186 pp.

        Education in Soviet Russia. New York: International Publishers. 159 pp.

        Glimpses of the Soviet Republic. New York: Social Science Publishers. 32 pp.

        The Law of Social Revolution (with others). New York: Social Science Publishers. 262 pp.

        Russia Turns East. New York: Social Science Publishers. 30 pp.

        Stopping a War: The Fight of the French Workers against the Moroccan Campaign of 1925. New York: Social Science Publishers. 31 pp.

        World Labor Unity. New York: Social Science Publishers. 31 pp.

1927   *The Economic Organization of the Soviet Union* (with Jack Hardy). New York: Vanguard Press. 245 pp.

        Where Is Civilization Going? New York: Vanguard Press. 110 pp.

        Whither China? New York: International Publishers. 225 pp.

1929   *Black America*. New York: Schocken (reprinted 1969). 275 pp.

1930   "An ABC of Communism" (N.pp., n.d., self-published in 1930?) 27 pp.

        The Twilight of Empire: An Economic Interpretation of Imperialist Cycles. New York: Vanguard Press. 349 pp.

1931   "From Capitalism to Communism." (Originally *An ABC of Communism*.) Washington, D.C.: World Events Committee. 23 pp.

War: Organized Destruction and Mass Murder by Civilized Nations. New York: Vanguard Press. 310 pp.

1932   *Free Born: An Unpublishable Novel*. New York: Urquhart Press. 237 pp.

The Decisive Year 1931: Capitalism, Imperialism, Sovietism before the Bar of History. New York: Urquhart Press. 30 pp.

Must We Starve? New York: Vanguard Press. 277 pp.

The One Way Out: An Answer to Hard Times. New York: Urquhart Press (n.d., 1932?). 42 pp.

Why Hard Times? New York: Urquhart Press. 30 pp.

1933   *Fascism*. Jamaica, Vt., n.pp. (Reprinted at Harborside, Me., in 1973 by Social Science Institute.) 56 pp.

1934   *Europe East and West*. Ridgewood, N.J. (N.pp., n.d., probably self-published in 1934.) 54 pp.

1936   "The European Civil War: The First Twenty Years, 1917–1936." Baltimore, Md.: Christian Social Justice Fund. 24 pp.

1940   "The Rise and Decline of Christian Civilization." Ridgewood, N.J. (n.pp.) 23 pp.

"The Second World War: An Evaluation." Ridgewood, N.J. (n.pp.) 8 pp.

1944   *United World*. Mays Landing, N.J.: Open Road Press. 265 pp.

1945   *Democracy Is Not Enough*. New York: Island Workshop Press. 153 pp.

The Soviet Union as a World Power. New York: Island Workshop Press. 105 pp.

The Tragedy of Empire. New York: Island Press. 168 pp.

1946   "Victory without Peace." Washington, D.C.: World Events. 15 pp.

War or Peace? New York: Island Press. 96 pp.

1949   "The New World Order: And Some of Its Immediate Problems." New York: World Events Committee. 22 pp.

"Sound the Alarm." New York: Monthly Review. 13 pp.

1950   *The Maple Sugar Book* (with Helen Nearing). New York: John Day. (Reprinted by Schocken Books, New York, 1971.) 273 pp.

1952   *Economics for the Power Age.* East Palatka, Fl.: World Events Committee. 190 pp.

1954   *Living the Good Life* (with Helen Nearing). Harborside, Me.: Social Science Institute. (Reprinted in 1970 by Schocken Books.) 213 pp.

        Man's Search for the Good Life. Harborside, Me.: Social Science Institute. 146 pp.

1955   *USA Today* (with Helen Nearing). Harborside, Me.: Social Science Institute. 254 pp.

1956   "To Promote the General Welfare." Harborside, Me.: Social Science Institute. 31 pp.

1959   "Our Right to Travel" (with Helen Nearing). Harborside, Me.: Social Science Institute. 24 pp.

        "Soviet Education." Harborside, Me.: Social Science Institute. 30 pp.

1961   "Economic Crisis in the United States." Harborside, Me.: Social Science Institute. 24 pp.

1962   *Socialism in Practice: Transformation in East Europe.* New York: New Century Publishers. 104 pp.

1963   "Cuba and Latin America: Eyewitness Report on the Continental Congress for Solidarity with Cuba." New York: New Century Publishers. 36 pp.

1965   *The Conscience of a Radical.* Harborside, Me.: Social Science Institute. 191 pp.

1972   *The Making of a Radical: A Political Autobiography.* New York: Harper & Row. 308 pp.

1973   "Peoples' China in 1973: A Group Report" (with others). Woodmont, Ct.: Promoting Enduring Peace; and Harborside, Me.: Social Science Institute. 24 pp.

1974   "The Good Life Universal." (Originally "A Memorandum for Right Living.") Harborside, Me.: Social Science Institute. 4 pp.

1975   *Civilization and Beyond: Learning from History.* Harborside, Me.: Social Science Institute. 263 pp.

1979   *Continuing the Good Life* (with Helen Nearing). New York: Schocken Books. 194 pp.

INDEX

Abyssinia, 210
Academic censorship, xiii
Academic freedom, 8, 61
    breach of, 7
"Acres of Diamonds," 3, 5
African Slave Coast, 168–70
Albania, xiv
All China Federation of Democratic
    Youth, 271
Allies, 126, 137
American Economic Association, 29
American Indians, 168
American Socialist, 82
American Socialist Society, 85
American Woolen Company (Law-
    rence, Mass.) strike, 31–32
Annapolis, 21, 188
Arden, Del., ix, 6, 7
    single-tax community, 5
Armour, Philip, 1
Athens, 180
Atomic bomb, 216
    Great Britain, 242
Augusta, Me., 272
Australia, 13, 59, 129
Austria, xii, 13
Autobiography, 278

Babylon, 180
Back to the land, 14, 253
Baker, Ray Stannard, 225
Baku petroleum, 140
Balkan Wars of 1912, 193

Baltimore, 51
Barnum, P.T., 114
Bavaria, 201, 214
Belgium, 48, 145
Berlin, 158–59
Bethel, Me., 282
Bible, 100
Bills of rights, 227
Black America, xiii, 11, 167
Black Shirts (Italy), 200
Board of Trustees
    U. of Pennsylvania, 7, 8
    U. of Toledo, 9
Bolsheviks, 151, 222
    Hungary, 201
Bolshevism, 158
Boston, Mass., 260, 262
    newspapers, 261
Bowles, Chester, 275
Boy Scouts of America, 17
Brady, Nicholas F., 111
The Brave New World, 267, 271
Breaker boys, 2, 6
Britain, xiv, 10, 62, 113, 122, 123,
    137, 145, 147, 153, 182
    atomic bomb, 242
    women's rights, 38
British Empire, 166, 168
Broun, Heywood, 143
Brown Shirts (Germany), 200
Bryan, William Jennings, 71, 143
Bryn Mawr College, 31
Buck, Pearl, 253

Canada, 129
Capitalism, xiii, 108, 110, 147, 150, 200
 and the church, 117
Caribbean, oil, 138
Carnegie, Andrew, 1
Censorship, 81–82
 academic, xiii
Census bureau. *See* U.S. Census Bureau
Central Manual Training High School (Philadelphia), ix, 3
Chamber of Commerce, 152
Chaplin, Charles S., 242
Chautauqua (N.Y.), x, 77
 summer school, 6
Chiang Kai-shek, 11, 160
Chicago, 51
 Garrick Theatre, 71
 race riots, 86
Chicago Herald, 7
Chicago Vice Commission, 56
Chicherin, 156
Child labor, xiii, 2, 5, 6, 8, 17–22, 51, 52, 56–57
 breaker boys, 2, 6
 causes, 19
Child Labor Committee, Pa., ix, 6, 17
China, xii, xiv, 11, 122
 Nearings travel to, 264, 267
 People's Party, 160
 revolution in, 23
China News Agency, 270
China Reconstructs, 271
"China's Good Earth," 271
"China Then and Now," 271
Chinese Embassy, Moscow, 270
Chinese People's Association for Cultural Relations with Foreign Countries, 271
Chinese Railway Administration, 11, 160
Chinese Republic, 160
Chinese Revolution
 forces of, 163–64
Christian Endeavor Society, 3
Christianity, 50, 59

Churchill, Winston, 143
Church members, 118
Civil Disobedience, 223
Civilization, 75
Civil Liberties Union, 179
Civil War, 1, 90, 170, 172
 cold, 263
Coal miners, Pennsylvania, 54
Cold War, 264
 civil, 263
Columbia University, 107
Communism, 147, 283
 church under, 117
 House Un-American Committee, 257
Communist Party, xi, xiii, 11, 135, 178, 221, 260
 expells Nearing, 112
 Nearing campaigns for, 167
 Nearing joins, 160
Community Church of Boston, xi
Community Church (New York), 114
Company town (Morris Run, Pa.), 2
Confederate North American States, 217
Conference at Genoa and Lausanne, 191
Conscience of a Conservative, 275
Conscience of a Liberal, 275
Conscription Bill, 81
Conservatism
 and the church, 119
Constitution (U.S.), 91, 93, 104, 117, 216–217, 262, 267, 284
 "General Welfare," 257
 "Preamble," 257
Conwell, Russell (Baptist minister), 1, 3, 5
Coolidge, Calvin, 143
Counterculture, 253
Cox, 118
Cromwell, Oliver, 150, 152
Cuba, xii, xiv
Czar, 104, 146. *See also* Tzar Nearing.
Czechoslovakian crisis of 1938, 210

Daily time schedule, 235–36
Daily Worker, 12, 178
Darrow, Clarence, 10, 71
Darwin, Charles, 72, 73
Davis, Richard Harding, 7
Dawes Report, 149
Debs, Eugene, 10, 85, 118
The Decadence of Europe, 149
The Decay of Capitalist Civilization, 149
Declaration of Independence, 96
Declaration of Korean Independence, 166
Delmonico's, 1
Democracy, 65, 71, 74, 76, 80, 86, 91–92, 94, 223
Depression, economic, 1, 12, 13, 179, 200
Dictatorship(s), 212
  Soviet form, 148
Disarmament
  Federal Council of Churches, 115
Disciplines, 227–33
Dodge, Cleveland H., 111
Dollar Diplomacy, 11
Dominican Republic, 62
Douglas, Paul, 9
Douglas, Stephen Arnold, 93
Du Pont, 187

Eastman, Max, 10, 85
East Prussia, 158
Economic divisions, world, 127
The Economic Organization of the Soviet Union, 11
Economics, 92–94
  ten first principles, 242, 243
  of war making, 189
Economics, 17
Edmonds, Franklin Spencer, 5
Education
  antidote for poverty, 23
  on marriage, 35–36
Eighteenth Amendment (Prohibition), 86
Eisenhower, Dwight D., 242, 261–62
Ellis, Havelock, 32, 143

Emerson, Ralph Waldo, 116
Empire(s), 168, 208, 216
Environment movement, 253
Espionage Act, xi, 9, 77, 85
Europe, 53
  WWI, 78
"Evolution" in schools, 71

Factory, 63
Far Eastern Affairs, 269
Fascism, 200
  Charter of Labor, 204
  definition, 202, 204
  Law of Corporations, 204
  nature of, 203
Facism, xiii, 10
Fascist party, 85
FBI, 259, 260
Federal Council of Churches of Christ in America, 115
Federal Grand Jury, xi, 9
Federal Reserve System, 41, 111
Federated Press, xi, xii
Federated world, 14, 206, 282
  constitution of, 284–85
Feudal system, 144, 146
Fields, Marshall, 1
Fifth Amendment, 259
Fifth Avenue (New York), 52
Financing the Wage-Earner's Family, 50
First Amendment, 82
First Congregational Church (Toledo, Ohio), 9, 61
Fish, Hamilton, 10, 179
Five-Year Plan of 1928–33, 184
Flagg system, stone and concrete, 239
Flagler, H.M., 136
Ford, Henry, 41
Forest Farm, xii, xiv, 14, 253, 275
Fourier, Charles, 47
France, xiv, 10, 34, 47, 83, 122, 145, 153
  Standard Oil Company, 137
France, Anatole, 143
Franco-Prussian War, 190
Franklin, Philip A.S., 111

Freedom, 223–24
French Revolution, 222
Friends' General Conference (Ocean
Grove, N.J.), 50
Friends of the Soviet Union, 160
Froebel, Friedrich Wilhelm August,
43

Gadski, Madame, 35
Gandhi, Mohandas K., 222
Gardening, organic, 253
Garland Fund, 178
Garrick Theatre (Chicago), 71
General Disarmament Conference of
1932, 210
General Electric, 257, 260
General Motors, 226
"General Welfare," 257
George, Henry, ix
Poverty and Progress, 5
Germany, xiv, 10, 13, 47, 48, 81,
104, 108, 113, 122, 123, 145,
147, 153
Brown Shirts, 200
coal, 137
oligarchy in, 226
The Germs of War, 96
God, 9, 58
Gold standard, 200
Goldwater, Barry, 275
Good Life Center, viii
Good Life Universal, xiii, 282, 285
Goodwin, Robert, 260–61
Gould Academy, 282
Gould, Jay, 1
Grace Baptist Temple, 3, 5
Grant, Stickney, 143
Great Depression, 12, 13, 179, 200
The Great Madness, xi, 9, 78, 85,
86, 95
Greece, xiv
Athens, 180
Green Mountains, 236, 241
Grundy, Joseph, 6–7

Hague Tribunal, 209
Hamilton, Cicely, 34
"The Hand of Fate" (painting), 61

Harborside, Me., vii, xi, xii, 14,
242
Harding, Warren, 118
Harkness, S.V., 136
H-bomb, 242
Hester Street (New York), 52
Hickey, Edward J., 267
Hill, Napoleon, 1
Hiroshima, Japan, 14, 216, 272
*A History of Panics in the United
States,* 110
Hitler, Adolf, xiii, 108, 200, 203
Holland, 145, 214
Holmes, Haynes John, 10, 114, 143
Homeless children, New York, study
of, 200
Homesteading, 220, 253, 254
Hong Kong, American consulate,
269
Honorary degree (U. of Pennsyl-
vania), 15
Hoover, Herbert, 186
Horthy de Nasybánya, Miklós, 203
House Un-American Activities Com-
mittee, 179, 257, 259
Hovet, Carl, 8
Hungary, 201, 271
Horthy, 203
Huns, 26
Hunting, 245
Huntington, Collis, 1
Huxley, Thomas, 72, 73

Immigration, low wages, 25
Imperialism, xiii, 11, 164–65, 178
capitalist, 222
Imperialism, 11, 178
Imperialists, 180, 184
in China, 161
Japanese, 165
Income, 23, 108–9
average total (1903), 20
1903, 27
India, xiv, 122, 270
Indians. *See* American Indians
Industrial regime, 62, 65, 67
Industrial Revolution, 1, 183
Inter-Church World Movement, 117

International Publishers, 11, 178
International Socialist Review, 82
International Workers of the World (IWW), 10, 77, 85
Interstate Commerce Commission (U.S.), wages, 54
Island Press, 220
Italians, New York, East Side, 26
Italy, 10, 122, 145
  Black Shirts, 200
IWW. *See* International Workers of the World

Jamaica, Vt., xi, 13, 200
Japan, xiv, 108, 122, 165
Jefferson, Thomas, 227
Jesus, 50–51, 56, 59, 73
Jews, 26
"Jim Crow" cars, 174

Kaiser, 104
Kansas
  wages in, 53
Kerensky, Aleksandr, 147
Ker, William Balfour, 61
The Kingdom of Man, 74
Knothe, Helen. *See* Nearing, Helen K.
Korea, 165–66
  war, 242, 258
Korea's Fight for Freedom, 166
Krishnamurti, 13
Krupp, 187
Ku Klux Klan, 108

Ladies' Home Journal, 6
La Guardia, Fiorello, xi
  campaign against, 9
Laissez-faire, 62, 227
Lankester, Ray, 74
Latin America, 122
Latvia, 158
The Law of Success, 1
Lawrence (Mass.) textile (American Woolen Co.) strike, 48
League for Public Discussion, 143

League of Nations, 122, 123, 141, 216, 217
  Covenant, 209
Lenin, Vladimir, 11, 143, 151, 178
Lexington Theatre (New York), 72, 107, 114
Liberty, 92, 103
Liberty bonds, 15
Liberty loan, 80–81
"A Life as Well as a Living," 234
Lincoln, Abraham, 93, 106, 109, 111, 168
Lippmann, Walter, 7–8
Lithuania, 158
Living the Good Life, 14, 253
  published, xi
Lochner, Louis, xi
London Armament Conference of 1930, 192
London, Jack, 225
Lower East Side (New York), xi, 9, 13, 26, 200
Loyalty tests, 259
Lynn, Mass., 257, 260

McCarthy, Joseph R., 257, 260, 261, 262
McDonald, Ramsay, 151–52
McKenna, Warren H., 271
McKenzie, F.A., 166
Macmillan Publishing Company, 10
Madison Square Garden, 9
Magnes, Judah L., 114
Maine, 14, 253, 272
The Making of a Radical, 15
Maloney, Sam, 5
Manchu dynasty, 23
Manchuria, 165, 210
Man's Search for the Good Life, 253
Mao Tse-tung, 160
Maple orchard, 14, 220
Maple sugar, 234
  orchard, 14, 220
The Maple Sugar Book, 14
Marot, Helen, 6
Marriage, 34–35
Martineau, Harriet, 38
Marxians, 242

Marx, Karl, 47, 150, 153
Massachusetts
  wages, 53, 54
Masses (journal), 10, 82, 85
Mays Landing, N.J., 206
Mesopotamia, 137
Metropolitan (New York), 7
Mexico, xiv, 62, 129, 140
Middle Ages, 148
Mill, John Stuart, 38, 44
Minimum wage, 43, 67
  New Zealand, 59
Minsk, Poland, 156
Monthly Review, xi, 14
Morgan, J.P., 1, 63, 111, 187
Morris Run Coal Company, 2
Morris Run, Pa., ix, 2
Moscow, 11, 15, 158, 160, 178,
  271
  Chinese Embassy, 270
  U.S. Embassy in, 268
Mussolini, Benito, 85, 150, 203

Nagasaki, Japan, 216
Napoleon, 43, 99
Napoleonic code, 34
(The) Nation, 107
National City Bank, Board of Direc-
  tors, 111
National Health Insurance Bill (En-
  gland), 23
Navy League, 101
Nazis, 200
Near East, oil, 138
The Nearing Case, 8
Nearing, Helen K., vii–viii
  ("Foreword"), xi, xiv, 13, 14,
  200, 220, 234, 253, 264, 269,
  282
Nearing, John Scott (son), x, 6, 15
Nearing, Louis (father), 2
  dies, xi
Nearing, Mimmie Zabriskie (moth-
  er), 2
  dies, xi
Nearing, Robert (son), x, 6, 15
Nearing, Scott
  academic freedom, breach of, 7

acquitted, 10
birthday (100th), vii
child labor committee, ix, 6, 17
Communist Party
  expelled, 12
  joins, 11, 160
  resignation, 178
Congress, xi, 9
dean, x, 8–9, 61
death, 16
degrees received, ix, x, xii
doctorate, x
  honorary, xii, 15
fired, x, 61
  U. of Pa., letter, 7
  U. of Toledo, 9
indicted, xi, 9
John (son), x, 15
Knothe, Helen (second wife). *See*
  Nearing, Helen K.
law courses, 3
pacifist, 10, 103
religion, 3
Robert (son), x, 15
Seeds, Nellie (first wife). *See*
  Seeds, Nellie
trial, 9–10, 77
Wharton School instructor, 6
Nearing, Winfield Scott (grandfather), 2
Negroes, 168
  business, 172
  laws for separation, 174
  laws restricting voting, 175–76
  servants, 169
New Economic Policy (Soviet),
  1921–22, 184
New England, 200
  wages, 53
New Freedom, 224
New Jersey, wages, 53
New Republic, 151
New World Review, 271
New York, 51
  homeless children, study of, 200
  Lexington Theatre, 72, 107, 114
  Lower East Side, xi, 9, 13, 26,
  200

slums, rent, 1
Waldorf-Astoria, 1
wealth of, 93
New York Call, 9
New York Edison Company, 111
New York Evening Post, 7
New York School for Social Work, 6
New York State Industrial Commission, 110
New York Stock Exchange, 167
New York Times, 112
New Zealand
minimum wage law, 59
Nineteenth Amendment, 32
Nitti, Signo, 149
Norris, George W., 78
North American (Philadelphia), 7
Nuclear weapons, 283

Ocean Grove, N.J., 50
Ogden, Armour, J., 111
Oil and the Germs of War, xiii, 135
Oligarchy, 226, 263, 279
Olympic Games, 209, 210
Open Road Press, Inc., 206
Organic gardening, 253
Oriental Development Company, 165
Owen, Robert, 47
Ownership, 243–52
individual, 250–51
of earth, 245–46
personalia, 247
social environment, 246

Pacifism, xiv
Pacifist, 10, 103
Panama Canal, 99
Parliament. *See* World Parliament
Parliament or Revolution, 151
The Paris Commune (1871), 224
Passport Office, 265–66, 268, 272
Passports
cancellation of, 274
denial of, 264
in China, 270
Pasteur, Louis, 43

Patten, Simon, 4, 6, 23, 29, 121
Peking, 160, 271
Pennsylvania Child Labor Committee, ix, 6, 17
Pennsylvania coal miners, 54
People's Council for Freedom and Democracy, 77
People's Party (China), 160
Pershing, John, 62
Persia, 137
Perth Amboy, wages, 25
Pettigrew (Senator), 109
Philadelphia, 3
Philadelphia Reading Coal and Iron Company, 113
Philadelphia School for Social Work, x, 6
Philippines, xiv
Pilsudsky, Poland, 203
Pittsburgh
overcrowding, 26
wages, 25
P.J.M. Railway (France), 126
Plutocracy, 152
Plutocrats, 78, 80, 81, 83, 84, 86, 89
Poland, 155–56, 158, 203, 210
Political bosses, 5
Portugal, 108
Post Office Department. *See* U.S. Post Office
Poverty, 23, 24, 57, 59, 62
belief in, 68
causes, 69
in the South, 167
Poverty and Progress, 5
Poverty and Riches, 61
"Preamble" (U.S. Constitution), 257
Preparedness, 77, 78–79
parades, 62
Presbyterianism, 116
Profit
opposition to, 255
Programme for Child Labor Reform, 21–22
Propaganda, 188–89
The Prospects of Industrial Civilizations, 149

298

Prostitution, 56
Protestant churches, 116
Proudhon, Pierre Joseph, 249
Pujo Committee, 111

Radical(s), xiii, 48, 49, 80, 82, 114, 179, 275, 277, 278
  Arden, Del., 5
  definition, 120
Rand, Carrie, 77
Rand School of Social Science, x, 9, 10, 77, 85, 86, 88, 91
Rebel, 82
Reds (film), xii, 15
Reed, John, xii, 7, 15
Reform Act of 1832, 38
Religion, 3, 5
Revolution(s)
  American and French, 76
  French, 222
  proletarian, 202
  See also Russian Revolution
Rhode Island, 124
Ridgewood, N.J., 13, 121, 135
Riga, 158
Riots, Chicago, race, 86
Rivera, Miguel Primo de, 203
Rockefeller, John D., 1, 63, 117, 135–36
Rockefeller, Percy A., 111, 112
Rockefeller, William, 111, 112, 136
Rolland, Romain, 143
Rome, 180
Roosevelt, Franklin D., 200
Roosevelt, Theodore, 7
Rotary Club, 152
Rothchilds, 187
Rowe, Leo, 5
Royal Dutch Shell, 113
Russell, Bertrand, 10, 143, 149
Russell, Charles Edward, 225
Russia, xiv, 13, 85, 104, 122, 146
  blockade by Western powers, 12
  Cromwell and, 150, 152
  education, 154
  socialism, 107
  Tsarist, 165

Russian Revolution (1917), xii, 15, 140, 154, 157–58, 210, 220, 221, 222
  (1905), 146
Russia Turns East, 11
Russo-Japanese War, 190

St. Louis Proclamation, 90, 96
Saint-Simon, Claude-Henri de Rouvroy, 47
Samaritan Hospital, University, 3
Sanger, Margaret, 143
San Remo agreement, 137
Schneider, 187
Scopes versus Tennessee trial, 71
Scranton, Pa., 51
Sebald, William, 269
Seeds, Nellie, ix, x, xi, 31, 121, 135
  dies, xi
  marries, 5
  separated, 11
Segregation law(s), 174
Selective Service Act, 86
Seligman, E.R.A., 107, 108, 110
Senate Permanent Committee on Investigation, 259–60
Seneca Falls, N.Y., 31, 38
Seoul, Korea, 166
The Shame of the Cities, 5
Shanghai, 160, 161–62
  massacre, 162
Shaw, George Bernard, 143
Shipley, Ruth, 265–66
Sinclair, Upton, 5, 225
Sixteenth Amendment, 41
Slave Belt, 167
Slavery, 93, 111–12
Slaves
  first black, 168
  in U.S., 170
Slavs, 26
Smith, Edgar F., 7
Smith, John, 119
Social Democrats, 184
Social insurance, 67

Socialism, xiv, 42, 47–48, 77, 147, 278, 283
  Russian, 107
Socialist (Cleveland, Ohio; Detroit, Mich.), 82
Socialist Party, x, xi, 9, 48, 77, 85, 90, 96, 135
  ticket, 47
Socialists, 87, 96, 97–98, 110
  ages of, 88
  World Events Committee, 220
Social Science Institute
  incorporates, xi, 242
South Africa, 97
South Bethlehem Steel Works, wages, 54
Southern Pacific Railroad, 1
Soviet Union, xi, xii, 10, 154–55, 184, 220
  proletarian revolution, 199
Spain, xiv, 10, 13, 108
Spanish Civil War, 210
Spencer, Herbert, 72, 73
Spinoza, Baruch, 72, 73
Stalinist "purge," 12
Stalin, Joseph, 12, 160
Standard of New Jersey, 136, 137
Standard Oil Company, 23, 113, 135, 140, 225–26
"The Star-Spangled Banner," 186
Stedman, Seymour, 88, 89, 92
Steel industry
  wages, 54
Steffens, Lincoln, 5, 225
Stockdale, Alan, 9, 62
Stockholders, 112–13
Stokes, Rose Pastor, 10, 85
Stolpce, Poland, 157
Stone house, xii, 15, 282
Stratton Mountain, 14, 236
Suffrage, 38–39, 49
Suffragette, 38
Summer, Walter T., 56
Sunday, Billy, 9
Sun Yat-sen, 222
Supreme Court. *See* U.S. Supreme Court

Swarthmore College, x, 5
Switzerland, 11
  Lenin's exile in, 178
Syndicalist movement, 48

Taiwan policy, 272
Tarbell, Ida, 225
Teaching, 279–80
Temple College, ix, 3, 5
Ten Commandments
  commercial value of, 1
Tenements (New York), 26–27, 52
  other cities, 51
Tennessee Valley Authority (TVA), 200
Terkel, Studs, vii
Teto, William, 260–61
Thebes, 180
Thomas, Norman, 135
Thoreau, Henry David, 223, 241
Toledo Public Forum, 61
Tolstoy, Leo N., xiv
Trans-Siberian Express, 160
Treason
  accusation of, 9, 62
  trial, 77
The Treaty of Protectorate, 165
Treaty of Versailles, 86, 158, 191
Truman, Harry S, 14, 257, 261, 272
Trusts, 63, 111
The Twilight of Empire, xi, 11, 12, 178
"Tzar Nearing" (Winfield Scott), 2

Unemployment, 283
Unions, 47, 48, 59
United Asia, 166
United Nations, 216, 217
  Declaration of Human Rights, 267, 269
United States, 51–52, 122
  depression, 1, 12, 13, 179, 200
  H-bomb, 242
  model for world organization, 212–13
  socialism, 48
  wages, 50

United States (*cont.*)
WWI casualties, 78
U.S. Army
Communists, 257
U.S. Census Bureau, 1, 17, 117, 173
church members, 118
U.S. Commissioner of Labor, 27
U.S. Department of Labor, 20
U.S. Food Administration, 93
U.S. Interstate Commerce Commission wages, 54
U.S. Post Office, 90–91, 225
U.S. State Department, 155, 257, 264, 273
passport policy, 265
United States Steel Corporation, 1, 51, 63, 98, 112, 141
U.S. Supreme Court, 23, 136, 242
United World, xiii, 13, 206
Universal Postal Union, 209
University Samaritan Hospital, 3
University of Chicago, 9
University of Pennsylvania, ix, x, xii, 3, 4, 7, 17, 50, 96
damage to reputation, 8
honorary degree, 15
University of Toledo (Ohio), x, 8, 61, 96
Ur, 180

Vanguard Press, 12, 178
Vegetarianism, xiv
diet, 253
Venezuela, xii, xiv
Vermont, 253, 254
Vickers, 187
Victorian woman, 31
Vietnam War, 14–15
Villa, Pancho, 62
Villard, Oswalk Garrison, 107
Vindication of the Rights of Woman (Mary Wollstonecraft), 38
Voting laws
restricting, 175–76

Wages, 20, 50, 66–67
immigration, 25
minimum, 53–57
Perth Amboy, 25
Pittsburgh, 25
remedies for low, 25
Wages in the United States, 1908–1910, 50
Waldorf-Astoria, 1–2
War, 125, 138–40, 186, 276, 283
capitalist, 87, 100, 113
cold, 264
definition, xiv, 188
economics of, 189–90
Korean, 242
list of, 192–93
of 1776, 213
social disease, 101
Vietnam, 14–15
Ward, Harry, 115, 162
Ward, Lester, F., 221
War: Organized Destruction and Mass Murder by Civilized Nations, 13
Warsaw, 156
Washington, D.C., 264, 265
travel to, 268
Washington, George, 74
Washington Treaties of 1921–22, 209–10
Watson, Frank, 17
Wealth, 43, 45–46, 66, 125, 181, 224
richest 1 percent, 1
Webb, Sidney and Beatrice, 149, 221
Welfare, 44, 46, 65
general, 257–58, 262, 274
Wells, H.G., 143
Western Federation of Miners, 47
West Point, 21, 188
Wharton School (U. of Pa.), ix, 3, 5, 6
Whither China?, 11
Wilson, Woodrow, 9, 41, 62, 101, 125, 191, 224
New Freedom, 224
Wisconsin, wages, 53
Witmer, Lightner, 8
Wollstonecraft, Mary, 38

Woman and Social Progress, xiii, 6
Woman's International League for
    Peace and Freedom, 77
Women, 48–49, 55–56
    economic power, 36–37
    political equality, 38–40
    Victorian, 31
Women's rights, 5, 31
    first convention, 31, 38
The Workers Party. *See* Communist
    Party
The Workers' University Society, 71
World Court, 209
World economic divisions, 127
World economy, 186, 198, 199
World Events, 14
    column, xi
    newsletter, xi
World Events Committee, 220

World federation, 128–33, 213–14,
    219
    similar to U.S. and Soviet Rus-
      sia, 131
World government, 133, 212, 216
    requirements, 217–18
Worldism, 208, 211
World Labor Unity, 11
World Parliament, 121, 197, 212
    structure, 131–33
World peace, 121, 122
World war, xiii
World War I, x, 78, 137, 184, 189,
    209, 222, 264
    opposition to, 9, 62
World War II, 13, 15, 216
Wright, Frances, 38

Zapata brothers, 222